# UNDERSTANDING
# DAVID FOSTER
# WALLACE

Understanding Contemporary American Literature
Matthew J. Bruccoli, Series Editor

**Volumes on**

Edward Albee • Nicholson Baker • John Barth • Donald Barthelme
The Beats • The Black Mountain Poets • Robert Bly
Raymond Carver • Fred Chappell • Chicano Literature
Contemporary American Drama
Contemporary American Horror Fiction
Contemporary American Literary Theory
Contemporary American Science Fiction
Contemporary Chicana Literature
Robert Coover • James Dickey • E. L. Doctorow • John Gardner
George Garrett • John Hawkes • Joseph Heller • Lillian Hellman
John Irving • Randall Jarrell • William Kennedy • Jack Kerouac
Ursula K. Le Guin • Denise Levertov • Bernard Malamud
Bobbie Ann Mason • Jill McCorkle • Carson McCullers
W. S. Merwin • Arthur Miller • Toni Morrison's Fiction
Vladimir Nabokov • Gloria Naylor • Joyce Carol Oates
Tim O'Brien • Flannery O'Connor • Cynthia Ozick
Walker Percy • Katherine Anne Porter • Richard Powers
Reynolds Price • Annie Proulx • Thomas Pynchon
Theodore Roethke • Philip Roth • May Sarton • Hubert Selby, Jr.
Mary Lee Settle • Neil Simon • Isaac Bashevis Singer
Jane Smiley • Gary Snyder • William Stafford • Robert Stone
Anne Tyler • Kurt Vonnegut • David Foster Wallace
Robert Penn Warren • James Welch • Eudora Welty
Tennessee Williams • August Wilson

# UNDERSTANDING
# DAVID
# FOSTER
# WALLACE

Marshall Boswell

University of South Carolina Press

Published in Columbia, South Carolina, by the
University of South Carolina Press

Manufactured in the United States of America

07   06   05   04   03       5   4   3   2   1

Library of Congress Cataloging-in-Publication Data

Boswell, Marshall, 1965–
  Understanding David Foster Wallace / Marshall Boswell.
    p. cm. — (Understanding contemporary American literature)
  Includes bibliographical references and index.
  ISBN 1-57003-517-2 (alk. paper)
  1. Wallace, David Foster—Criticism and interpretation.
  2. Modernism (Literature)—United States. I. Title. II. Series.
PS3573.A425635 Z53 2003
813'.54—dc22

                                                        2003

Grateful acknowledgment is made to the following publishers for permission to reprint copyrighted material:

From *The Broom of the System* by David Foster Wallace, copyright © 1987 by David Foster Wallace. Used by permission of Viking Penguin, a division of Penguin Group (USA) Inc. From *The Girl with Curious Hair* by David Foster Wallace. Copyright © 1989 by David Foster Wallace. Used by permission of W. W. Norton & Company, Inc. From *Infinite Jest* by David Foster Wallace. Copyright © 1996 by David Foster Wallace. By permission of Little, Brown and Company, (Inc.). From *A Supposedly Fun Thing I'll Never Do Again* by David Foster Wallace. Copyright © 1997 by David Foster Wallace. By permission of Little, Brown and Company, (Inc.). From *Brief Interviews with Hideous Men* by David Foster Wallace. Copyright © 1999 by David Foster Wallace. Used by permission of Little, Brown and Company, (Inc.).

# UNDERSTANDING
# DAVID FOSTER WALLACE

# Series Editor's Preface

The volumes of *Understanding Contemporary American Literature* have been planned as guides or companions for students as well as good nonacademic readers. The editor and publisher perceive a need for these volumes because much of the influential contemporary literature makes special demands. Uninitiated readers encounter difficulty in approaching works that depart from the traditional forms and techniques of prose and poetry. Literature relies on conventions, but the conventions keep evolving; new writers form their own conventions—which in time may become familiar. Put simply, *UCAL* provides instruction in how to read certain contemporary writers—identifying and explicating their material, themes, use of language, point of view, structures, symbolism, and responses to experience.

The word *understanding* in the titles was deliberately chosen. Many willing readers lack an adequate understanding of how contemporary literature works; that is, what the author is attempting to express and the means by which it is conveyed. Although the criticism and analysis in the series have been aimed at a level of general accessibility, these introductory volumes are meant to be applied in conjunction with the works they cover. They do not provide a substitute for the works and authors they introduce, but rather prepare the reader for more profitable literary experiences.

M. J. B.

# CHAPTER 1

# Cynicism and Naïveté
## Modernism's Third Wave

Born February 21, 1962, two years after the publication of John
Barth's *The Sot-Weed Factor,* David Foster Wallace came into
the world at more or less the moment American postmodern
fiction came into its own. Astounding as it may seem, Wallace's
novel *Infinite Jest* (1996) is as far away chronologically from
Barth's groundbreaking work as Barth's book was from James
Joyce's *Ulysses* (1922). As a result, although Wallace is often
labeled a "postmodern" writer, in fact he might best regarded as
a nervous member of some still-unnamed (and perhaps unname-
able) third wave of modernism. He confidently situates himself as the direct heir to a tradition of aesthetic development that
began with the modernist overturning of nineteenth-century
bourgeois realism and continued with the postwar critique of
modernist aesthetics. Yet Wallace proceeds from the assumption
that *both* modernism and postmodernism are essentially "done."
Rather, his work moves resolutely forward while hoisting the
baggage of modernism and postmodernism heavily, but respect-
fully, on its back.

David's parents, James Donald and Sally Foster, were both
teachers and writers: his father, a philosophy professor, is the
author of *Virtues and Vices* (Cornell University Press, 1978),
a slim yet provocative work of moral philosophy, while his
mother—a community-college English professor who, in 1996,
was selected by the Council for Advancement and Support of

Education as the National Professor of the Year and who, in 1998–99, was the recipient of a Pew National Fellowship from the Carnegie Mellon Foundation—is the author of the remedial writing textbook *Practically Painless English* (Prentice Hall, 1990), a now standard textbook in the field. David was born in Ithaca, New York, where his father was completing his Ph.D. at Cornell University, alma mater of Wallace's great literary forbear Thomas Pynchon and one-time employer of grand master Vladimir Nabokov. Sometime la · while David was still an infant, the family moved to Philo, Illinois, so that his father could begin work as an assistant professor at nearby University of Illinois at Urbana-Champaign. Wallace's most extensive fictional treatment of his native Midwest can be found in the novella "Westward the Course of Empire Takes Its Way," most of which takes place in "Collision, Illinois," a windswept hillless expanse of dust and corn, "the most *dis*closed, open place you could ever fear to see."[1] Elsewhere he has said that his native topography, when "seen from the air, strongly suggests a board game . . . laid down special, as if planned."[2]

David and his younger sister, Amy, grew up amid the rambunctious middle-class bohemia of modern-day academia, in a house full of books and afghan blankets where dinner conversation was a coded affair of private jokes and insular slang. One can possibly glean faint hints of Wallace's childhood via the family portraits he has placed at the center of his two major novels thus far: both the Beadsmans of *The Broom of the System* and the Incandenzas of *Infinite Jest* are comically dysfunctional, fiercely self-involved, and engagingly cerebral. In a recent *Harper's* essay on language and usage, Wallace, in a footnote, provides a funny and self-mocking portrait of his family as a group of SNOOTs, where SNOOT stands for the reviewer's nuclear family's *nickname à clef* for a really extreme usage fanatic, the sort of person whose idea of Sunday fun is to look for mistakes in Safire's column's prose itself. This reviewer's family is roughly 70 percent SNOOT, which term itself derives from an acronym, with the big historical family joke being that whether S.N.O.O.T. stood for "Sprachgefuhl Necessitates Our Ongoing Tendance" or "Syntax Nudniks of Our Time" depended on whether or not you were one.[3]

In addition to being an acknowledged math and verbal whiz, David, like Hal Incandenza, his youthful protagonist in *Infinite Jest,* was also a tennis prodigy, spending the bulk of his middle- and high-school years competing in junior tennis tournaments. In "Derivative Sport in Tornado Alley," an insightful autobiographical essay about his childhood career as a "near-great tennis player," Wallace reports that, at fourteen, he "was ranked seventeenth in the United States Tennis Association's Western Section." He also describes how, in 1977 at the age of fifteen, he realized his athletic development had suddenly and inexplicably plateaued. "My vocation ebbed," he writes. "I felt uncalled." This event Wallace calls his "initiation into true adult sadness." Fortunately, his tennis game, as he describes it, was enhanced by a preternatural gift for geometric thinking, that is, "the ability to calculate not merely your own angles but the angles of response to your angles": hence, just as he was realizing his career as a "near-great" juniors tennis champion was coming to an end, he "discovered definite integrals and antiderivatives and found [his] identity shift from jock to math-wienie."[4]

In 1980, Wallace began his studies at Amherst College, his father's alma mater. While there he pursued a major in philosophy, with a specialization in math and logic. He has affirmed that he was particularly gifted at technical philosophy and was for a short while convinced that he had found his calling. During this period he also first encountered the work of Ludwig Wittgenstein, whose philosophical ideas would exert a lasting influence on his later fiction. Then, quite unexpectedly, as with junior tennis, he abruptly lost interest in his new calling—this despite the "buzz" he once got from solving mathematical or logical problems. This sudden change threw him into "kind of a mid-life crisis at twenty," because, as he puts it, "I was suddenly not getting joy from the one thing I was clearly supposed to do because I was good at it and people liked me for being good at it." Depressed and confused, he took a leave of absence from college, went home to Illinois, and began writing fiction. He quickly found that he got the same sort of buzz from writing fiction that he once got from doing technical philosophy, a conflation of apparently competing experiences he explains thus: "What I didn't know then was that a mathematical experience was aesthetic in nature, an epiphany in Joyce's original sense."[5]

By the time he graduated from Amherst in 1985, Wallace had completed the rough draft of a novel. This draft manuscript was instrumental in securing his admittance into the M.F.A. program at the University of Arizona, where, on a basketball court, he met fellow fiction writer Robert Boswell, author of such critically acclaimed novels as *Crooked Hearts* and *Mystery Ride*. Boswell encouraged Wallace to start submitting his novel to agents and even showed the young author how to write a cover letter. That cover letter, plus the writing sample Wallace included, caught the eye of New York literary agent Bonnie Nadell, who instantly took on the book and sold it to Penguin

Books, which was still flush with the recent and surprising success of another twentysomething writer, Bret Easton Ellis. Wallace's completed book eventually came out in 1987 under the title *The Broom of the System*. Unlike the thin, anemic work of Wallace's fellow "brat pack" novelists, *Broom* was a five-hundred-page declaration of independence by a young writer who considered himself not the peer of the decade's media darlings but rather the inheritor of a venerable literary tradition stretching back at least to the William Gaddis of *The Recognitions*. Wallace has also called the novel "a coded autobio that's also a funny little post-structural gag."[6]

Meanwhile, the short stories he produced while at Arizona began to appear in such high-profile journals as the *Paris Review, Playboy, Conjunctions* and *Harper's*. "Little Expressionless Animals," the piece he published in the *Paris Review* won the John Traine Humor Prize in 1988, while "Here and There," originally published in *Fiction,* was selected for *Prize Stories 1989: The O. Henry Awards*. These stories, plus a groundbreaking novella, formed his second book, the story collection *Girl with Curious Hair* (Norton 1989). Because of its repeated and insistent use of "real-life" celebrities as fictional characters—Jack Lord, Pat Sajak, Merv Griffin, David Letterman, Keith Jarrett, among others—the book's publication was delayed for a little over a year while lawyers secured copyrights and Wallace made revisions. The book's concluding novella, "Westward the Course of Empire Takes Its Way," set in a writing workshop and at an amusement park, enacts a rewriting of John Barth's "Lost in the Funhouse" and thereby outlines a way, possibly, to transcend mere self-reflexivity. It remains Wallace's clearest, most programmatic explanation of the next step he is proposing to take.

While working on *Girl with Curious Hair,* and watching his first novel catapult him into fame (in 1987, the book won the prestigious Whiting Writers' Award from the Mrs. Giles Whiting Foundation) Wallace apparently fell victim, once again, to doubt and depression. A second novel, set in a prep-school tennis academy, refused to come alive on the page, and Wallace kept restarting and then abandoning the project. According to some reports—variously affirmed and denied by Wallace himself—this period was also marked by excessive drug use and sexual promiscuity. He carried these doubts and destructive habits with him to Harvard University where, in 1989, he began graduate work in philosophy, studying logic, semantics, and math. Uninspired and adrift, he left Harvard after a year of course work. In 1990, he moved back home to the significantly named Normal, Illinois, where he accepted the post of assistant professor of English and located the creative life current for the once stillborn followup to *The Broom of the System.* He also took time out during this period to publish, with old Amherst friend Mark Costello, a nonfiction book on hip-hop culture titled *Signifying Rappers: Rap and Race in the Urban Present* (Ecco Press). In 1993 he moved to Bloomington, Illinois, with his two Labrador retrievers, Jeeves and Drone, and continued his duties as an English professor at Illinois State University. Now teaching and writing full time, Wallace directed the bulk of his creative energy to his new novel project.

In 1996 the 1,079–page novel *Infinite Jest* finally emerged. It instantly became a publishing phenomenon. The book's publication spawned the overnight creation of a constellation of Wallace-oriented Web sites, a high-profile appearance on *The Charlie Rose Show,* and a flurry of magazine puff pieces, including a major spread in the *New York Times Magazine.* Before the book even had a chance to go into its first paperback printing, Wallace learned that he had been awarded a six-figure "genius grant" from the John D. and Catherine T. MacArthur Foundation.

While working on *Infinite Jest,* Wallace continued to publish award-winning short stories in the *Paris Review, Conjunctions,* and elsewhere, while on the strength of *Signifying Rappers, Harper's* magazine began sending him out on unconventional journalistic assignments. In 1995, *Harper's* named him a contributing editor. These pieces, as well as a few others, he gathered together to form the bulk of his 1997 nonfiction collection, *A Supposedly Fun Thing I'll Never Do Again: Essays and Arguments.* Two years later, he issued his second story collection, *Brief Interviews with Hideous Men* (Little, Brown, 1999), a somewhat uneven assortment that nevertheless served as the touchstone for a lengthy career-spanning appraisal by A. O. Scott in the February 10, 2000, issue of the *New York Times Review of Books.* The essay even featured a David Levine cartoon of the Celebrated Author: Wallace is portrayed as an unwashed, grunge-era bookworm, complete with his characteristic razor stubble and his trademark bandana, his unkempt hair falling in a chaotic cascade across both his glasses and the pages of a massive dictionary over which he is wearily poring. Without question, Wallace had arrived.

After *Brief Interviews with Hideous Men,* Wallace involved himself in a number of unconventional side projects that served to keep his name firmly planted in the public consciousness. In winter 2000 he climbed aboard Senator John McCain's "Straight Talk Express" to cover, for *Rolling Stone* magazine, the Arizona Republican's presidential campaign. The resulting essay was a by-now typically entertaining and insightful Wallace journalistic effort, with characteristically Wallace-like meditations on pundits, cable network news coverage, spin, and political cynicism. Behind the sophisticated analysis lay a passionate call to Wallace's young readers to overcome their own cynicism and indifference and get out there and vote. *Rolling Stone* published the piece in the magazine's April 13, 2000 issue; later that summer, in an effort to get the essay widely disseminated before the November 2000 elections, Wallace sold an expanded version of it to TimeWarner Books, which published it as a cheap, downloadable "eBook" titled *Up, Simba! Seven Days on the Trail of an Anticandidate.*

Finally, in February 2001, in an intriguing example of Wallace's professional career imitating his quirky art, Pomona College announced that Wallace had been hired as the college's Disney Professor of Creative Writing. The endowed chair was established by Roy Edward Disney, Walt Disney's nephew and a 1951 graduate of the college. Few journalists could resist noting the delicious irony of such a position going to the pop-culture obsessed author of *Infinite Jest*—a novel that, among many other things, parodies corporate sponsorship in all its forms, even creating an alternative near future in which calendar years are no longer assigned numbers according to the Roman calendar but are rather named after the companies that "subsidize" them. Wallace also contributed a brief essay in *Rolling Stone*'s October 25, 2001, special issue commemorating the September 11, 2001, terrorist attacks on the United States. In spring 2002 Wallace sold his third short story collection to Little, Brown, with publication planned for 2004.

Like most serious—and even less serious—accounts of Wallace's work, A. O. Scott's *New York Times Review of Books* essay attempts, somewhat tentatively, to explain exactly *how* Wallace's distinctive work moves beyond postmodern self-reflexivity. Scott follows in the wake of a number of public declarations of Wallace's innovative importance. In 1996, for instance, upon publication of *Infinite Jest,* Wallace edited a special edition of the *Review of Contemporary Fiction* titled "The Future of Fiction." Similarly, in 1997 *Time* magazine published an article titled "Fiction's New Fab Four," in which Wallace was elected as the most visible member of a new literary vanguard, if not a of coherent new literary movement.

Though neither of the above two treatments arrives at concrete definition of this new movement, Scott comes very close with his probing analysis of Wallace's 1993 essay "E Unibus Pluram: Television and U.S. Fiction," originally published in the *Review of Contemporary Fiction* and later collected in *A Supposedly Fun Thing I'll Never Do Again: Essays and Arguments.* This essay, one of the most important pieces in Wallace's growing corpus of nonfiction, preceded the publication of *Infinite Jest* and in many ways prepared the way for that career-making book. In intent and subject matter, it functions as one of the most direct articulations of Wallace's particular take on postmodernism and the unique challenges facing writers of his generation. As such, the essay has the same centrality in unfolding the shape of Wallace's career as John Barth's famous 1968 essay, "The Literature of Exhaustion," had in shaping the career of Wallace's primary fictional father. Indeed, "E Unibus Pluram" is in many respects a "response," one generation later, to Barth's "response" to his modernist forbears. Before addressing "E Unibus Pluram" directly, then, it is important to outline how Barth's essay conceives of the relationship between these two heterogeneous literary movements.

Modernism refers to the literary dominant of the first half of the century, a dominant often defined as an expression of crisis, specifically the crisis of the Word, as George Steiner has it.[7] Modernism confronts the world that emerged following Friedrich Nietzsche's "death of God": meaning and certainty had been severed from their long-held metaphysical grounding, while all the old certainties of Western culture had been destroyed, from Darwin's unseating of the Hebraic creation myth to Freud's replacing of the soul with the internal combustion engine of the three-part psyche. In the absence of objective certainty, modernist writers, like their painter contemporaries, abandoned the outdated mode of nineteenth-century "objective" realism in favor of a new valorization of individual subjective experience. The new subject became the individual in isolation, the new agenda the intense tracing of consciousness in all its contingent manifestations.

Brian McHale argues that modernist fiction is essentially epistemological: it inquires into the mechanics of knowing and privileges perceived over objective truth. In rejecting Victorian/Edwardian conventions of linear, cause-and-effect narrative, modernist fiction affirms the discontinuous, the private, the subjective. Still, modernism regards this shift toward epistemology as a *crisis*, for in valorizing the subjective and the provisional it also, by extension, announces the loss of transcendent universals. In response to this loss, modernist writers propose new universals that are paradoxically allied to subjective experience. Marcel Proust's inquiry into the transcendent nature of memory, Joyce's much-lauded mythic method, William Faulkner's Bergsonian distinction between time and *duré*: all of these innovations stand as courageous artistic attempts to connect private experience with some nontemporal universal.[8]

Postmodernism is both a subtle critique of modernism and a direct extension of it. In effect, postmodernism shifts the emphasis from epistemology to ontology, that is, to the study of metaphysical grounds, essentially of being. Whereas modernists sought to approach the metaphysical via the epistemological, postmodernists examine the ontological ground of modernist epistemology. Or, as Wallace more clearly puts the case, "It's almost like postmodernism is fiction's fall from biblical grace. Fiction became *conscious* of itself in a way it never had been."[9] This shift in emphasis is the direct result of a fatal flaw in the modernist project. In *The Five Faces of Modernity*, Matei Calinescu cites as one of the chief characteristics of modern consciousness—regarded here as the consciousness of the post-Renaissance West—the haunting sense of an unrepeatable, one-way vector of linear time.[10] Connected to this new sense of time is the widespread acceptance of *progress*, whether with regard to art or technology or politics. Modernist literature—that is, literature of high distinction produced between 1900 and 1945—assumes as its chief raison d'être the need for newness and innovation, for further refinement and complexity. Unavoidably linked with this agenda is an implicit faith in the possibility of perfection, in the achievement of an end. Eliot's *Four Quartets* tries to approach the final limits of language, and John Cage's *4'33''* dramatizes the logical end of avant-garde abstraction, for example. In other words, modernism, in addition to exploring the full range of epistemological doubt, also sets artistic development on a road to death, affirming an endpoint that is, in the final analysis, a zero-point, a peace that passeth understanding. All of which begs the question, What is one to do next?

Barth's "The Literature of Exhaustion" remains the most cogent account of what it might have felt like to be a young postwar writer confronted with the burden of following the modernists, a task that was tantamount to proceeding past the zero point.[11] According to Barth, the modernist novel so thoroughly interrogated the nature of perception and the limits of literary representation that it effectively exhausted the form. Not only was nineteenth-century bourgeois realism dead, but so also was modernist innovation. All the advances in novelistic technique introduced by the modernist masters—from stream-of-consciousness to spatial form—were originally designed to provide a more accurate access to reality, albeit a reality now understood to be principally the product of subjective experience. But by the time Barth took up his pen, these same innovations had become, from overuse, simply more new literary conventions, neither more nor less "accurate" than bourgeois realism and only slightly more current. For Barth, the task of the *post*-modernist writer was not to develop additional new methods of rendering the act of perception but rather to examine the relationship between literary method and the reality it sought to depict. As he argued, the postmodern novel would employ literary conventions ironically, in the form of parody, thereby undertaking a self-reflexive inquiry into the ontological status of literary inquiry itself.

Wallace, a young writer who cut his teeth not only on the work of John Barth and Thomas Pynchon but also on twentieth-century philosophy, is more than fleetingly aware of the modernist/postmodernist debate as outlined here; in fact, he is directly engaged in moving beyond it. For him, the self-referential quality of John Barth's work, the way it unseats our belief in literature's ability to address directly the world outside itself and replaces epistemology with temporal ontology, serves as a necessary and even useful response to the modernist project. He is also attentive to the way in which Barth's strategy follows Heidegger's existentialist critique of metaphysics, ungrounding certainties and producing in the reader both a sense of endless possibility and anxiety, since the text is now grounded in nothing beyond itself. Barth's job was to yank the ground from underneath the writers of his era, to produce that anxiety (the recognition that nothing is beneath us) and create a new zone of pure possibility. In part, this process of un-grounding represents "the frankly idealistic" rationale that Wallace feels inspired the metafictional project in the first place. In a famous interview, Wallace has even called this process "the postmodern founders' patricidal work."[12] But Wallace also recognizes that for all the liberation produced by this "patricide," there is also a concomitant sense of isolation and anxiety.

In "E Unibus Pluram," he accuses television as being the primary cause of this shift from a liberating to an isolating anxiety fueling the postmodern project. The essay primarily seeks to demonstrate how current trends in television have succeeded in dissolving the subversive power of postmodern metafiction. First he explains that the original intention behind postmodern irony was "to illuminate and explode hypocrisy." Postmodern writers called attention to their fictional devices and undermined our faith in the truth-value of various interested conventions because these writers were, in Wallace's term, "frankly idealistic; it was assumed that etiology and diagnosis pointed toward cure, that revelation of imprisonment led to freedom."[13] The prison we were in was the prison of naive belief; the freedom they were offering was the intellectual and spiritual freedom of the cynic to see hypocrisy wherever it was at work. Unfortunately, by 1990 the once subversive strategies of postmodernism—self-reflexivity and irony—had been co-opted by television, even by television advertising, to such an extent that these same strategies had been sapped of their revolutionary power.

For instance, television commercials are now largely self-reflexive in the way they cunningly call attention to the hokey emptiness of advertising, as in the Joe Isuzu ad where a fast-talking car salesman is shown clearly to be lying. In Wallace's clever analysis, the ads "invited viewers to congratulate Isuzu's ads for being ironic, to congratulate themselves for getting the joke, and to congratulate Isuzu, Inc. for being 'fearless' and 'irreverent' enough to acknowledge that car ads are ridiculous and that Audience is dumb to believe them." The result is that "it is now *television* that takes elements of the *postmodern* —the involution, the absurdity, the sardonic fatigue, the iconoclasm and rebellion—and bends them to the ends of spectation and consumption." And now that irony and cynical sophistication have become the primary weapons of mass culture, these same strategies have become agents not of rebellion but rather of "great despair and stasis in U.S. culture." What's more, "for aspiring fiction writers they pose especially terrible problems."[14] In Wallace's view, we are all horribly alone in our sophisticated irony: so preoccupied are we with *getting the joke* that we never allow ourselves to feel anything directly, for "fear of ridicule." Whereas the original metafictionalists exploded conventions and employed irony to blast the naive hypocrisy of mass culture, writers of Wallace's generation are confronted with the dilemma of devising a way to analyze the culture that neither reclaims discredited realism nor resurrects irony and self-reflexivity, the weapons of the enemy.

Scott, in his analysis of Wallace's theory, focuses on the essay's final paragraph, where Wallace forcefully declares,

It's entirely possible that my plangent noises about the impossibility of rebelling against an aura that promotes and vitiates all rebellion say more about my residency inside that aura, my own lack of vision, than they do about any exhaustion of U.S. fiction's possibilities. The next real literary "rebels" in this country might well emerge as some weird bunch of *anti*-rebels, born oglers who dare somehow to back way from ironic watching, who have the childish gall actually to endorse and instantiate single-entendre principles. Who treat of plain old untrendy human troubles and emotions in U.S. life with reverence and conviction. Who eschew self-consciousness and hip fatigue.[15]

Scott wonders if this passage isn't an indirect description of Wallace's own method, and an indicator that his work should be read alongside such works as Jedediah Purdy's 1999 critique of postmodern irony, *For Common Things*. Is Wallace simply an "anti-ironic anti-rebel"? Scott wisely rejects this assessment. As he puts it, "If one way to escape from the blind alley of postmodern self-consciousness is simply to turn around and walk in another direction . . . Wallace prefers to forge ahead in hopes of breaking through to the other side, whatever that might be." That final phrase—"whatever that might be"—is telling, for Scott, like most of Wallace's critics, seems befuddled when it comes to describing what fiction from the "other side" of postmodern fiction might look like, even though they all seem convinced that Wallace's work is an example of that kind of fiction. The best description that Scott offers is to call Wallace's work "meta-ironic. That is . . . to turn irony back on itself, to make his fiction relentlessly conscious of its own self-consciousness, and thus to produce work that will be at once unassailably sophisticated and doggedly down to earth."[16]

In fact, Scott almost has it, right there: the essence of Wallace's innovation. To complete his analysis, Scott quotes Wallace on David Lynch, whose films, Wallace asserts, possess "bothness." Scott goes on to say that Wallace wants to be "at once earnest and ironical, sensitive and cerebral," and here, too, Scott has Wallace almost exactly right. Wallace himself defines the multiplicity he wants to embody as a joining of "cynicism and naïveté." He uses these specific terms in three of his major works, including the "E Unibus Pluram" essay, his novella "Westward the Course of Empire Takes Its Way," and *Infinite Jest*. In all three cases, Wallace links the two concepts while outlining the exhausted vitality of postmodern irony. What's more, he repeats phrases and terms in such a way as to suggest that here is a core idea—perhaps *the* core idea—behind the work itself. "Culture-wise," he writes in "E Unibus Pluram," "shall I spend much of your time pointing out the degree to which televisual values influence the contemporary mood of jaded weltschmerz, self-mocking materialism, blank indifference, and the delusion that cynicism and naïveté are mutually exclusive?" Similarly, in "Westward," the narrator remarks that D. L., the novella's resident postmodern metafictionalist, suffers from the delusion "that cynicism and naïveté are mutually exclusive." Finally, in *Infinite Jest,* amid a long digression told from the point of view of Wallace's autobiographical doppelgänger Hal Incandenza on the most recent "Romantic glorification of *Weltschmerz,* which means world weariness or hip ennui," the narrator speaks about "that queerly persistent U.S. myth that cynicism and naïveté are mutually exclusive."[17]

Typically, the passage from *Infinite Jest,* thus far the culmination of Wallace's corpus, provides an illuminating and more thorough explanation of what Wallace has in mind when he speaks of this "delusion" or "myth," a delusion, obviously, that his work seeks both to embody and to explode: "Hal, who's empty but not dumb, theorizes privately that what passes for hip cynical transcendence of sentiment is really some kind of fear of being really human, since to be really human (at least as he conceptualizes it) is probably to be unavoidably sentimental and naïve and goo-prone and generally pathetic." Wallace's work, in its attempt to prove that cynicism and naïveté are mutually compatible, treats the culture's hip fear of sentiment with the same sort of ironic self-awareness with which sophisticates in the culture portray "gooey" sentimentality; the result is that hip irony is itself ironized in such a way that the *opposite* of hip irony—that is, gooey sentiment—can emerge as the work's indirectly intended mode. For if irony, as Wallace explains in "E Unibus Pluram," is a means of "exploiting gaps between what's said and what's meant, between how things try to appear and how they really are," then Wallace uses irony to disclose what irony has been hiding.[18] He does not merely join cynicism and naïveté: rather, he employs cynicism—here figured as sophisticated self-reflexive irony—to recover a learned form of heartfelt naïveté, his work's ultimate mode and what the work "really means," a mode that Wallace equates with the "really human." The work is both as diagnosis and cure. As he succinctly put it in a long and significant interview with literary critic Larry McCaffery, "In dark times, the definition of good art would seem to be art that locates and applies CPR to those elements of what's human and magical that still live and glow despite the times' darkness. Really good fiction could have as dark a worldview as it wished, but it'd find a way both to depict this dark world *and* to illuminate the possibilities for being alive and human in it." Wallace, certainly by the time of *Infinite Jest* but in significant ways before that as well, has found that way. His method allows him to fulfill what he regards as the primary job of all fiction, that is, to articulate "what it is to be a fucking *human being*."[19]

In devising this ingenious narrative strategy, Wallace is doing much more than simply diagnosing a peculiar form of alienation that haunts contemporary culture. Rather, as Scott implies in his overview, this strategy stands as Wallace's solution to the apparently indissoluble dilemma that sits at the center of his historical situation as a serious literary artist: how to follow postmodernism without merely rejecting it and returning to the mode of the prepostmodern, or even the premodern. His clever conjoining of "cynicism and naïveté," of irony and sentimentality, is grounded in his keen understanding of, and participation with, the intellectual, aesthetic, and philosophical trajectory that characterizes the movement from modernism to postmodernism. Furthermore, his use of irony and self-reflexivity places him squarely within the discourses of existentialism, structuralism, and poststructuralism. Consciously or not, Barth's critique of modernism shares affinities with poststructuralism, specifically with the project termed "deconstruction," generally associated with the French philosopher Jacques Derrida and allied with the work of German philosopher Martin Heidegger. One of the key ways in which Wallace intervenes in this philosophical dialogue is, in effect, to abandon Martin Heidegger and Jacques Derrida in favor of Heidegger's celebrated contemporary, Ludwig Wittgenstein. Wallace has said that he regards Wittgenstein, and not Heidegger, as the "real architect of the postmodern trap," that is, the "trap" of alienated self-referentiality. He also regards Wittgenstein as a "real artist" because Wittgenstein understood that "no conclusion could be more horrible than solipsism." Wittgenstein's central argument in his famous posthumous work *The Philosophical Investigations*—a book Wallace praises as "the single most comprehensive and beautiful argument against solipsism that's ever been made"—is that language, as Wallace puts it, is "always . . . a function of relationships between persons" and is "dependent on human community."[20] This argument, though grounded in many of the same premises that guide Heidegger and Derrida in their deconstructive project, marks a decisive break with poststructuralism and also allows Wallace to use his ironic method both to disillusion his readers and at the same time to *connect* with them.

Wallace's work is steeped in Wittgenstein's ideas, from the actual appearance of Wittgenstein in *The Broom of the System* to *Infinite Jest*'s lexicon of specially coined futuristic jargon and its extensive use of hypertext-like endnotes. The work both articulates Wittgenstein's ideas and tries to employ those ideas in the many specially designed formal strategies Wallace has designed over the course of his career. In a very real sense, reading a David Foster Wallace novel, short story, or essay is tantamount to learning the "rules" of his game, yet once the reader learns those rules his texts succeed in creating a special, surprisingly intimate zone of communication, of subjective interaction, that is unlike anything else in contemporary literature.

Since *Infinite Jest*, a whole new group of emerging young writers has copied the elusive Wallace "tone," that paradoxical blending of cynicism and naïveté, as well as Wallace's use of self-reflexivity for the purposes of moving beyond irony and parody. The most visible and successful writer of this group is the young essayist Dave Eggers, whose memoir *A Heartbreaking Work of Staggering Genius,* shot to number one on the nonfiction bestseller list and helped transform his underground literary magazine, *McSweeney's* (to which Wallace has frequently contributed) into the flagship publication of a growing publishing imprint specializing in funny, heartbreaking "post-postmodern" works such as *The Neil Pollack Anthology of American Literature*. Similarly, Jonathan Franzen, a close acquaintance and friendly rival (Wallace and Franzen have contributed blurbs to each other's books), freely admitted that the publication and surprising success of *Infinite Jest* almost single-handedly jolted him out of a protracted period of doubt and depression and thereby inspired him to finish his runaway bestseller, *The Corrections*. From its ingenious blending of an almost Victorian interest in "character" to its up-to-the-minute cultural and aesthetic sophistication—a sophistication that is sharply reminiscent of Don DeLillo's *White Noise*—*The Corrections* stands as perhaps the most prestigious confirmation of Wallace's revolution in literary sensibility. Wallace's special innovations have been so formative for contemporary fiction that his biggest problem at this stage of his career is overcoming his own immense influence. Then again, any writer with the talent, discipline, and courage to produce a work as breathtaking as *Infinite Jest* is certainly up to the task.

# CHAPTER 2

# The Broom of the System

## Wittgenstein and the Rules of the Game

Wallace's first novel, *The Broom of the System,* tells the story of Lenore Stonecipher Beadsman, Jr., a twenty-five year-old switchboard operator and reluctant heir to a baby-food empire who undertakes a fruitless search for her great-grandmother, also named Lenore Stonecipher Beadsman, a ninety-year-old nursing-home deserter and former student of Ludwig Wittgenstein's. Aiding but not really abetting Lenore in this search is her lover, an overcompensatingly verbal magazine editor named Rick Vigorous, who helps Lenore through her ordeal principally by telling her fantastic stories. Published in 1987, the novel was set three years in the future, in an imaginative and slightly askew 1990s Ohio. Though in many ways a compendium of gags (some of which are laugh-out-loud funny), the novel is at once both a slapstick bildungsroman and a serious inquiry into language and its relationship to the observable world. More important, it uses the techniques of self-reflexive metafiction—that is, fiction that dramatizes its own status as fiction—to explore self-consciousness, solipsism, and signification writ large.

In this latter respect, it owes more to the great postmodernist novels of the 1960s and 1970s than to the "brat pack" novels—Bret Easton Ellis's *Less Than Zero* and Jay McInerney's *Bright Lights, Big City* being the principal two—with which it was originally linked. Few of the book's original reviewers failed to invoke such figures as John Barth, Thomas Pynchon, and

William Gaddis, all of whom Wallace himself has acknowledged as formative influences. Still, even in this early work, Wallace proves himself impatient with mere homage, for *The Broom of the System* does more than continue the work of its postmodern forebears: it also charts a bold next step beyond metafiction and self-reflexivity. The book uses the strategies and techniques of metafiction because these techniques undermine the "picture-theory" of language—that is, the theory that words name objects in the world, and that sentences are combinations of such names.[1] Rather, metafiction emphasizes the chasm that separates fictional conventions from the "real world" to which they refer. At the same time, Wallace is uneasy with the way earlier metafictional works of his forebears tended to create hermetic, enclosed, and self-referencing fictional structures that alienated readers. Instead, he uses these same conventions—all of which have the shared quality of being "honest" about their status as conventions—to propose an *open* system of communication. In place of alienating self-reflexivity, the book proposes a communal approach to communication (note the shared root words), one that operates not between word and object, or Self and Other, but between two equal and interactive participants, a dynamic carried over onto the novel's relationship with its own reader. The book also updates Thomas Pynchon's exploration of entropy—both thermodynamic and informational—in such a way that this proposed "open" system emerges as the most viable model by which to combat not only solipsism and loneliness but also the "death of the novel," as outlined by Pynchon's postmodern partner, John Barth.

This is a weighty agenda, to be sure, yet Wallace manages to pull it all together via the novel's simultaneously learned and entertaining allusions to the great Cambridge philosopher

Ludwig Wittgenstein, whose presence can be felt everywhere in the book. The title itself is a complex allusion to Wittgenstein. At first glance it looks like a play on the phrase deus ex machina, which means "god from the machine" and refers to the moment in a play when an unanticipated agent intervenes in the plot. In this novel, Wittgenstein is that intervening agent. Significantly, he never actually appears but is rather "represented" by one of his students, Lenore Stonecipher Beadsman, the protagonist's great-grandmother, who, of course, starts the machinery of the plot by disappearing. Among the things the grandmother takes with her is her beloved copy of Wittgenstein's late masterpiece, *The Philosophical Investigations,* a book that seeks to demonstrate the almost unlimited influence of language in our everyday life. Rick Vigorous, Lenore's lover, uncharitably describes Wittgenstein as a "crackpot genius . . . who believed that everything was words," and yet he is not entirely wrong, nor is he off the mark when he characterizes Lenore Sr.—called by her great-granddaughter "Gramma"—as someone "obsessed with words."[2] Indeed, words were the obsessive preoccupation of Wittgenstein's life-work, and they are also the primary focus of Wallace's first novel. Rick Vigorous accuses Gramma Beadsman of teasing Lenore Jr. "with a certain strange book, the way an exceptionally cruel child might tease an animal with a bit of food, intimating that the book has some special significance" (73). This "strange book" is Wittgenstein's *Philosophical Investigations,* and it has more than "some special significance" for Lenore: it is also the key to understanding Wallace's audacious first novel.

Wittgenstein published only one book in his lifetime, a brief but important text titled *Tractatus Logico-Philosphicus* (1921).

This compact treatise—broken up, like most of his completed work, into short, numbered aphorisms—seeks to reduce language to its core and thereby locate the irreducible constituent parts upon which all communication is based. From the moment it first appeared, the *Tractatus* was an instant sensation in philosophical circles—it is generally cited by critics as the central inspiration for the philosophical school called "logical positivism"—and yet Wittgenstein remained unsatisfied with the work, going so far as to give up philosophical work for nearly a decade. Unexpectedly he returned to teaching in the late 1920s and kept at it until his death in 1951. In tortuously deliberate classroom discussions with student/disciples (one of whom, Wallace would have us believe, was Gramma Beadsman herself) Wittgenstein radically altered his view of language, as well as his approach to analyzing the subject. The gist of these classroom discussions was distilled into his second philosophical work, *The Philosophical Investigations,* published posthumously in 1953.[3]

In this latter book, Wittgenstein affirms that his earlier method was too simplistic, that perhaps it was a mistake to believe that the bewildering heterogeneity of language could be pared down to some irreducible core, some minute and indivisible atomic structure. Instead, he argued, the multiple aspects of language might best be imagined as a "complicated network of similarities overlapping and criss-crossing: sometimes overall similarities, sometimes similarities of detail." Wittgenstein famously compared these similarities to "family resemblances": members of a family may look and act alike, but not because they share some common denominator—a single trait, for instance, or a single, common ancestor. Similarly, a language is not built around some core or essence nestled in its interior like a peach pit. Rather, all the uses of language are linked the same way continuously overlapping fibers form a thread.[4]

Early in the *Investigations* Wittgenstein proclaims that there is no way to get at the essence of language except by means of language. That is why he declares that philosophers concerned with language "must do away with all *explanations,* and description alone must take its place." "Explanations" fall victim to the illusion that we can determine a "meaning" separate from the language we are using—the money that helps us buy the cow, as he puts it—whereas Wittgenstein argues that most philosophical problems arise from a misunderstanding about language, usually a misunderstanding predicated on the word-object illusion. Instead he proposes that we cease thinking of words as having meanings in and of themselves and begin to conceive of them as having functions in various real-life situations, which he liked to call "games." The meaning of a word is therefore determined by its use in a given situation, say, a sentence.

For instance, how does one teach a child the concept of the number five? Though you can point to five apples—this is Wittgenstein's example—there is no way to ensure that the child understands that the word "five" means the number of objects and not the objects themselves. Perhaps the child takes "five" to mean "red" or "round." The only way the child will grasp the concept—and almost every child eventually does—is if she already understands the surrounding language situation in which the demonstration takes place. In short, she has now understood the function, rather than the meaning, of the word "five," which designates the number of objects. Similarly, the function of the word "red" is to designate the color, while the function of the word "apple" is to designate the kind of fruit.

In order for someone—a reader, say—to grasp the manner in which a word is being used, that person must know the "rules of the game" being played. Grammar is one component, but so is the real-life situation in which the sentence is being uttered, plus the sociohistorical moment, the country, and so on. Further, language can *mean* only when the rules are agreed upon by more than one person. Or, as Wallace himself put the case in a recent essay on usage published in *Harper's* magazine, "A word like *pain* only means what it does for me because of the way the community I'm part of has tacitly agreed to use *pain*."[5] Language cannot be separated from the real world in which it is used, for it is inextricably bound up with what Wittgenstein calls "the forms of life." And without a "community" in which the rules are generally known, there can be no meaning, no communication at all.

Wallace uses Wittgenstein's elegant model to escape from what he regards as the dead end of postmodern self-reflexivity, particularly as practiced by John Barth. (Wallace would later devote the bulk of his second major a work, the novella "Westward the Course of Empire Takes Its Way," to a sustained critique of John Barth's theories about the function of literature in the postmodern era.) As numerous critics have already shown—Charles Harris chief among them—Barth's approach to language in such works as *Lost in the Funhouse, Chimera,* and *LETTERS*—all of which have exerted a formidable influence on Wallace—borrows much from the continental poststructuralists, chiefly the deconstructionist philosopher Jacques Derrida and the psychoanalytic theorist Jacques Lacan.[6] Like these thinkers—and much like Wittgenstein—Barth affirms that words—and, for that matter, novels as well—have no direct connection to the objects they would ostensibly name. Rather, in Barth's view, language always *replaces* the reality that it seeks to articulate. But since the words on the page do not point directly to a stable reality, how then do they achieve their meaning? Somewhat like Wittgenstein and his theory of "function," Barth might argue that the words achieve their meaning by virtue of their proximity in the sentence to other words. To put it another way, language for Barth is inherently self-referential, which is to say it always refers back to itself rather than to the world.

Derrida is generally credited with popularizing this latter theory of language. His most direct description of this idea can be found in an essay titled "*Différance,*" the title of which refers to a complex term Derrida coined to encompass the multiple ways in which language achieves meaning. As Derrida puts it, "The signified concept is never present in and of itself, in a sufficient presence that would refer only to itself. Essentially and lawfully, every concept is inscribed in a chain or in a system within which it refers to the other, to other concepts, by means of the systematic play of differences."[7] Because the words in a sentence have no direct relationship to the things to which they refer (Derrida's "signified concept"), they achieve meaning only by interacting one with another in an ongoing system of contrast, one word with the other. The "world" has been shut out from the sentence, which is now wholly self-referencing. A similar line of argument supports Barth's metafictional strategies. By insistently calling attention to what he is doing even as he does it, Barth foregrounds the artificial means by which literature creates an illusion of reality; as such, he acknowledges the unbreachable gap between text and world—or, to use Derrida's terminology, between signifier and signified concept.

In making this same acknowledgment, however, Barth also dramatizes two paralyzing problems for the contemporary writer. The first involves the writer's function, which is to depict "reality" in language, a tool that by its very nature alienates us from reality. And to be sure, Barth's heroes—many of them writers themselves—*are* often alienated. His metafictional strategies serve both as badges of honesty (I am declaring right up front that I am under no illusions about the supposed "reality" of fictional worlds) and as declarations of despair (This is futile, reader; we're just playing with words). The second problem involves Barth's historical situation. Having declared that language is ultimately self-referential, Barth has also affirmed that novels themselves, because they do not refer directly to a knowable reality, unavoidably refer instead to other novels. This latter idea directly informs his essay "The Literature of Exhaustion," discussed at greater length in chapter 1. Briefly, Barth argues that all the advances in novelistic technique introduced by the modernist masters—from stream-of-consciousness to spatial form—were originally designed to provide a more accurate access to reality. Now that "reality" is understood to be nothing more than a construct of language. Since all literary conventions have been "exhausted" from overuse and have been undermined by recent theories concerning the relationship between language and the world, the postmodern novel would employ literary conventions self-consciously, thereby warding off the "death of the novel" by writing novels that dramatize that death. The end result would be a fiction that overcomes exhaustion by dramatizing it. Or, as Barth explains, "An artist may paradoxically turn the felt ultimacies of our time into material and means for his work—paradoxically, because by doing so he transcends what had appeared to be his refutation, in the same way that the mystic who transcends finitude is said to be enabled to live, spiritually and physically, in the finite world."[8]

There would seem to be no way out of this series of dilemmas, a distressing prospect for a writer like David Foster Wallace to confront, coming, as he does, after Barth, after the only marginally postponed death of the novel. And yet Wallace has found a way out, and Wittgenstein has shown him the way. For Wallace does not wish simply to "overcome" Barth, to dispense with his theories and return to the good old days of uncomplicated "realism." Much of what Barth says—about the inherent artificiality of literary devices, about the self-referencing web that language creates over the reality it would seek to illuminate —has profound merit for Wallace. And Wittgenstein, Wallace's guide, agrees with Barth in many respects. In Wittgenstein, for instance, the meaning of a word is not the "thing" it refers to but rather its function in the language-game of which it is a part. Similarly, in Barth's Derridean concept of language, meaning in a sentence is generated not by the correspondence of words to their referents but rather by what Derrida calls "the play" of possible meanings along the "chain of signifiers": meaning, ambiguous and unstable, flickers in the spaces between the words in the sentences.

Nevertheless, even here we come upon the crucial difference between Barth's poststructuralist vision of language and Wallace's Wittgensteinian one, and the difference lies in the terms "game" and "play." A language-game in Wittgenstein must be played by more than one participant, whereas "play" in Derrida is a dynamic property of language itself. If signs could be shone to correspond directly to their referents in the outside world, then we would have no trouble determining the meaning of a sentence or a paragraph, since we would merely need to know the "things" to which all the words in the text refer. Conversely, Derrida argues that there is no way to shut down the play of meanings along the chain of signifiers, because meaning is not grounded in a stable outside reality but rather generated by the interaction of the signs themselves, wherein a dizzying (Derrida would say "infinite") number of possible interacting combinations can be detected, brought out, interpreted. Signs also carry with them "trace" elements of unintended meanings and defining oppositions, of past texts and ideological underpinnings, all of which increase the text's potential for play. Amid all this multiplicity and fecundity, however, the one thing that is lost is the world itself: rather, the text displaces the outside world in exchange for the self-referential universe of signs. For all its dynamic energy and instability, the text in Derrida's vision remains always shut off and alienated, helplessly incapable of saying what it intends or of intending what it says.

Wittgenstein—if he were he alive now to address Derrida directly—might object that language is not a "chain" but rather "as much a part of our natural history as walking, eating, drinking, playing." Our primary, even primitive relations to one another give rise to the game of language, and this game involves, as critic Michael Weston puts it, "a shared, or sharable, way of taking certain expressions, which *consists* partly in agreeing as to the *truth* of a certain range of judgments." These shared ways of taking expressions represent the rules of the game, and the rules are justified by their results. One can, in Wittgenstein, arrive at a final justification for the meaning of some expression, but only through an exhaustion of the possible available justifications; this final justification, however, is not a center or an essence but merely a provisional end for that particular rule. The point here is that for Wittgenstein, language does not displace us from the world but rather takes place "in" that world, specifically among people in language-game situations. Far from alienating us from others, language can only exist as a product of communal agreement between others.[9]

Hence, for Wallace, the job of the post-*Barth* novelist is to honor the master's insight into the inherent artificiality of novelistic conventions but to overturn the related insistence that texts are "closed systems" that produce their own meaning through endless self-reference. Rather, the self-conscious metafictional novel, in David Foster Wallace's hands, becomes an open system of communication—an elaborate and entertaining game—between author and reader.

Because *The Broom of the System* is first and foremost a work of metafiction, it is fitting that the protagonist, Lenore Stonecipher Beadsman, suspects that she is less a person in the world than a construct of language. In this respect she recalls other famous protagonists from the metafictional canon, including Barth's Ambrose Mensch (*Lost in the Funhouse*), Pynchon's Tyrone Slothrop (*Gravity's Rainbow*), and any number of Vladimir Nabokov's magnificently mad heroes and humberts. "To the extent that she understands herself," Rick Vigorous explains at one point, "it's as having a literary sensibility" (259). In numerous comic conversations with her "psychiatrist," a genuine crackpot named Dr. Jay, she explains that she probably acquired this sensibility from her great-grandmother, the Wittgensteinian, who told her "really convincingly that all that really exists of [her] life is what can be said about it" (119).

Unfortunately, this insight, if true, also implies for Lenore that her life is absolutely no different from that of a fictional character in a story, since a character in a story also consists of "exactly what's said about her. . . . Nothing more at all. And same with me, seems like" (119). Just as a fictional character acts according to the needs of the story, so, too, does Lenore sense that everything she does has "some sort of . . . function beyond herself" (66). The word "function" clearly tells us we are in Wittgensteinian territory, as does the narrator's explanation elsewhere that this floating conviction is much different from that of a Calvinist, who can assign final responsibility for all action to "something objective, impersonal"—that is, God. Lenore simply feels "as if she had no real existence, except for what she said and did and perceived and et cetera, and that these were . . . not really under her control" (66). What does control these things are the various language-games that give them meaning—which, here, is the same thing as an assigned function —since, as Gramma Beadsman would say, "any telling automatically becomes a kind of system, that controls everybody involved" (122).

So Lenore is "controlled" from without by the language-games she inhabits, like it or not. But she is also, both literally and figuratively, controlled by her Gramma Beadsman, who, we learn late in the novel, has actually been living underneath the very building where Lenore works (see 455–57). Notwithstanding Lenore's insistence that her paranoia is "not a plot thing" (66), Gramma is, in fact, the ghost of this book's plot machinery,—that is, the broom of the system—for not only does she inaugurate the narrative by mysteriously disappearing, but she also keeps it going by living, ghostlike, in the telephone tunnels that wind confusingly beneath the Bombardini building. Her influence reaches even further than that, because, with the help of her former neighbor at the Shaker Heights Home, Mrs. Yingst, she is also using Dr. Jay and Lenore's own father, Stonecipher Sr., to further her elaborate plans (see 309–11). Indeed, nearly every major plot development in the novel eventually points back to her.

Yet inasmuch as Gramma is the novel's deus ex machina, she is also the monkey wrench in the complex machinery of Lenore Jr.'s identity. As Rick explains, in addition to suspecting that she has no control over her life, Lenore also suffers from "feelings of disorientation and identity-confusion" (61), and these feelings, like her sense of being controlled from without, are once again attributable to Gramma. It is hardly accidental, for instance, that the two women share the same name. Lenore's identity problems stem from the fact that her name, the foremost signifier of who she is, points to someone else. All of this goes a long way toward explaining why Lenore, an abnormally bright young woman gifted with "a quality that attracts men" (72), works at a menial job far beneath her intellectual abilities and settles for a largely one-sided relationship with a lover, Rick Vigorous, who is neurotic, needy, overbearing, insecure, not to mention both sexually and emotionally inadequate. Lenore does not know what to do with herself; she does not know, to use Wittgenstein's term, what her *function* should be, largely because she feels her primary function has already been preempted by Gramma Beadsman. Lenore's brother LaVache also regards Gramma as the source of Lenore's problems, telling her, "You're the one on whom the real brunt of the evil . . . of this family has fallen. Evil," he goes on to clarify, "in the form of these little indoctrination sessions with Lenore" (248). By disappearing, Gramma removes the outside "other" against whom Lenore has been defining herself and thereby clears the way for Lenore to take possession of both her name and her identity.

Conversely, most members of the Beadsman family assume Gramma leaves because she feels "useless . . . as if she had no function, over there, in the nursing home" (15). Given her adherence to Wittgenstein's language theory, this interpretation makes sense, for, by Gramma's own reasoning, a life without use is a life without meaning.[10] In this sense, Gramma makes herself *useful* by disappearing, and the person who benefits most from this act is Lenore. Even more important, Gramma can also correct an error Lenore has been making all along, chiefly of imagining the meaning of her name, and hence her life, as founded on outside referents rather than on its own function within a system. Now that false referent is gone, and in the absence thereby created Lenore encounters what Gramma has been leading her toward all along: the wide-open space of Wittgenstein's language-game, where meaning is achieved through functional and constructive interaction with others rather than through the referential connecting of words to their objects.

The Great Ohio Desert, in addition to being one of the Wallace's more inspired comic inventions, also embodies the novel's dim view of referent-based signification. Designed and built by a company called "Industrial Desert Design," the Great Ohio Desert consists of a hundred miles of scorching black sand—a void, in other words. Raymond Zusats, the then governor of Ohio who spearheads the project, sees the desert as a necessary "point of savage reference for the good people of Ohio. A place to fear and love. A blasted region. . . . An Other for Ohio's Self" (54). Significantly, most of the characters refer to the Great Ohio Desert by its initials, G.O.D. Here Wallace seems to be poking fun at what Derrida would call a *logocentric* view of language, or what we might more usefully call "referent-based signification." *Webster's Tenth New Collegiate Dictionary* defines "Logos" as "the divine wisdom manifest in the creation, government, and redemption of the world and often identified with the second person of the Trinity"—that is, Jesus. In most English translations of the Bible, Logos is typically translated as

"The Word," as in the famous preamble to the Gospel of John, which reads, "In the beginning was the Word, and the Word was with God, and the Word was God." God is the creator of all things, so all created things ultimately have him as their referent and ground: the Logos, then, is the ultimate referent point for all meaning, the transcendental signified, the broom of the universal system, and logocentrism is the view that linguistic systems have at their center some core, indivisible object of reference on which their meaning is based. In this novel, however, the Logos is a vast void, an emptiness—literally a desert.

Again, Wallace emphasizes this essential point through Lenore and Gramma's shared name. In our waking life, we generally assume that proper names "mean" the persons to which they refer, yet Wittgenstein, throughout the *Investigations,* demonstrates why this cannot be so. A person's name, he argues, does not "mean" that person. Otherwise, a name would lose its meaning the moment the bearer of that name died, and clearly this is not the case, since we continue to *use* the name to refer to that dead person.[11] Lenore's name can refer to both her and Gramma; its meaning is defined not by its referent but by its context; that is, by its use within a particular language-game. Take, for example, the nonexistent psychiatric theorist, Olaf Blentner, whom Lenore's psychiatrist Dr. Jay cites as the pioneer of his so-called "hygiene anxiety" theory. When Dr. Jay, who is being retained by Gramma Beadsman to aid her in her plot, tells her spokesperson Mrs. Yingst that he can no longer sustain the Blentner fiction (largely because Rick is "going to want to read something by Blentner. He's a reader. He's going to want to lay eyes on Blentner's actual texts"), Mrs. Yingst blithely tells Jay, "There can be a Blentner if you want there to be, if you need there to be" (311). How so? Simple: all Jay has to do is "make up something and attach a name to it" (311). The fact that there is no actual "Blentner" in the world of real things is entirely irrelevant. Because the name "Blentner" possesses meaning so long as it maintains a viable function within a game—the game here being Jay's sessions with Lenore and Rick—a Blentner "text," spurious though it may be, can only enhance that function. Similarly, when Gramma disappears, Lenore begins to understand Wittgenstein's crucial insight that the meaning of her name does not depend on the existence of some stable outside referent—here, the great-grandmother—but rather on its own volition within a system of relations.

And what a richly suggestive name it is. In a letter to Lance Olsen, the author of the only sustained critical article on *The Broom of the System,* Wallace reveals that Gramma is based on a former Smith College professor named Alice Ambrose who actually *had* been one of Wittgenstein's students.[12] In Marshall McLuhan's *Gutenberg Galaxy,* moreover, we are reminded of that memorable moment in St. Augustine's *Confessions* (a book also cited significantly by Wittgenstein in the *Investigations*) in which the narrator, stunned and amazed, first sees St. Ambrose reading *silently.* Lenore Sr. is therefore modeled after someone who was not only Wittgenstein's actual student but also connected with the historical figure first associated with the silent reading.[13] What's more, that bewildering middle name, Stonecipher, suggests an elusive, secret message carved in stone. A cipher, for instance, is the secret part of an encrypted message, where alternate letters, words, numbers, or other signs stand for the plain-text alphabet. It is a message that can signify only for those people who know the rules of the game—that is, the formula that unlocks the cipher. Still, no message in Wallace's novel can be carved in stone, for meaning is fluid, a product of function rather than one-to-one correspondence with a referent. So clearly Lenore's name—and hence her identity, her function in the world—is an elaborate, fluid "cipher" that she must decode: all she needs to do is determine the rules of the game and locate the proper partners with whom to play it.

Unfortunately, for most of the novel one of those partners is her lover, Rick Vigorous, whose name translates essentially into "overactive penis" (Rick=Richard=Dick). This name is painfully ironic, for, among his many problems, Vigorous is seriously underendowed in the area of sexual apparatus. Like Lenore, Rick also mistakenly clings to the word-object conception of language. A "man of letters," according to Dr. Jay (356), Rick seeks to fill with *words* the enormous gap left by his small penis. "Damned if you're not the most articulate little rooster I ever heard crow," observes Andrew "Wang-Dang" Lang, and he is right: Vigorous is tirelessly, hysterically articulate, the one figure in the novel through whom Wallace exhibits the full range of his astonishing syntactical dexterity. Vigorous also provides Wallace with a means by which to parody the patriarchal conflation of the penis and the pen, a symbolic gesture that Rick takes literally. "Rick wants to *talk* all the time," complains Dr. Jay. "Talk talk talk. Tell tell tell" (120). Instead of making love to Lenore, he tells her stories, long entertaining stories in which he tries, through the transforming power of fiction (the power of his pen), to reconfigure the reality of their doomed relationship. All his stories are basically retellings of their love affair. Ultimately, he wants to confine words to their objects, for in this way he hopes to control the objects themselves. "Meaning exactly what?" he asks Lenore at one point, the implication being: meaning should be exact, should be referential (285). Language for Vigorous is not a Wittgensteinian game played by equal partners; it is a weapon of control, and the person he most wants to control is Lenore.

A single example of Rick's stories should suffice to show how he uses his "pen" to redirect Lenore's affections. One of the more memorable pieces involves a man who lacks the "love-discrimination mechanism," which would allow him to "decide whom and on the basis of what criteria to love" (183). As a result, he falls instantly and head-over-heels for every woman he meets. On the advice of his therapist, this man begins a friendship with a conspicuously unattractive woman holding a Thermos and wearing "Coke-bottle glasses" and a thick scarf around her neck. We soon learn that the Thermos woman—so named—hails from an "unspecified area in Eastern Europe, in which area the people have always stood in really ambiguous relations to the world outside them, and that the area's families were internally fiercely loyal, and their members were intimately and thoroughly connected with one another" (189). We also learn that one of the ways these Eastern Europeans maintain their family loyalty is for each member to keep a tiny animal living in his/her neck. The woman's tiny animal, it turns out, is a tree toad. This tree toad is "the thing that has kept the Thermos woman from connecting emotionally with the world outside her" (187), and after revealing her secret to the man she finds that she no longer wants to be so unconnected. The result is that "the very thing that has made the woman unconnected when she wants to be connected and so has made her extremely unhappy is also the center of her life, a thing she cares a lot about, and is even, in certain ways the man can't quite comprehend, proud of" (188). Confused about what to do, the woman throws herself in front of the subway, and the man ends up serving as caretaker for the toad.

Although Rick insists that all of the stories he tells Lenore actually come to him as unsolicited submissions at the *Frequent Review,* a literary quarterly he edits, in fact, he simply makes them up. The man with the overcharged "love-mechanism" and the faulty "love-discrimination mechanism" is clearly a fictional version of himself, while the Thermos woman, with her dysfunctional yet insular family, is Lenore. The therapist is Dr. Jay, of whom both Rick and Lenore are patients. (Not surprisingly, all of Rick's stories involve a couple and a therapist.) The story, then, is Rick's way of suggesting to Lenore that one of the "things" keeping her from giving herself entirely to him is her confused loyalty to her family, particularly her great-grandmother, the "tree toad" living like a vampire on Lenore's neck. Lenore has made Gramma "the center of her life" when in fact she should make Rick that center. If not, he implies, tragedy will result.

But just as no cipher can be carved in stone, so can there never be one simple interpretation of a story, and this piece, like all of Rick's stories, carries second-order significance as well. Rick is wrong in wanting Lenore to make him his "center," for, as the story clearly demonstrates, *any* time we make something outside ourselves the center of our existence, we are not connecting. Lenore is, for him, "the object of [his] adoration and the complete reference and telos of every action of [his] whole life," and yet Dr. Jay calmly reminds him that "an object and reference are intrinsically and eternally Other" (347). So no matter how much he wants to make Lenore *his* center (and vice versa), he will fail for the simple fact that Lenore, too, must always remain eternally Other. Nevertheless, he continues to pursue his great ambition, specifically through the medium of language, which he still imagines operates according to the word-object dynamic: by "writing" Lenore with his pen/penis, he and his object can become one. Knowingly or not, he discloses this very hope in the pseudonym he uses for those of his stories he actually writes down with his pen: Monroe Field-binder. As Fieldbinder, Rick can cast himself as one who *binds* the world to his word, who controls the *field* of play. For even Gramma admits that "any telling automatically becomes a kind of system"—a field of play—"that controls everybody involved" (122). What Rick does not want to admit is Gramma's related assertion that "the telling makes its own reasons." Rather, he wants to control the meaning, and the only way to do that is to bind words to their objects. In short, to *objectify*.

Throughout the novel Wallace freely puns on the word "object," which denotes not only a referent in a logocentric vision of language but also an inanimate thing. In *The Broom of the System,* the two meanings are never very far apart. Whenever the characters invest meaning in things—that is, in referents rather than in the interactive production of functional signification—they inevitably succumb to loneliness and solipsism. We have already seen how the Thermos woman in Rick's story makes the tree toad her center and referent and in the process undermines her ability to "connect emotionally with the world outside her" (187). Similarly, Mr. Bloemker, the director of Gramma's retirement home, conducts an entire conversation with Lenore in the company of a remarkably lifelike inflatable woman named Brenda, while Lenore's brother, LaVache Beadsman, who has renamed himself the Antichrist, creates a campus identity focused entirely around his artificial leg, in which he hides drugs acquired in exchange for research papers and test answers. "It's my thing," he explains to Lenore. "Everybody here has a thing" (239). Both the name change and the predominance of his artificial leg succeed in alienating LaVache from his family, who know him as Stoney. "Stoney reminds me I'm probably just a part in a machine I wish I wasn't part of. . . . As the Antichrist I have a thing, and it's gloriously clear where I leave off and others start" (250). Stoney grounds his Antichrist identity on its referent—the artificial leg, an object rather than a system of relations such as a family—with the result that he has quarantined himself from a complex web of responsibilities and relations. "No one expects me to be anything other than what I am," he concludes, "which is a waste-product, slaving endlessly to support his leg" (250). So if the Antichrist's referent-based identity succeeds in alienating him from his family, it is a pyrrhic victory in every other way, for it leaves him reduced to an inanimate object, a dead thing, a waste product. Similarly, Rick's referent-based love of Lenore transforms her into an object, a dead thing. As Lang explains to Lenore late in the novel, "R.V. sat there in that plane . . . and just flat out and told me you were *his* . . . Like you were his car, or a TV" (405).

Wallace also broadens this objectification motif to encompass a large-scale feminist critique of literary misogyny writ large. Two writers in particular seem to be targets here: John Updike and Vladimir Nabokov. The Nabokov critique is contained primarily in the overarticulated, purple-tinged Vigorous sections, which in many ways read like parodies of Nabokov's parodic prose. For example, there is this: "[Lenore's] lips are full and red and tend to wetness and do not ask but rather demand, in a pout of liquid silk, to be kissed. I kiss them often, I admit it, it is what I do, I am a kisser, and a kiss with Lenore is, if I may indulge a bit for a moment here, not so much a kiss as it is a dislocation, a removal and rude transportation of essence from self to lip, so that it is not so much two human bodies coming together and doing the usual things with their lips as it is two sets of lips spawned together and joined in kind from the beginning of post-Scarsdale time, achieving full ontological status only in subsequent union" and so on and so forth, for pages and pages. In passages such as this—and they are everywhere in *The Broom of the System*—Rick becomes a pale shadow of Nabokov's Humbert Humbert, transforming his fairly simple, objectifying lust into lilting, languorous language. Lenore's first name can even be glossed as an incomplete anagram for Dolores/Lolita, while Rick admits at one point to a decades-long obsession with his former thirteen-year-old nymphet neighbor, the "unbelievable undulating" Mindy Metalman, whose last name clearly identifies her as a human-turned-object (metal+man): "Heavy of necktie," Rick writes at one point, "I rise from the plume over baby Vance's crib to see Mindy Metalman, and yes perhaps two or three incidental neighborhood children around her, for decoration, doing her Circe dance around Rex Metalman's sprinkler" (373). Even the "decorative" neighborhood children—no nymphets they—sound a pitch-perfect Nabokovian note. Finally, during one of his characteristically unsettling arguments with Lenore, she pleads, "Stop trying to *pin* me, Rick. I feel like a butterfly on a board" (287), a clear allusion to Nabokov's lepidoptery.

The Updike parodies are largely confined to the Andrew Lang plot line; like the Nabokov allusions, they associate sexist objectification with the phallic conflation of pen with penis. Lang first appears as a drunk Amherst student, in the opening chapter, set in 1981. Fifteen-year old Lenore has gone to Mount Holyoke College to visit her sister, Clarice, her roommate Sue Shaw, and their dorm neighbor, the same Mindy Metalman of

Rick Vigorous's Nabakovian obsessions. For several hours the four women lie around, stoned, talking aimlessly but playfully, even toying with certain words—"blasphemous," for instance—in a spirit of Wittgensteinian play. All at once "Wang-Dang" Lang and his friend Biff Diggerence appear in the doorway with a forceful and threatening demand that the girls, as part of a fraternity hazing ritual, sign their bottoms (17). In so doing the women inscribe themselves not only as objects of the males' control but also as recipients of their excrement.

That Wallace wants us to associate this scene with Updike becomes clear when Lang reveals that his partner, Biff Diggerence, hails from Shillington, Pennsylvania, a remarkably small and insignificant suburb of Reading famous for one reason only: it is John Updike's hometown, the real-world model for the "Olinger" of the short stories and the "Mt. Judge" of the Rabbit tetralogy. Moreover, Updike's first novel, *The Poorhouse Fair,* was also set in the near future and featured an old folks' home, this one located not in Ohio but in yet another fictionalized version of Shillington. Finally, Lenore will later recall Biff Diggerence's "bottom, and his playing with Sue Shaw's hair" (411), an image that seems to have been lifted from a central moment in *Rabbit, Run,* where Rabbit asks his lover, Ruth, to fellate him.[14]

The most damning Updikean echo, however, is purely symbolic. Diggerence, Lang tells us, is incapable of vomiting, no matter how ill or bloated he might be, a physiological oddity that eventually results in his remaining henceforth alone in his room, "never seein' anybody, never talkin' to anybody. Just locked up in his room with the door locked" (410). Diggerence here dramatizes what Wallace regards as Updike's debilitating solipsism. Wallace has repeatedly faulted Updike for his narcissism and solipsism, most spectacularly in an extended parody of the Rabbit tetralogy that he published in a 1992 issue of *Harper's,* wherein he describes Rabbit's famed interiority as "a solipsist's heaven, full of his own dead perceptions," and, second, in a polemical attack on Updike's 1997 novel, *Toward the End of the Time,* in which he declares, "No U.S. novelist has mapped the solipsist's terrain better than John Updike, whose rise in the '60s and '70s established him as both chronicler and voice of probably the single most self-absorbed generation since Louis XIV." In both pieces, Wallace betrays his complex feelings about Updike and his influence on his own work. Declaring in the latter review that he is "probably classifiable as one of very few actual sub-40 Updike fans," Wallace nevertheless sees a direct correlation between Updike's preoccupation with his Self and the long-standing charge against Updike of misogyny. What's more, in his dismissal if *Toward the End of Time* he makes overt the same tacit argument that runs through *The Broom of the System,* namely that solipsistic, phallocentric writing of the sort Updike is alleged to practice corresponds directly to the (false) belief that the Western novel is heading toward exhaustion and death. "Mailer, Updike, Roth," he declares in the review's opening sentence, "the Great Male Narcissists who've dominated postwar realist fiction are now in their senescence, and it must seem to them no coincidence that the prospect of their own deaths appears backlit by the approaching millennium and on-line predictions of the death of the novel as we know it. When a solipsist dies, after all, everything goes with him."[15]

Lang, however, is the real brunt of the Updike critique, for it is he who marries the objectified Mindy Metalman, significantly the first of the four women in the dorm room to consent to the boys' demand. In an episode that viciously rewrites the opening of *Rabbit, Run,* Lang abruptly leaves Metalman because, as he puts it, "You've just run out of holes in your pretty body, and I've run out of things to stick in them" (176). Here we are meant to recall Rabbit's conflation of sex and sports, and specifically his description of "the high perfect hole" of the basketball rim with its "pretty skirt of net." Also like Updike's Rabbit, who, upon leaving his wife Janice, runs to his old basketball coach, Tothero, Lang runs first to *his* old high-school lacrosse coach, Zandagnio (269). Finally, when he explains to Vigorous, sometime later, that he left Mindy because, as he puts it, "To my mind there's just this temporary lack of wonderfulness about our whole relationship" (269), Wallace invites us to remember Rabbit's similarly worded explanation to the Reverend Eccles for leaving Janice: "I played first-rate basketball . . . and after you're first-rate at something, no matter what, it kind of takes the kick out of being second-rate. And that thing with Janice, well, boy was that second-rate."[16]

These two narrative lines—the Nabokovian and the Updikean, respectively—join together, not coincidentally, in a gay bar in Amherst called the Flange, where Rick Vigorous, on a visit with Lenore to his alma mater, happens to meet Andrew Lang, on a visit to same. They have both come to the Flange to see if their initials are still scrawled on the club's bathroom wall. The implications here are plain yet at the same time rich in interpretive resonance. Like Vigorous, Andrew "Wang-Dang" Lang is endowed with a name that firmly implicates him as a walking phallic symbol; also like Vigorous, he has scrawled a "cipher" of that name—that is, marked his territory—in a place reserved for depositing wastes. The pen/penis axis holds firm, as does the writing/fecal matter motif established in the novel's opening scene. This bathroom scene also foreshadows Lang's imminent role as Rick's rival for Lenore, specifically when Rick notices, with regret, that in the bathroom stall where he was sure he had left his initials he finds "instead of an R.V., a deep, wickedly sharp set of W.D.L., long since filled in with violet pen" (232). In effect, Lang here "erases" Rick as the primary inscriber of Lenore, who is present in the form of the "violet" ink, violet also being the color of a dress Lenore is wearing when Lang first meets her (see 12) and which later becomes a fetish object of both Lenore's roommate, the ever-available Candy Mandible (another humorous Wallace name) and Lang's estranged wife, Mindy (see 378–80). True to Eve Sedgwick's great insight in her book *Between Men,* Lenore is less the object of the two men's desire than a displaced byproduct of what is essentially a form of homoerotic competition.[17] Not surprisingly, Rick instantly asks Lang to return with him to Ohio, where they can work together, in secret, on a project hatched by Lenore's father that requires their "translating" into idiomatic Greek a pamphlet outlining the pineal-gland discovery made by Lenore Sr.

As if all of this were not clear enough, Rick has a dream that makes it all even clearer, a dream, moreover, that overtly establishes the fact that Rick sees his relationship with Lenore solely in terms of a word-object dynamic. Immediately after meeting Lang, he watches Lenore sleep and declares, "lying on her side, defined by the swell of a breast and the curve of a hip, she is an S," while in a fetal position she "becomes variously a question mark, a comma, a parenthesis," until finally, while "spread out before [him], open, wet, completely and rarely vulnerable . . . she is a V" (235). These observations come back to haunt him in his dream, in which he imagines himself sitting in an office with Lang, "the translation between us" (324). Both men are nude, thereby suggesting that the translation is none other than Lenore herself. Lang then begins an erotic drawing of Lenore on the back of one of Rick's Fieldbinder manuscripts —a story titled "Love," about which more anon—inspiring in Rick an unexpected erection. "Lang," Rick tells us, "sucks at the pen, periodically" (324). In a clear reference to Rick's own erotic penmanship, Lenore, in the drawing, is described as "a Vargas girl, a V" (324), whereupon Lang carves in his initials "in the side of Lenore's long, curving leg." Then an even stranger thing happens: as Lang's initials burrow deeper into Lenore's sketched leg, Lenore herself emerges, in three dimensions, from the page. Mindy reappears outside, jumping through the sprinkler, as Lenore begins initialing Lang's rear end, whereupon Vigorous, helplessly watching all this from behind his desk, begins to urinate in a "fan of uncountably many lines," leaving him "trapped behind [his] fan" (325).

Nothing particularly subtle is going on here, as Wallace very well knows. Indeed, the entire sequence is a playful parody of the Freudian dream. Yet it still signifies, it still tells us what we need to know. Dr. Jay even provides a reading for us, which we are not to dismiss out of hand, particularly since he is on retainer by the novel's deus ex machina. According to Jay, the fan of urine is clearly Rick's own blanket of words, all of them issuing from his pen and all of which ultimately keep him separate from Lenore, since she is reduced to a thing outside him. The initials that Lang scrawls on her two-dimensional legs Dr. Jay interprets as "his Self, his self, of which the initials are an elegantly transparent signal and flag" (344). Unlike Vigorous, Lang is here seen bringing "himself within" Lenore, rather than making her an object and referent point for his own self, and in so doing Lenore "becomes real, Rick. She becomes free" (344). And she, of course, reciprocates. Meanwhile Rick is left outside, watching, much as he did with Mindy Metalman, the objectified nymphet who, not surprisingly, reappears here. A solipsist and an objectifier of woman like Rick can never lend himself openly to a lover, as he also concedes. "I cannot possibly satisfy you," he tells Lenore. "We cannot unite. The Screen Door of Union is for me unenterable. All I can do is flail frantically at your outside. Only at your outside" (286). He lacks, as Dr. Jay explains, "the wherewithal to allow that Other to be a Self" (347). Therefore he can do little else than "soil" his beloved. "From the Outside," Dr. Jay concludes, "you can influence only by soiling, dirtying" (345).

But what of Lang, the novel's original soiler? Unexpectedly —and somewhat unconvincingly—Lang turns out to be a better person than Wallace initially wants us to believe. He is young, for one thing, and, as Bloemker points out, the young are in a much better position to change for the simple reason that the young have a more elastic relationship to the past than do the old. "As people age," Bloemker argues, ". . . their sense of history tightens, narrows, becomes more personal . . . Objective events and data become naturally more and more subjectively colored" (369). Lang, however, is young and thus open to change. And one of the events he definitely wants to change is his initial encounter with Lenore. He wants, according to his wife, Mindy, "to go back to a branch in the tree of his life, the branch nine years ago . . . and just take a different path from the same branch" (381). In short, he sees "in this Lenore person a chance to change the past" (381).

In many respects he succeeds. Essentially, Lang functions as Rick's negative double, the Wang-Dang Lang to his Vigorous Rick. Rick is physically inadequate, while Lang is fully-fleshed and complete. Rick is incapable of union, while Lang is a regular cocksman of the first order. He is, as Rick laments, a veritable catalogue of desirable features and, therefore, "features-love-deserving" (288). But Rick's sense of Lang's appeal is typically object oriented, based solely on "features and qualities"—things, in other words—none of which have managed to impress Lenore thus far. Rather, Lenore suggests a "reversal" concept of attraction to which Lang eventually measures up. "It's not that you love the person because of certain things about the person anymore," Lenore explains; "it's that you love the things about the person because you love the person. It kind of radiates out instead of in" (287). Rick, with his object-centered vision of language and the world, is always already "outside" his beloved, whereas a lover who can communicate from a position of Self-to-Self rather than Self-to-Other can earn Lenore's "reverse" love. And that is what Lang, eventually, manages to do. In the only act of healthy lovemaking in the novel, Lenore and Lang lie in bed together, "cuddling," which, in contrast to Rick's in-bed storytelling (he tells, Lenore listens), involves both partners communicating back and forth, as two selves. During this same scene, Lang also admits that his "good old boy" persona is really a false front, a manifestation, his "thing" back at Amherst —much like the Antichrist's "thing"—and therefore as limiting and alienating as Rick's fan of urine. Here in bed with Lenore, however, as they cuddle, the front collapses.

Even Lang's name signals to us that he is Lenore's more suitable, "reverse" lover. His middle name, Sealander, suggests that he contains within him the possibility of genuine union, an ability to link up opposites, such as sea and land, male and female, self and other. The novel's recurring preoccupation with his initials also directs us to perhaps another secret cipher that Lenore—or, at least, the reader—is expected to decipher. In his good-old-boy persona he is W.D.L., the initials he superimposes over Rick's faint "R.V.," yet behind that persona he is A.S.L., for Andrew Sealander Lang. Interestingly, Lenore's initials are L.S.B. (Lenore Stonecipher Beadsman), which are almost a reverse mirror image of those of her reverse lover, the only difference being that Lang is an "A" to Lenore's "B." They form a nice yin-and-yang, an image that appears throughout the novel and which will be taken up at greater depth in the final section.

One thing more: Lang's success seems to have been anticipated and designed, in advance, by Gramma Beadsman. All the various coincidences of the plot serve both as playful metafictional emblems and as further evidence of Gramma's control. Gramma first designs the verbal-skills enhancing formula, then disappears. Next, Lenore's father (who also seems to be in on the "plot") hires Rick to compose three "product-information packages" detailing the wonders of the new product, requesting in the same contract that Rick first retain "some personnel familiar with the culture and language of the inhabitants of the island of Corfu" and, second, accompany Lenore to Amherst "for a trip to see her brother" (168–69). Once at Amherst, Rick just so happens to meet Lang, who also just so happens to be "intimately familiar with the culture and language of the inhabitants of the island of Corfu" and who is "furthermore as of now probably unemployed, and chafing for some sort of at least temporary change in [his] geographical, professional, and personal circumstances" (235). What is more, Lang's father built the G.O.D., this novel's primary symbol for the emptiness of logocentric thinking. If all of this is starting to sound like the plot of a Pynchon novel, then it should: Wallace is certainly paying homage here to one of his most decisive influences. Yet, once again, there is a difference. In Pynchon's work, the paranoid elements of the plot are always left unresolved at the end, thereby forcing the reader to choose between a paranoid reading (everything here is connected; some sort of conspiracy is at work) and an open-ended reading (none of this adds up; nothing is connected to anything). In this way, Pynchon calls attention to the artificiality of his textual world and also to the ways in which our experiences with texts might control the way we "read" lived experience. Wallace's plot is as self-consciously artificial as Pynchon's, but without the anxiety-producing ambiguity. There *is* a god in this machine, yet all she is trying to do is bring two people together.

Wallace also borrows Pynchon's interest in entropy. Entropy is a complex idea that, in both Pynchon and Wallace, has two primary applications, thermodynamic and informational. Perhaps Pynchon's most concise exploration of entropy can be found in his second novel, *The Crying of Lot 49,* a book that bears a number of striking similarities to *The Broom of the System:* in both novels, a young, female protagonist embarks on a search for someone missing, only to uncover a larger plot, the source of which remains elusive; both protagonists leave behind inadequate lovers and also seek solace in untrustworthy psychiatrists; and each novel connects its respective conspiracy motif to the concept of entropy, which, broadly defined, measures the amount of disorder within a closed system.[18] Typically, though, Wallace uses entropy in a slightly different way than does Pynchon, tying it once again to his Wittgensteinian argument about language-games and ambiguity and communication. By conceiving of the Self/Other dynamic as an inside/outside dialectic, Wallace links the science of open and closed systems to the themes of identity, community, and signification.

As we have seen, Rick Vigorous's referent-based thinking has trapped him in a lonely and alienated Self-Other dynamic from which he cannot escape, and yet, in various ways, all the major characters suffer from this same misconception about their place in the world and their unavoidable connectedness to others. LaVance "the Antichrist" Beadsman changes his name as well as the name of his telephone—he dubs it a "lymph node" —in order to avoid contact with his family, while the Thermos woman clings to her "tree toad" in order to hide from the outside world. In both cases the characters waver between identifying themselves as individuals and asserting their membership in a family. Perhaps taking his cue from Wittgenstein's famous "family resemblances" metaphor, Wallace carefully charts the way families both nurture identities and stifle growth. As Wittgenstein shows us, our connection with other members of our family does not hinge on a common denominator but rather represents a "complicated network of similarities overlapping and crisscrossing: sometimes overall similarities, sometimes similarities of detail." Problems arise when we become trapped in the illusion of a common denominator, yet another instance of logocentric thinking that ultimately leads to insularity and loneliness.

Lenore is both trapped by her identity within the family and also estranged from her brothers, her father, and most especially her mother, who has been languishing for decades in a psychiatric facility in Wisconsin. Lenore's sister, Clarice, has similar family issues of her own. In one of the novel's more heavy-handed satirical set pieces, Clarice and the rest of her family —all of them portrayed by Wallace as paradigm middle-class suburbanites—engage in an elaborate family-therapy ritual in which members don masks of their own faces and then reenact their shared problems before a television screen on which is projected a recorded tape of an audience. In the play, the members of the family declare that they all once thought of themselves "more as members of the family than as real people who were special individual people" (167). To combat this problem, the various members began "attaching themselves to things in the world, extrafamilial objects and pursuits" (169), a gesture that resulted in an even bigger problem since, as one of the children explains, "things couldn't be people, not even the people they belonged to" (170). So "they found that what they needed to get their feelings of being themselves from was themselves" (172), whereupon the members take off their masks and "[stare] deeply into the empty eyeholes of their own faces" (173). The episode plays out in miniature the novel's critique of logocentric thinking: like Lenore, the members of the family first look outside themselves to other family members for identity, a move that leads inexorably to the reduction of meaning to objects and objectification and concludes with empty solipsism.

The point here is that Wallace wants us to regard such solipsism as a "closed system," which, according to the Second Law of Thermodynamics, always tends toward disorder. Entropy is the measure of that disorder. In Wallace's world, the solipsism of the logocentric thinker is a closed system that always results in a symbolic sort of heat death, figured here as a gradual transformation of a living entity into an inanimate object. And because solipsists cannot recognize a larger system outside their own closed system, they try to combat this heat death—the ultimate form of psychic loneliness—by bringing *others* into their closed system. As Rick laments, "My inability to be truly inside of and surrounded by Lenore Beadsman arouses in me the purely natural reactive desire to have her inside of and contained by me" (72). Meanwhile, Norman Bombardini, the obscenely overweight financier and owner of the building where Lenore and Rick both work, undertakes Project Total Yang, developed in response to his unsuccessful experience with Weight Watchers. Weight Watchers, Bombardini explains, holds "as a descriptive axiom the transparently true fact that for each of us the universe is deeply and sharply and completely divided into for example in my case, me, on one side, and everything else, on the other" (90). Bombardini visualizes this Self-Other dynamic as a Yin and Yang. Weight Watchers seeks to cure obesity by convincing the overweight person that he or she simply needs "to have as much Other around as possible, so that the relation is one of minimum Self to maximum Other" (90–91). Bombardini rejects this solution in favor of its mirror opposite, namely to maximize Self by eating himself to infinite size. In this way he hopes to create universe of one, a closed system with nothing in it but his Self. And in a grisly reenactment of Rick's own veracious solipsism, Bombardini undertakes a campaign to ingest Lenore.

Even Dr. Jay's preposterous "hygiene anxiety theory" taps into this inside/outside motif. Though clearly a parody of psychoanalytical master-theories in general, the Blentner hygiene theory is also, in some ways, the novel's own master-key, a clear instance of Wallace using the discrete parts of his game in such a way that they function seriously in the larger game of the novel's total vision. As Dr. Jay explains, "Hygiene anxiety is identity anxiety" (120). The individual imagines his or her identity as a closed system, figured in Jay's term as an organism with a nonpermeable membrane. Any fear of the outside world *entering* through a fissure in that membrane is tantamount to worrying about the hygiene of that membrane. A nonpermeable

membrane is a clean membrane. Dr. Jay uses this model to analyze, among other things, the significance of Lenore's obsession
with showers, which symbolize Lenore's fear of connecting with
others—or, in Dr. Jay's terminology, of opening her membrane
or entering the membrane of another. "What does the Outside
do?" Jay asks in another, but related, context. "It makes you
unclean. It coats Self with Other. It pokes at the membrane. And
if the membrane is what makes you you and the not-you not
you, what does that say about you, when the not-you begins to
poke through the membrane? . . . It makes you *insecure,* is what
it does" (136). So she showers away the outside and keeps her
Self clean and unsoiled.

He also uses hygiene theory to interpret all of Rick's
extraordinary anxiety dreams, including the one outlined above
involving Lang, Lenore, and the fan of urine. In that session, Jay
repeatedly returns to his theory to convey to Rick what one suspects Gramma has retained him to say all along: "Are you helping her? Are you concerned with her needs? Are you engaged in
the sort of discriminating, mature love that focuses primary
attention on the needs and interests of the beloved?" (342).
Clearly the answer is no, and to emphasize this point, Jay pulls
out all the stops in his hygiene arsenal, concluding his analysis
with this delightful yet insightful harangue: "Do we love an as
yet two-dimensional membrane enough to afford that membrane entry into validity, reality, three-dimensionality, to afford
it an escape from the very flattening context exclusively within
which the original love can be exercised and pseudo-recipro-
cated? Do we, recognizing our inability to enter and fertilize and
permeate and validate a membrane, an Other, let that Other out,
back outside, to a clean, odor-free place where she can find
fullness, fulfillment, realness?" (347). In non-Blentnerian jargon,

Rick sees Lenore as merely a flat, two-dimensional object outside himself that he cannot penetrate (figuratively and literally) and so wants to bring "inside" his own system through his logocentric language. Only as a Self, rather than as an Other, an Object, will Lenore find fulfillment, yet in granting her this status Rick must relinquish his control of her. He does not love truly, for true love is between a Self and a Self. In other words, let her go, Vigorous.

Similarly, Dr. Jay uses hygiene theory to analyze Lenore's various identity issues. Whereas Rick suffers from an inability to allow the Outside world to enter his membrane, Lenore operates under the opposing assumption that her "own natural desires and inclinations and attractions" are "somehow being directed at and forced on [her] from outside, from *Outside,*" which fear Jay predictably declares is "exhaustively reducible to and explainable in terms of membrane-theory" (330). In his diagnosis of her problem—and, again, we can feel the guiding hand of Gramma Beadsman here—Lenore needs to understand that all those same desires and attractions come from "inside her." By recognizing this fact, Lenore will be able to "withstand the onslaught of the countless Other-set, ceaselessly battering," for "the strong, clean membrane chooses what to suck inside itself and lets all the rest bounce dirtily off" (330). Jay goes on to propose a sperm-ovum model in which Lenore must recognize that she is made up both of her mother's ovum (a self-contained but permeable membrane) and her father's sperm (the outside Other battering its way in), all of which is tantamount to saying that her identity is a product of both nature and nurture, genes and environment, Inside and Outside.

In the end, Dr. Jay's "hygiene anxiety" jargon affirms a vision of "open systems" interacting one with another within the free space of an even larger open system, that of some encompassing human community. Although disorder might ensue from these fissures in our systems, the resulting increase in entropy is offset by the potential for more work via the interaction with other open systems. We succeed or fail insofar as we understand this essential trade off. "We are helpless and inefficacious as parts of a system," Jay concludes, "until we recognize the existence of the system" (333). Typically, Wallace conceives of this entropic disorder in linguistic terms; in so doing, he joins the thermodynamic conception of entropy to its more arcane application in the complex field of information theory. As a double philosophy and mathematics major at Amherst, Wallace might well be familiar with the work of mathematician Claude E. Shannon, the pioneer of information theory. Shannon adapts many of the mathematical formulas associated with thermodynamics to analyze language systems, all with an eye toward determining the total amount of disorder and redundancy in various linguistic structures. His formulas have proved invaluable to computer programmers, for example, who want to maximize the amount of information they can send through the limited space of an Ethernet connection, the size of which is determined by bandwidth. These same formulas have also shed valuable light on Wallace's intriguing conflation of Ludwig Wittgenstein and arcane science.

To understand how entropy functions in this communication theory, substitute discrete symbols, such as the words used to form this sentence, for the hot and cold molecules we usually associate with thermodynamics. To communicate, we must select symbols that effectively convey our idea. Entropy would measure the total amount of free choice we have in selecting these symbols, with "choice" here understood as "randomness" or disorder. Though it might seem counter-intuitive at first, Shannon demonstrates that higher entropy (randomness) results in greater information flow. Conversely, "redundancy" refers to those parts of the message that are not freely chosen but are rather predetermined by standard linguistic practice. These parts could presumably be eliminated from the message without any loss of essential information and so are "redundant" in the truest sense.[19]

In a perfectly successful linguistic utterance, one with maximum information flow, each word in the sentence would be so perfectly tailored to the idea being conveyed that the auditor could not reasonably predict the next word in the sentence: this inability to predict or anticipate where the message is heading serves as a marker of the message's high entropy, that is, its randomness. As one might say of an Emily Dickinson poem, every word counts. Yet redundancy, here understood as "predictability," is hardly without a purpose since it allows the auditor to fill in "gaps" and correct possible misunderstandings that might arise in the linguistic encounter. This explains why much of our verbal communication is awash in redundancy, for, unlike Emily Dickinson, we rarely say exactly what we mean with the absolute minimum of words. A computer programmer seeks to eliminate as much of this redundancy as possible so as to maximize the total amount of space used in the bandwidth, whereas in our daily communications we might *need* this redundancy to help our auditor understand what we are saying, particularly if that auditor is not familiar with the specialized vocabulary we are using, or does not have the leisure to sit down and carefully review the message, the way a reader of a Dickinson lyric might pore over every well-chosen word.

Wallace would surely recognize the possible connections between Shannon's theory of redundancy and Wittgenstein's attempt, in the *Tractatus,* to pare language down to what he called "elementary propositions," which are such because no other elementary proposition can contradict them. An elementary proposition is that core part of language that can not be broken up any longer into constituent parts and is therefore free of any redundancy. It is significant that Shannon's theories have been useful in the development of *mechanical* communications systems, such as computers, whereas Wittgenstein, in the *Investigations,* abandons his search for "elementary propositions" in view of the multifarious ambiguity of "language-games," which exist as "forms of life." Wallace seems to have something similar in mind in his own affirmation of communication disorder which, as in Wittgenstein, is a necessary product of vital human interaction.[20]

Once again, Dr. Jay's hygiene theory illustrates how the theory of communication entropy works in the novel. Early in the book Rick has a dream in which he stops at a hotel in dirty, dusty Mexico and encounters a mouse working as the concierge. The air conditioning is not working. When the mouse shows Rick his room, Rick remarks, "There are no sheets on this bed," to which the mouse responds, "Señor . . . if you sheet on my bed, I will kill you" (132). Dr. Jay predictably interprets the dream in hygiene jargon, seeing the broken air conditioner as symbolic of Rick's fear of the "Outside getting in." The net result of this puncture in Rick's insular sense of self is "communication breakdown" (136), which "again simply reinforces the idea of the hygiene-identity-distinction membrane being *permeable*—permeable via *uncleanness*—permeable via *misunderstanding*—which are ultimately, according to Blentner, not coherently distinguishable" (137). A break in the closed system causes disorder, that is, the potential for misunderstanding. At the same time, this potential for misunderstanding is also linked to *freedom* and multiplicity of meaning, whereas a closed system provides either order and no potential for work, or disorder and ultimate heat death.

This final model functions as the book's overarching guiding principle, for it points to a way out of Barth's argument for the literature of exhaustion. An exhausted literary tradition, in Wallace's terms, is a closed system—that is, entirely self-referential—one that, as Barth points out, inevitably tends toward heat death (exhaustion). Wallace would level the same charge at the solipsistic, self-obsessed work those "great male narcissists," John Updike, Norman Mailer, and Philip Roth. As Wallace argues, the work of these writers, so preoccupied with subjectivity and private experience—the Inside of things—must also obey the law of closed systems.

Surprisingly, none other than Rick Vigorous himself provides the clearest explanation of Wallace's counter theory. In the one Fieldbinder story we get to read in full, a couple learns that the lonely and private old man who lived next door had been sustaining for years an unseemly sexual obsession with their son, Steve. The story is about solipsism and fetishism—the old man collects such items as Steve's baseball cards and used Kleenex tissues—and yet it also dramatizes Wallace's own "open" system of self-reflexive literature. The story, Rick says, is "about neighborhood obsession," but it is also about how each "neighbor is shut away inside his own property, his house, surrounded by a fence" (336). The story only emerged when "the Private leaked out . . . and became Incident. And that perceived incident became Story" (336). A story comes alive when there is a puncture in the closed system; this puncture creates disorder, which here might be understood as conflict or drama. The larger implication is that the story gets transmitted to the reader, who is outside the story. Although the interaction of reader and text is a relationship fraught with ambiguity and misunderstanding, since there are so many choices for interpretation, it is nevertheless the vital energizing force that keeps the story alive. Interpretation is open and never complete, yet that is also the very source of its vitality.

Conversely, in "Westward the Course of Empire Takes Its Way" Wallace characterizes the "preceding generation of cripplingly self-conscious writers" as being "obsessed with their own interpretation," much the way Rick Vigorous is obsessed with controlling Lenore through the power of his pen.[21] In this way, Wallace associates solipsism and self-consciousness with Shannon's concept of "redundancy," which measures those parts of a message that are predetermined rather than freely chosen. Barth's crippling self-consciousness is a form of redundancy because it leads him to believe that any literary device he might choose has already been calcified and exhausted by overuse. The autobiographical preoccupations of Updike and Roth are equally redundant in the way they limit their choice of subject matter and restrict their interaction with the world outside the Self.

Gramma Beadsman, then, is not only the novel's deus ex machina but also its heroine, for her selfless gesture of disappearing models Wallace's own larger agenda for this novel: both Gramma and Wallace are seeking to restore vitality to a prematurely closed system. Gramma herself is an open system, for, as we are told early in the novel, she suffers from a physical oddity whereby she lacks "any kind of body thermometer" and must therefore depend "for her body's temperature on the temperature of the air around her" (39). That is why any room she lives in must be kept at precisely 98.6°. This fact also explains one of the novel's central mysteries: why the Bombardini Building switchboard system has broken down. Peter Abbott, the maintenance worker whose thankless job it is to fix the system, explains that the switchboard operates via a complex system of "tunnels" underneath the building. These tunnels, or phone lines, are "just basically lines of heat" (455). For the information passing through those tunnels to remain *ordered,* the temperature must be kept at sixty to sixty-five degrees: this temperature keeps the lines discrete and staves off the disorder that might result if the information were allowed to flow freely through the lines. "The upshot here," he explains near the end of the book, "is that your particular line tunnel looks likes it's kind of decided it's a real freakin' human being or something," because a series of diagnostic tests reveals that the tunnels are in fact at "a perfect ninety-eight point six" (457). In other words, Gramma Beadsman has been living underneath the building all this time—the deus ex machina is revealed at last—with a series of interesting results: communication has broken down in the system, and yet, as a result, Lenore is free of Rick Vigorous, not to mention her great-grandmother's limiting influence. The machine has been made human, the closed system has been opened.

Though the chapter in which all of this is revealed marks the novel's climax, Wallace is careful to cast the episode in the form of an elusive *anticlimax.* Gramma never appears, for instance—she might very well be dead down there—nor does anyone in the novel draw the (obvious) conclusion that she has been residing in the tunnels all along. All the major figures from the novel reappear, yet Wallace never actually pulls back the curtain to reveal Gramma as the real Wizard of Oz. As with a mathematical differential, we approach the zero point of the novel but never actually get there. The black arrows that head each new chapter division serve as emblems of this strategy: all movement tends toward the revelation of the god in the machine only to reveal that this same god or logos is a black void, like the Great Ohio Desert itself. Similarly, Wallace gives the final word in the novel to Rick Vigorous, and that word is "word," as in the *word* "word"—except that Rick never actually *says* the word. Rather, the final sentence reads: "'You can trust me,' R.V. says, watching her hand. 'I'm a man of my      '" The novel ends with a blank space. The system remains open.

Instead of comforting closure, then, we get a transcript of the Reverend Sykes's *Partners with God Club* cable television program, on which Lenore's cockatiel, Vlad the Impaler, has been spouting nonsense for dollars. Of course, Vlad the Impaler, being a cockatiel, has no idea what he's saying: he simply repeats what he hears without understanding or meaning a single word. None of this, however, stops Reverend Sykes from believing that the animal has been inspired directly by God himself. On the one hand, Sykes allows Wallace to poke easy fun at televangelists, the same way Dr. Jay provides him with an occasion to satirize the psychiatric profession. On the other hand, like Dr. Jay, Sykes also functions as a serious (albeit unwitting) spokesperson for Wallace's various themes. Sykes is certainly mistaken about Vlad's "inspiration," since we know, first, that the God of this novel is a black void and, second, that the real reason for Vlad's verbal dexterity lies in his having ingested Gramma Beadsman's pineal-gland-enhancing chemical. So he is free to believe (because it is profitable for him to do so) that the meaning of Vlad's words results from their having come directly from the capital-L Logos itself, but the fact remains that whatever sense Vlad's random outbursts manage to achieve comes from their accidental function within some larger context—and a context, in this novel, is the same thing as a system.

It is no accident, moreover, that the name of the Reverend's program is *Partners with God,* for partnership is what Wallace wants to establish between himself and his reader, an interactive relationship in the language-game of the text in which both parties remain open to each other. For although Rick Vigorous does get the last (unspoken) word in the novel, it is Reverend Sykes who ultimately speaks for Wallace himself. Rev. Sykes' final benediction can even be read as Wallace's final blessing on his reader: "Use me, friends. Let us play the game together. I promise that no player will feel alone. You see my hand? Here it is. I hold it out for you to touch. Touch it. Lay your hands in the soil and touch me. Here I am for you. Friends, I sense we are all ready tonight" (466). Everything is reprised here—the concept of the language "game," the strategy of metafictional self-consciousness (showing your hand), the penetration of closed systems and its resulting vitality, a call for partnership between reader and text. Though not without its flaws—a great deal of the humor is juvenile in the end, for instance, while the novel goes on a bit too long, as does most of Wallace's output—*The Broom of the System* stands as one of the more confident and audacious first novels in recent memory, an assessment that seems even more sound in view of what has followed in its wake. At the age of twenty-five, in his first attempt, Wallace managed not only to produce a rich, provocative, and entertaining work that established him as one of the leading talents of his generation, but also to set forth in a dramatically powerful way a full outline of his own unique and significant aesthetic agenda.

# CHAPTER 3

# *Girl with Curious Hair*

Inside and Outside the Set

Of his own experience as a devotee of popular culture, Wallace has said, "I think it's impossible to spend that many slack-jawed, spittle-chinned, formative hours in front of commercial art without internalizing the idea that one of the main goals of art is simply to *entertain,* to give pleasure." Then he adds, "Except to what end, this pleasure-giving?"[1] In *Girl with Curious Hair,* Wallace seeks to answer that second question. He proceeds from the assumption that the old dichotomy between pop and high art has now been successfully dissolved, thanks to the pioneering work of such postmodern forebears Thomas Pynchon, Donald Barthelme, and others. His job in these stories is to use pop culture not as an ironic lens or as a symptom of cultural decline but rather as a regenerative means of communication between himself and his readers. Far from being an exercise in self-satisfied irony and pop culture in-jokes—the very things that would come to characterize the so-called Generation X, of which Wallace is an uneasy member—*Girl with Curious Hair,* despite some of its faults, succeeds as a cogent and prophetic diagnosis of irony and its discontents.

Wallace is hardly the first postmodern writer to create fictional characters from living media figures. *Girl with Curious Hair* certainly owes a respectful debt to such trailblazing works as Robert Coover's *The Public Burning* (1977), a flamboyantly stylized retelling of the 1951 trial of "atom spies" Ethel and

Julius Rosenberg, as narrated by Richard Nixon, and Don DeLillo's *Libra* (1988), a fictionalized depiction of the assassination of John F. Kennedy told from the point of view of Lee Harvey Oswald. Similarly, by littering his work with up-to-the-minute pop culture references, Wallace places himself firmly in the milieu of such 1980s minimalists as Bret Easton Ellis and Bobbie Ann Mason. The book's particular innovation resides in the way it employs the philosophical premises underlying the work of Coover and DeLillo to critique both the postmodernism of those very same authors as well as the bleak and emaciated fictional worlds of Ellis and Mason. When Robert Coover makes Richard Nixon a fictional character and the Rosenberg trial a cartoonish spectacle with equal parts P. T. Barnum and Marvel Comics, he is making a by-now orthodox postmodern inquiry into the ways in which various ideologically interested discourses—Hollywood and comic books, for instance—get mistaken for "reality," here the "actual" trial of Julius and Ethel Rosenberg. The book tries to demonstrate how history is primarily a text, a constructed narrative that is less about truth than about the will to power. Conversely, Ellis and Mason, two darlings of the 1980s minimalist school, littered their anemic narratives of post-sixties ennui with up-to-the-minute pop culture artifacts in order to depict, in a more or less conventionally "realistic" way, the emptiness and superficiality of that same post-sixties world. Wallace's work takes the next step. He *parodies* the use of up-to-the-minute pop culture references in order to show that even *this* technique, really a late variation on the Coover and DeLillo strategy, is itself a construction, perhaps even a symptom of the very problem such work is trying to diagnose. In these stories, Wallace does not merely seek to call attention to the ways in which our immersion in pop culture and mediated narratives alienates us from reality; he also wants to show how it is actually our *awareness* of this immersion that alienates us.

A brief note included on the book's copyright page provides a helpful insight into Wallace's peculiar aims. The note, quoted in part, reads, "These stories are 100 percent fiction. Some of them project names of 'real' public figures onto made-up characters in made-up circumstances. Where the names of corporate, media, or political figures are used here, those names are meant only to denote figures, images, the stuff of collective dreams; they do not denote, or pretend private information about, actual 3–D persons, living, dead, or otherwise."[2]

The disclaimer's somewhat defensive tone might be attributed to the difficulty Wallace had in getting the book vetted for publication: apparently, several of these "corporate, media, or political figures" took issue with being turned into fictional entities, so much so that Wallace and his publisher were compelled to delay the book's publication while lawyers from both sides combed through the intricacies of copyright law. Yet the disclaimer is also a clue to how Wallace wants his readers to understand these "real" public figures: they are, in short, "the stuff of collective dreams." Pop culture is our new mythos, the source of our contemporary archetypes. This means, in turn, that "David Letterman" is both a real person and an emblem of some archetypal idea shared by the culture, the same way mythic characters like Odysseus and Perseus represent, as Joseph Campbell would argue, archetypal ideas stored in the *Spiritus Mundi*

Not surprisingly, Wallace also declares, later in this same disclaimer, that portions of the book are "written in the margins of John Barth's 'Lost in the Funhouse'" (vi). Barth's story was originally included in a collection of the same name that sought to move beyond the vaunted "mythic method" of such modernists as William Faulkner and James Joyce. Hence *Girl with Curious Hair* stands as Wallace's attempt to enter into and at the same time revise a tradition that begins with Joyce's *Ulysses* and carries through to Barth's *Lost in the Funhouse* and *Chimera*. All three works employ mythic archetypes as "a way of controlling, of ordering, of giving shape and significance to the immense panorama of futility and anarchy which is contemporary history," as T. S. Eliot once famously put it.[3] Moreover, these works mark three decisive turns in literary sensibility: *Ulysses* is the Bible of literary modernism, Barth's *Lost in the Funhouse* is American fiction's paradigmatic work of postmodern metafiction, and Wallace's book is perhaps one of the first works in this tradition to suggest the next step.

In *Ulysses,* Joyce arranges Leopold's Bloom's circuitous journey through the city of Dublin so that it corresponds, scene for scene, with Odysseus' famous journey in Homer's *Odyssey;* by this means, he seeks to connect the resolutely unheroic and unspectacular events of Bloom's day to a timeless archetypal past. The mythic mode both lifts Bloom's daily life to a cosmic, epic level of importance and locates a transcendent structure in the everyday. Barth reverses Joyce's strategy: instead of writing more or less realistic fictions "which point always to mythic archetypes," Barth composes narratives involving mythic characters (Perseus, Bellerophon, Narcissus, and so on) that point to the contemporary everyday. In his words, he takes up the other "end of the mythopoeic stick."[4] By self-consciously rewriting the archetypes themselves, Barth situates text prior to so-called transcendent truth and demonstrates that perhaps the reality we see around is shaped by narrative, rather than vice versa.

In Wallace's book, which is as much a direct "response" to Barth's two works of myth narrative as Barth's work was to

Joyce's Stephen Dedalus novels, the realm of the mythic is constructed from mass media. Wallace is happy to concede to Barth his argument that we shape our myths rather than vice versa. He also aligns himself with Barth's notion that this reversal on Joyce's method makes us all paralyzed with self-consciousness, since we no longer have any faith in a "reality" prior to our conventionalized rendering of it. He goes Barth one step further by treating the "real" figures of mass media the same way Barth treats the great figures from Greek, Roman, and Persian myth, that is, as archetypal characters who point to the modern everyday. Similarly, Wallace understands that the paralyzing self-consciousness that Barth depicts in his mythic narratives is now directed at this *same* self-consciousness, which is to say we are no longer in need of Barth's analysis of our paralysis, since we are doubly paralyzed by our *knowledge* of that analysis. Hence Wallace's stories have a twofold agenda. First, in treating pop-cultural figures as fictional constructs, they disclose the manner by which the objects of mass media have become the stuff of our collective unconscious. Second, the stories highlight, after Barth, the numerous ways in which this same collective unconsciousness itself is a construct. The book holds a mirror up to our mirror, and in so doing seeks a way out of the postmodern dilemma, a way out that allows us to recognize the omnipresence of mediated reality while at the same time pointing *away* from the mediated reality and toward some undepicted, yet still vital, reality—the reality *surrounding* those two mutually reflective mirrors.

The first nine stories are arranged in a sort of freestyle contrapuntal system of contrast and comparison. Wallace follows lengthy pieces with short experimental sketches, then contrasts more or less "serious" stories with extravagant and comic treatments of the same theme. In addition, he employs a wide range of styles and techniques, and indulges in a fair amount of literary pastiche and parody. With the possible exception of "Lyndon," none of the pieces could be called "traditional," while all nine share a refusal to resolve in a satisfying—Wallace would derisively say "soothing"—fashion. Rather, the collection comes to a thematic and programmatic "resolution" only in the concluding novella, which reprises all the numerous themes and innovations that preceded it. In this novella, the collection's most significant achievement (though not its most successful story), Wallace both explains the numerous unconventional methods already employed and also outlines the shape and purpose of his future work.

## "Little Expressionless Animals"

"Little Expressionless Animals," the opening piece from *Girl with Curious Hair,* takes as its protagonist an orphaned savant named Julie Smith who pulls off a seven-hundred-episode sweep of the television game show *Jeopardy!* The story also serves double duty as the book's overture, a composite of themes and techniques that the rest of the volume will take up one by one. Written in an incisive and damning parody of the minimalist style of the 1980s—with its short declarative sentences and its air of cold objectivity—the story, light and comic though it principally is, also manages to address such weighty issues as popular culture and its complex ideology; the fluidity of boundaries like self-and-other and hetero- versus homosexual desire; and poststructuralist conceptions of presence and absence.

The opening sentences immediately announce the story's minimalist style: "It's 1976. The sky is low and full of clouds. The gray clouds are bulbous and wrinkled and shiny. The sky looks cerebral. Under the sky is a field, in the wind" (3). Lance Olsen connects this passage, and the story that contains it, to "the methodical, clean, subject-verb-predicate sentences of [Wittgenstein's] *Tractatus*" and concludes that Wallace intends this style of writing to serve negatively in his corpus as an example of a naïve belief in language as "a mirror held up to reality." Wallace indirectly confirms Olsen's insight when he affirms that the story conversely employs "flashcuts and the distortion of linearity" to "prohibit the reader from forgetting that she's receiving heavily mediated data, that this process is a relationship between the writer's consciousness and her own, and that in order for it to be anything like a real full human relationship, she's going to have to put in her share of the linguistic work." He goes on to contrast these "distortions" with the much more opaque technique employed by television, whose whole reason for existence, he explains elsewhere, "is reflecting what people want to see. It's a mirror."[5] The story contrasts these competing stylistic strategies—opaque prose and deliberately distorted chronology—to blur and complicate the traditional boundary between phenomenal reality and the mediated world of television or language.

For a number of reasons, *Jeopardy!* turns out to be the perfect vehicle through which to enact this blurring of fact and fiction. First, it is a "game show" that tests the contestants' knowledge of facts; second, it is set apart from other trivia-based programs by its "distinctive . . . inversion by which the host 'asks' the answer and the contestant supplies the appropriate question" (16). The show is all about inversion, then, and about the fluidity of rules, of binaries. For instance, Julie's unstoppable run of victories runs against one hard-and-fast rule of the game, as spelled out by the show's director: "Five slots, retire undefeated, come back for Champion's Tourney in April. Annual event. Tradition . . . Fairness to whole contestant pool. An ethics type of thing" (24). Merv Griffin, the show's producer, shoots back, "See that window? . . . That's where the rules go. Out that window" (25). The window image is central to the story, as it invokes, both visually and conceptually, the television screen: outside the window is the real, while inside the window is "the game." Somewhat like his fictional Merv Griffin, Wallace is interested in breaking through that window, in throwing out the rules that govern "the real" and the "fictive" and instead creating a fluidity between the two; at the same time, Wallace also dramatizes that this "fluidity" occurs *only* within the story, which is irrevocably cut off from the real world. In other words, the story paradoxically proposes that fluidity in order to prove the impossibility of *actually* breaking through.

Alex Trebek, the show's host, tells his psychiatrist that his favorite word "is *moist* . . . especially when used in combination with my second-favorite word, which is *induce*" (19). Accordingly, Julie functions as the story's primary "moist" figure, a person of blurry and permeable boundaries who possesses an uncanny ability to transmit some mysterious quality through the television screen. Her skin, we are told, "has the texture of something truly alive, an elastic softness, like a ripe sheath, a pod. It is vulnerable and has depth. . . . Everything about her is sort of permeable" (13). Similarly, before each *Jeopardy!* taping and during commercial breaks, she stares at the audience with no expression whatsoever, her face a blank surface concealing a mysterious and unknowable interior, and yet "something happens to Julie Smith when the red lights light. . . . Every concavity in [her] now looks to have come convex. . . . Her face, on-screen, gives off an odd lambent UHF flicker; her expression, brightly serene, radiates a sort of oneness with the board's data" (17). The shift from concavity to convexity suggests an interior bursting outward—the "interior" in this case residing within both Julie and the television set the viewers at home are watching. Griffin posits that this "something" in Julie "is the capacity of facts to transcend their internal factual limitations and become, in and of themselves, meaning, feeling. . . . This girl informs trivia with import. She makes it human, something with the power to emote, evoke, induce, cathart. She gives the game the simultaneous transparency and mystery all of us in the industry have groped for, for decades" (25). In a sense, Julie does to cold "facts" what Wallace does to the cold, "factual" minimalist style that this story seeks to explode once and for all: through its permeable movement from the world of "reality" to the world inside the television, as well as its use of "flashcuts and distortions," the story "breaks through" minimalism's internal limitations and, paradoxically, reaffirms the text as a site of human interaction between author and reader.

The "concavity/convexity" motif also invokes one of the story's declared source texts, John Ashbery's famous "Self-Portrait in a Convex Mirror." In the book's already cited disclaimer, Wallace admits that the story "makes use" of that poem's third stanza. Ashbery is perhaps the chief postmodern poet of our time; his poetry, in the words of critic David Shapiro, "is humorously and melancholically self-reflexive and sees itself as a provisional, halting critique of naïve and degraded referential poetries. The sign in Ashbery's collages is eminently cut off from the world." Fittingly, Ashbery's famous poem is both a "self-portrait" in a warped, bulging mirror but also a "reflection" on a Parmigianino painting of the same name, itself a mirrored reflection of a mirrored reflection. In the painting, Parmigianino depicts his portrait as it appears in the round, convex mirror, his hand prominently out front and, in obedience to the law of perspective, larger even than the head. The portrait in the painting as well as in the poem is "life englobed"—that is, life transmitted into mediated territory— and although "One would like to stick one's hand / Out of the globe, . . . its dimension, / What carries it, will not allow it." The world within the text/poem looms out into the world but cannot break through. As Shapiro remarks, "To believe that one can escape the text, get out of it as into a realm of existence beyond language, is an impossibility filled with pathos." "The surface is what's there," the poem declares, "And nothing can exist except what's there." In the crucial third stanza, the poet argues that the stylized "forms" in the painting "nourish / A dream which includes them all, as they are / Finally reversed in the accumulating mirror," and yet the impossibility of breaking out of that dream world and into the real world is hardly cause for unhappiness, "since / Dreams prolong us as they are absorbed[.]/ Something like living occurs, a movement / Out of the dream into its codification."[6] Like Wallace's story, then, Ashbery's poem both entertains the fantasy of escaping textuality, of breaking through, and rejects it simultaneously. In an elegant paradox, this final rejection preserves the integrity of the world outside the text, where "something like living occurs."

Ultimately, the television screen is the story's—indeed, the entire collection's—"convex mirror." If television's purpose is "reflecting what people want to see," then, Wallace goes on to argue, "television's real pitch . . . is that it's better to be inside the TV than to be outside, watching."[7] One of the story's characters speaks about people who watch television so much that it "comes to be their whole emotional world, . . . their whole way of defining themselves as existents, with a distinct identity, that they're outside the set, and everything else is inside the set" (31). These same people are sometimes driven mad when they accidentally get "on TV": "They go home and plunk right down in front of the set, and all of a sudden they look and they're *inside* the set" (31). Television might compel us to "come inside," but once we get there we recognize that our status as "existents" is firmly grounded in that unbreachable chasm between reality and text.

Fittingly, Julie gives all her earnings from the show to a psychiatric hospital where her brother is a patient suffering from a condition in which he "has trouble living in the world" (25). The hospital "specialize[s] in sort of . . . *yanking* people outside themselves. Into the world" (20). What is more, Julie's one area of nonexpertise involves animals, "because animals' faces have no expression" (41). She ends her streak when this same brother appears on the show as a challenger and answers a run of questions involving animals. The implication is clear: the inside/ outside motif applies also to the psychic split between surface and interior, and Julie, with her curious ability to transform the concave into the convex, refuses to compete with her beloved, troubled brother, who, like the "expressionless animals" of the title, cannot accept the lessons of Ashbery's poem concerning the slippery but ultimately unbreachable movement from interior to exterior, between self and other.

Similarly, Julie runs into difficulty with her lover, Faye Goddard, who, among other problems, does not like poetry because she sees it as "nothing more than a really oblique way of saying the obvious" (13). Faye is troubled by her homoerotic passion for Julie, for not only is she unsure whether she "is" a lesbian or not, but she is also concerned about what to tell others about their relationship, which makes perfect sense on the "inside" but resists lucid explanation to those on the "outside." "Say lesbianism is simply one kind of response to Otherness," Julie tells her. "Say the whole point of love is to try to get your fingers through the holes in the lover's mask" (32). Unsatisfied with Julie's response, Faye then joins Julie in a "game" of making up "pretend reasons for being a lesbian" (39). Near the end of the story, after running through a list of "reasons" that have tenuous connection to various "realities" offered up within the narrative, Julie asks Faye to regard their passion as like an ocean they used to watch early in their relationship: "Our dawn ocean, that we loved? We loved it because it was like us, Faye. The ocean was *obvious*. . . . Oceans are only oceans when they move. . . . Waves are what keep oceans from just being very big puddles. Oceans are just their waves. And every wave in the ocean is finally going to meet what it moves toward, and break. The whole thing we looked at, the whole time you asked, was obvious. It was obvious and a poem because it was us. See things like that, Fay. Your own face, moving into expression. A wave, breaking on a rock, giving up its shape in a gesture that expresses that shape. See?" (42). The image recalls Ashbery's "Self-Portrait," with its references to "our / Landscape sweeping out from us to disappear / On the horizon," and it also serves as the story's oblique conclusion. Julie, a master at conveying the illusion of breaking through the breach between inside and outside, here explains that what she truly affirms is the movement *toward* that breakthrough, like the outstretched hand in the Parmigianino painting. Ultimately, the story is an "ocean"—not a space filled with elements of fiction and reality but rather all fiction, all "waves," in effect all *language,* which moves toward its signifier but "breaks up" before it can make contact. But as Ashbery says, in this process "Something like living occurs, a movement / Out of the dream into its codification."

## "Luckily the Account Representative Knew CPR"

Less a story than a sort of recitative between the book's overture and its title piece, "Luckily the Account Representative Knew CPR" picks up the implications of Julie's ocean-wave motif and rethinks them in terms of "parallel lines." With obsessive precision, the narrator follows the movement from office to underground parking garage of two businessmen leaving work late at night amid the eerie barrenness of an empty office building. Though one man is a "newly divorced" Account Representative and the other an elderly, grandfatherly "Vice President in Charge of Overseas Production," the narrator insists that "there were between these last two executives to leave the Building the sorts of similarities enjoyed by parallel lines" (45). These similarities include such things as shared reactions to the empty building, matching brief cases, and "pain, though of course neither knew" (48). Much like Julie's waves and their destinations, or words and their referents, parallel lines never meet, and yet in this story the lines meet horribly, as the Vice President suffers from a heart attack and the Account Representative rushes to help. At that moment the Vice President's life falls "literally" in the hands of the lonely Account Representative, and the two people are last seen "bent to what two lives required, below everything" (52).

Slight though the piece is, Wallace here first announces a theme that will assume central importance in *Infinite Jest,* namely that our isolation from one another as well as our inability to access the interior of others causes us the sort of pain that paradoxically joins us together. As Hal Incandenza will say in that novel, "We're all on each other's food chain. . . . We're each deeply alone here. It's what we all have in common, this aloneness."[8] It is what we share, "below everything," and alleviating that loneliness through the CPR of fiction is what Wallace's fiction will henceforth attempt.

"Girl with Curious Hair"

Whereas the theme of "Luckily the Account Executive Knew CPR" is resuscitation, the theme of the book's title story is death, both literary and cultural/political. The story is dedicated, in part, to 1960s psychoanalytical theorist Norman O. Brown, author of *Life against Death* and *Love's Body*, two works that combine Freudian and Marxist methodologies to produce a psychological history of Western neurosis. *Life against Death* bears a special weight on this disturbing story, particularly in its extended treatment of "anality" and Freud's preoccupation with the symbolic axis of money/feces. Still, it is probably a mistake to interpret the story through the lens of Brown's colorful theories, for the second dedicatee is purse-lipped conservative pundit William F. Buckley. Taken together, the dedications are clearly ironic.

Rather, as he did in "Little Expressionless Animals," Wallace once again sets his sights on 1980s minimalism, with a more precise target this time out, chiefly the work of Bennington College "brat pack" novelists Bret Easton Ellis and Jill Eisenstadt, whose Joan Didion–inspired novels *Less Than Zero* and *From Rockaway* became minor literary sensations around the same time that Wallace published *The Broom of the System*.

In one of the book's numerous instances of striking prophecy, the story eerily forecasts Ellis's 1991 slasher novel *American Psycho,* the story of a wealthy, emotionless New York yuppie who spends his days buying designer clothes and skin emollients and his evenings brutally torturing women—a novel, in other words, that actually *does* invite an interpretation indebted to Norman O. Brown. Wallace's hero, meanwhile, is Sick Puppy, a chillingly unemotional Yale graduate and corporate liability attorney who relates, in a grisly and hilarious pastiche of Ellis' preposterously benumbed prose, the events surrounding an evening at a Keith Jarrett concert with his punk rock friends Gimlet, Mr. Wonderful, Grope, Tit, and Cheese. By placing his wealthy WASP narrator alongside these angry, disaffected punks, Wallace decisively explodes the vacuity of Ellis and Eisenstadt's phony nihilism. A somewhat bewildering curiosity now, "Girl with Curious Hair" was a genuine watershed in 1989, the story that announced to all who were listening that the 1980s were officially dead.

Wallace has never been shy about his disgust with Ellis's work. In a far-ranging interview with Larry McCaffery, he contends that Ellis's flat characters and their emotionless response to the crass emptiness of contemporary culture can hardly be regarded as "a mordant deadpan commentary on the badness of everything," as Ellis himself would contend. Rather, Wallace argues that "if the contemporary condition is hopelessly shitty, insipid, materialistic, emotionally retarded, sadomasochistic and stupid, then I (or any writer) can get away with slapping together stories with characters who are stupid, vapid, emotionally retarded, which is easy, because these sorts of characters require no development." Ellis, in his view, is simply a bad writer who has managed to hoodwink his audience into thinking that "bad writing—flat characters, a narrative world that's clichéd and not recognizably human, etc.—is also a description of today's world."[9]

"Girl with Curious Hair" neatly exposes this deception. Among his myriad oddities, Sick Puppy "cannot become high from ingesting drugs," even though his friends spend most of the story tripping on LSD. Nothing, in fact, can "affect [him] or [his] state of normal consciousness" (58), not even his friend Gimlet's hairstyle, which is a Mohawk shaped into an enormous penis atop her otherwise bald head. He also cannot engage in normal sex; rather, he can only become aroused by burning his partner with a match and then letting this same partner/victim fellate him, this apparently owing to an incident from his childhood in which his military father caught him in incestuous congress with his sister and burned his own penis in punishment, a tale he relates in his inimical zombielike style. He is Ellis's flat, inhuman WASP personified. And like all of Ellis's protagonists, Sick Puppy is rich, privileged, and vapid.

Set in contrast to Sick Puppy are his friends, the punk rockers, who seem to enjoy Sick Puppy both for his emotionlessness and his unlimited cash flow. The one exception to this rule is Cheese, the youngest of the pack, who, midway through the story, pulls Sick Puppy aside and asks him how he "had become friends with [his] punkrocker friends in Los Angeles . . . since [he] did not look like them nor did [he] dress like them or have a distinctive punkrocker hairstyle, nor was [he] poor or disaffected or nihilistic" (64). Cheese goes on to affirm that "punkrockers were children born into a very tiny space, with no windows, plus walls all around them made of concrete and metal . . . and that as adults they were trying to cut their way out of the walls"; that this was why they "all felt as if they had nothing and would always have nothing [and] therefore they made the nothing into everything" (67). Conversely, Cheese wonders why Sick Puppy, "who already had everything," would want to trade "[his] big everything for a big nothing" (68). Cheese's questions also seem to be Wallace's questions to Ellis and his ilk.

And during all of this, jazz improvisational pianist Keith Jarrett is performing in the background, linking "little melodies" together and arranging them in his "sub-conscious," thereby creating "a little life story of [his] special experiences and feelings" (66). Jarrett, in fact, works within the story as yet another counterpoint to Sick Puppy and all he represents. Jarrett, Cheese marvels, "not only played the little tunes with skill but also joined them together in unique and interesting ways, improvisationally, so that each of his piano concerts was different from all others" (66). The performance, moreover, is "like a line instead of a composed and round circle" (66). Much like those incessant waves in "Little Expressionless Animals" that give up their shape in a gesture that expresses that shape, Jarrett's jazz performance can be read as a self-reflexive description of Wallace's art, which, in this case, uses pastiche and virtuosity to move fiction forward toward an open reengagement with the emotions.

## "Lyndon"

Whereas "Girl with Curious Hair" takes on Reagan-Bush conservatism, the following story, "Lyndon," reverses thrust in a way, taking up Democratic politics during the Cold War. The story's narrator, David Boyd, relates his experience working as an aide to Lyndon B. Johnson from roughly 1954, sometime after the Rosenberg trial, to 1968, the final year of Johnson's first full term as president of the United States. Also in contrast to the previous story's surreal prose pyrotechnics, "Lyndon" is told straight, in a reasoned, eloquent voice that stands alone in Wallace's growing oeuvre for its conventionality. Nevertheless, the story bears traces of Wallace's trademark inventiveness and love of stylistic play, namely in its nonlinear chronology, its use of actual and made-up "quotations" from the public record, and in the imaginative fun Wallace clearly takes in characterizing the famously irascible Johnson. In this latter regard, the story betrays perhaps the book's most direct debt to Coover's *Public Burning,* with its own curiously sympathetic portrayal of an anal-retentive and paranoid Richard Nixon.

The story answers "Girl with Curious Hair" in a number of other ways as well. Boyd is Sick Puppy's direct opposite, both in his emotional clarity and in the fact that he is a homosexual. Likewise, he describes his parents, and their reaction to the news of his sexuality, with empathy and objectivity. His most intense feelings, however, he reserves for the charismatic title character, referred to throughout simply as "Lyndon." Boyd wrestles throughout the story with his feelings for his overworked, over-achieving boss, never fully admitting but also never altogether dismissing the possibility that what he ultimately feels for Lyndon is love. Love, in fact, is the story's unexpected theme—love as a concrete fact, love as an abstract illusion, love as a political construct. As a result, Lyndon B. Johnson emerges in these pages as both a creature of vast political manipulation and a real person deserving of our empathy. In the end the story explores how, or perhaps even whether, these competing forms of love can be reconciled.

In one of the many quotations sprinkled throughout the story—each new section is headed by one or two such passages

—a "former aide" remarks of Johnson, "I never saw a man with a deeper need to be loved than LBJ" (90). Another aide speaks of Johnson's terrible fear of being alone, of his need always to be surrounded by aides, coworkers, constituents, and voters. The awful irony for Johnson—and for any president, surely—is that this need to be loved fuels the voracious desire for a political office that leaves each holder horrifyingly isolated and alone. At one point Johnson walks out of his office late one night and finds Boyd, another lonely soul hungry for love, also working late. Embarrassed to be caught out in this way, Johnson defends himself by saying, "You give your life to other folks, you give your bodily health and your mind in your head and your intellectual concepts to serving the people, you and your wife got to carry each other inside, 'matter from how far away, or distant, or alone" (89). In a related passage, Lady Bird explains that she and Lyndon are so much "inside" each other that they "do not properly *love* one another anymore." She goes on: "Because we ceased long ago to be enough *apart* for a 'love' to span any distance. Lyndon says he shall cherish the day when *love* and *right* and *wrong* and *responsibility,* when these words, he says, are understood by you youths of American to be nothing but arrangements of distance" (115).

The "youths of America" she means here are the baby boomers of the 1960s, who, late in the story, have turned on Johnson, on his presidency and his war in Vietnam, all in the name, as the Beatles taught them, of love. Clearly, then, Wallace wants to disclose the "distance" between a genuine love between two people and the "love" ideology of the 1960s, and yet this critique also applies to Johnson himself, whose love is also one of distance, as Lady Bird admits. Isolated and powerful, he is as englobed as the stylized figure in Parmigianino's painting. Indeed, in the opening quotation Johnson, "campaigning by helicopter for U.S. Senate, 1954," yells, "Hello down there. This is your candidate, Lyndon Johnson." Later, in 1968, with protesters gathering daily outside the White House, Johnson, looking ruefully out the window, admits, "I believe I am out of touch with the youth of America. I believe that they cannot be touched by me, or by what's right, or by intellectual concepts on what's right for a nation" (106). Boyd then describes Johnson sorrowfully pressing his nose against the glass, an image that gives Boyd "a quick vision . . . of children and candy stores" (107).

Ironically, Johnson, even in his isolation, insists that for those youths, "right and wrong is *words*," while for him they are "feelings. In your guts and intestines and such. . . . They're inside you" (107). This is Johnson's tragedy, as Wallace portrays it: he is a man of feeling who is turned into an abstraction. Another aide, in yet another quotation, remarks of Boyd's homosexuality that it "is kind of abstract, . . . and LBJ hated abstractions. They were outside his ken" (94). This same aide calls Johnson "a genius and a gorilla at the same time" and goes on to contrast Johnson's "animalism" with Boyd's "abstractness," citing specifically the way Boyd "could be in a room with you and you'd never even notice him in the room" (93). Their relationship, then, represents the story's central dialectic, between real animal love and death—that is, "feelings. In your guts and intestines and such"—and abstractions like political power, war strategies, casualty lists. Johnson, late in presidency, has been displaced so completely from the realm of real, genuine feelings that the only thing he *does* feel is a palpable, crushing sense of "responsibility," which he cannot actually describe as a feeling but rather compares to "the sky." "It's there, over your ass, every fucking day" (108).

In the story's somewhat murkily dramatized final movement, Lady Bird, responding to her husband's pain as his presidency winds to its ignominious conclusion, summons Boyd to the White House for tea, right at the same moment that Boyd's lover, Rene Duverger, ill with a mysterious disease, suspiciously disappears. A creature of Washington, Boyd draws any number of paranoid conclusions, even suspecting Nixon's people at work—the 1968 election is looming, after all—and rushes to his meeting with Lady Bird. After their discussion, he goes to Johnson's bedroom and finds the president in bed, surrounded by the innumerable "notecards" Boyd had filled with Johnson's inspirational maxims through the years, and accompanied by Duverger, whose hands covers the President's face "as in an interrupted caress" (117). Johnson's eyes are "yolked with a high blue film of heartfelt pain" (118), and his last words are an inversion of his first words in the story: "Hello up there" (118). Johnson thus ends the story completely enclosed in his isolation, having betrayed the one person, Boyd, who even Lady Bird admits had "been his sole comfort for almost a decade" (115). With this final image, then, Wallace deliberately undercuts the piece's principal playful illusion, namely its promise to "get inside" and treat as "real" someone as public and unknowable as Lyndon B. Johnson.

## "John Billy"

Arriving like a burst of manic comic relief following the sober seriousness of "Lyndon," "John Billy" employs the full range of Wallace's linguistic virtuosity. The story is a dramatic monologue in a mock Faulknerian mode, with the title character relating in breathless open-eyed wonder—and more than a little syntactical inventiveness—the story of Minogue, Oklahoma's favorite son, a man of mythic force and power named Chuck Nunn, Junior, equal parts Thomas Sutpen and Paul Bunyan, "more God than not to those of us peers that lived for whiff of his jet trail" (123). The proprietor of Minogue's most successful sheep ranch and the husband of the town's most desired woman, "the illegally buxom and tall Glory Joy duBoise" (125), Nunn runs afoul of the area's "malignant and malevolent" sheep mogul, T. Rex Minogue, who, in his jealousy, dynamites Nunn's sheep farm to smithereens. In his attempt to exact revenge, Nunn suffers a head-on collision with T. Rex's alcoholic brother, V. V. Minogue, with the result that his eyeballs become dislodged from their sockets. The event damages Nunn such that "something inside Nunn got left by the impact askew," rendering "his sense of right and wrong and love and hate smithered to chaotic" (131). Whenever Nunn subsequently lost his temper "he lost the sucker real and true. It became gone. Absent. Elsewhere" (132). Though the plot is as bizarre and delightful as the story's irrepressible narrative voice, the piece nevertheless serves as a serious attempt on Wallace's part to explore the role of myth and the metaphysics of identity.

Everything about Nunn invokes mythic archetypes. He is a Christ-like shepherd, he walks like "a man who is in communion with Forces" (122), and he recovers from his accident on "the seventh day" (131). Similarly, John Billy tells his story "one fine dark day a pentecost's throw from Ascension" (146). His principal audience is a "damaged dust-scout" named Simple Ranger who, Odysseuslike, turns out to be C. Nunn himself, secretly returned to Minogue to hear the tale of his own attempt to exact final retribution on T. Rex. These numerous mythic echoes do not add up to a single, unified ur-myth, which means the story cannot be read as a retelling of a myth in the manner of Joyce or Barth. Whereas Joyce used myth to give a transhistorical grounding to his contemporary tale, and Barth directly transformed mythic characters into contemporary figures in order to undercut any notion of myth as transhistorical, Wallace uses myth in a spirit of joyful play that suggests both an understanding of Joyce and Barth and also a recognition that their differences can now be reconciled.

For instance, John Billy is fully aware that his story has a mythic component, for he says as much, repeatedly, as when he has Glory Joy describe Chuck Nunn's rage as "something mythopoeic, thunderous, less man or thing than sudden and dire force, will, ill" (133). The gag here is that neither Glory Joy nor John Billy would be aware of such terms as "mythopoeic," yet the other gag is directed at John Barth's self-conscious mythic characters, who are also aware of such terms. Barth's stylistic tic, in *Lost in the Funhouse,* of using "etc." over and over again also gets parodied throughout. Hence this fanciful tall tale parodies both Joyce and Faulkner's attempt to raise the modernist contemporary world to the realm of the mythic and also Barth's attempt to reinscribe the mythic into the world of postmodern self-consciousness and self-reflexivity. Eventually, however, the myth turns into a literal "community dream" of Chuck Nunn and all he represents to the town. His life is a living myth set within a story that makes no claims to be "realistic" at all, realism in any form being an illusory mode already effectively exploded by postmodern metafiction. John Billy serves as the story's communal voice, and via his narrative the mythic importance of Chuck Nunn's tale emerges as a self-contained archetype that also borrows freely and playfully from the canon of Western myth. From the ashes of Barth's attempt to exhaust modernism and its illusions of transcendence, Wallace story rises like a phoenix.

Indeed, "rising" and transcendence turn out to be the story's primary theme, thanks to its repeated motifs of dust-bowl destruction and the literal levitations that take place at the story's conclusion. As T. Rex remarks near the end, the story of his battle with Chuck Nunn "ended where all things titanic end. In meadowphysics. We done some together, that day. Some macrocosmic speculation" (143). Instead of "metaphysics," the story offers up a vision of transcendence grounded literally in the arid land of the Oklahoma dust bowl: literally a "meadow-physics." "Remember what's the next world and what ain't," T. Rex advises, a buzzard sitting symbolically on his shoulder. "See you selves. You, me, the corporeally phenomenal Glory Joy, the Ranger especially, we been swirling and blowin' in and out Minogue land since twinkles commenced in our Daddies' eyes" (144). Their transcendence is grounded in the very ground beneath their feet, and their myth is the stuff of local legend, but myth all the same.

Eyes and seeing are also central to the story, since Chuck Nunn—sometimes punningly called "C. Nunn" (See None)—suffers, after his accident, ongoing problems with his eyes: specifically, when his eyes were resewn into their sockets they "was left smaller" so that whenever he coughed or was slapped on his back the eyeballs again popped out of his head. At the cri-sis moment, in fact, T. Rex slaps Nunn on the back and dis-lodges his eyes. The two then look "down at what the life and death of every soul from Comanche to Nunn done gone to fer-tilize and plenish" (144), an experience that gives Nunn a moment of insight properly understood as sublime: "When the high winds blew off Country . . . I was able to hear the infinitely many soft sounds of the millions of delicate petals striking and rubbing together. They joined and clove together in wind. My eyes was blowing everywhere. And the rush of perfume sent up to me by the agitation of the clouds of petals nearly blew me out that window. Delighted. Aloft. Semi-moral. New" (145). This moment serves as an unexpectedly serious and poetic conclusion to a story that, up till now, has been hysterically absurd, which is precisely Wallace's intent—to arrive at a vision of the sublime by way of the comic and to reclaim the metaphysical claims of mythic connectivity for self-reflexive fiction, all without forgetting for a moment the postmodern critique of mythic transcendence.

"Here and There"

Continuing with the collection's ongoing strategy of contrast and continuity, the next story brings readers back down the ground with a thump. "Here and There" is a love story, of sorts, a piece of "fiction therapy" (153) that is both innovative in its technique and also an important touchstone for *Infinite Jest.* Picking up where "Lyndon" left off, the piece reengages the themes of love, loneliness, and distance, but does so in a much more open and vulnerable way such that one can almost see the faint outline of Hal Incandenza coming into focus in Wallace's imagination. Alone among the stories in *Girl with Curious Hair,* "Here and There," like the Hal sections in *Infinite Jest,* invites an "autobiographical" reading, if only because the hero, a twenty-two-year-old electrical engineering graduate from MIT named Bruce, shares a great many biographical details with his brainy creator. Not only does Bruce describe himself as "a hulking, pigeon-toed, blond, pale, red-lipped Midwestern boy" (153), but he also admits that he wants to be "the first really great poet of technology" (155). The story additionally distinguishes itself from others in the collection in its relatively traditional subject matter: in a nutshell, "Here and There" is a college breakup story. As is usually his way, however, Wallace employs these banal tropes of apprentice fiction self-consciously, so that the resulting story becomes a critique of the very same exhausted conventions that the piece simultaneously reconfigures and reinvigorates.

The breakup in question involves Bruce and an unnamed woman from his hometown, "a certain cool, tight, waistless, etcetera, Indiana University graduate student" and "the object of [his] theoretical passion, distant affection, and near-total loyalty for three years" (153–54). Though their affair is a relatively standard college long-distance relationship, one that falls apart, almost predictably, as both college and late adolescence come to an end, Bruce insists on regarding his own failure to sustain the affair in complex, abstract terms that stubbornly resist simple analysis. An engineer with a scientist's love of clarity and precision, Bruce also hopes to write literature someday that is "mathematical and technical," in which "meaning will be clean" (155). He remarks at one point, "I admit to seeing myself as an aesthetician of the cold, the new, the right, the truly and spotlessly *here*" (155). Bewilderingly, he finds he can only feel what he imagines to be "love" for his lover when she is *not* here, but rather *there*, back home, away from his study carrel at MIT with its promise of cold precision and friction-free isolation. He even prefers kissing her photograph to kissing the girl herself, since during the latter he would feel "vaguely elsewhere" (151). The story, then, allows Wallace not only to exorcise his own private demons but also to explore the chasm between the cold logic of science and the intractable, elusive ambiguity of interiority and emotion.

The story's innovative structure provides a resourceful means by which Wallace can pull off this two-part agenda. It is a two-part dramatic monologue, in which Bruce and his lover take turns narrating their own respective versions of the affair to an offstage therapist who, near the end, begins breaking into the story and offering her own observations. In keeping with the title, the two narrators are apparently not in the same room, even though their alternating narratives occasionally take on the nature of a give and take. Wallace thereby accepts the premise that the story is at root a piece of "fiction therapy"—"This kind of fiction doesn't interest me" (153), mutters morose Bruce—so much that it takes the charge and makes it an overt component of the story's structure. But even here Wallace seeks to move beyond the "fiction-as-therapy" convention already established by Philip Roth and J. D. Salinger, for in this piece, as the therapist explains, the therapy scenario "must locate itself and operate within a strenuously yes some might even say harshly limited defined structured space. It must be confronted as text, which is to say fiction, which is to say project" (153). The lover whose memory he is trying to exorcise, moreover, becomes in this "defined structured space" at once reader (of Bruce's justifications), object (of Bruce's narrative), and subject (of her own narrative). The story therefore creates a "space" that contains and ultimately collapses such dichotomies as reader versus text, self versus other, and here versus there—the very dichotomies that the text is in fact exploring.

According to both lovers, the relationship finally ends when, on the final Christmas break before graduation, Bruce asks her not if she would marry him but if he could ask her someday, and when she responds tentatively—"All I said to him then was do you think we could do it" (154)—Bruce gets moody and "distant," and the relationship never fully recovers. According to Bruce, he took off because at that exact same moment he had "gotten, suddenly . . . an idea for a truly central piece on the application of state variable techniques to the analysis of small-signal linear control systems" and so rushed off to his father's university office and thence to MIT to work on the problem. "She regarded the things that were important to me as her enemy," he complains, "not realizing that they were, in fact, the 'me' she seemed so jealous to covet" (154). The therapist counters that perhaps Bruce turned away because he did not get the answer he assumed he would get. "Bruce," the therapist asks, "why not just admit that what bothers you so much is that she has given irresistible notice that she has an emotional life with features that you knew nothing about, that she is just plain different from whatever you might have decided to make her into for yourself" (156–57). In other words, despite the fact that Bruce once, by his own assessment, "could unlock her like a differential," he must confront the fact that she is not a "formula" with rules that he can master.

The story concludes with an extended, lovingly described account of Bruce's visit to the house of his aunt and uncle in Maine, where he comes to grips with his confusion and loss. He begins to realize that his inarticulate feelings of dejection are "the creative products of something outside" him, specifically "a nascent emotional conscience" (165). One day while his uncle is out, his aunt asks him, the celebrated electrical engineer, to fix their ancient stove, symbol of the couple's warm and nurturing relationship. Rejecting his aunt's suggestion that "it was just a matter of a screw to be tightened or something that had to be given a good knock," Bruce proceeds to take apart the primitive wire system, and quickly finds that this simple mechanical device has stumped him. "At the cutting edge of electrical engineering," he admits, "almost everything interesting is resolvable via the manipulation of variables" (170). Yet the simple problem before him is beyond his ability, much the same way Bruce's brother accuses him of "playing games with words in order to dodge the real meanings of things" (166).

And the real meaning here is that Bruce, all along, only knew how to want his lover from a distance, and not to *have* her, this complex Other outside his control. "I think he really likes to want," she speculates at one point (159). Similarly, the whole time Bruce is deep in the bowels of the stove suffering from a panic attack, his aunt is in the kitchen preparing for a French class she is taking, that day's lesson concentrating on the conjugation of the French verb *venir,* "to want." The story, then, with its elaborately diffused structure, also plays "games with words" both to dramatize how its hero tries to "dodge the real meanings of things" and also to direct the reader, indirectly and obliquely, *toward* the story's final vision of desire as an insistent urge that must be reconciled with the fact that we cannot contain or finally possess the things or people we desire. This is not a blinding or necessarily original insight, of course, and Wallace knows it. His job in this story—and, later, in much of *Infinite Jest*—is not to create new truths but rather to recover old truths that postmodern sophistication—of which Bruce's "poet[ry] of technology" is a species—might have dismissed prematurely.

## "My Appearance"

Originally published in *Playboy* as "Late Night," "My Appearance" is the most important and successful story in *Girl with Curious Hair.* Like its companion piece, "Here and There,"

"My Appearance" forecasts many of the themes and concerns that will occupy Wallace in *Infinite Jest,* yet it also serves as Wallace's most concise formative illustration of how he hopes to move past postmodern self-reflexivity. Some six years after this story's first appearance in print, he revisited and expanded its central ideas in the form of the long essay "E Unibus Pluram"; as lucid and rich as that essay may be, however, it still reads like a footnote to "My Appearance."

The story opens with a precise statement of fact: "I am a woman who appeared in public on 'Late Night with David Letterman' on March 22, 1989" (175). The woman in question is a middle-aged television actress named Edilyn, a forty-year-old mother of four kids who, by her own clear-eyed appraisal, will "never be recognized seriously for [her] work as an actress" (179). This latter fact does not seem to bother her, as she prides herself on being a woman who is direct and knowable. "I am a woman who lets her feelings show rather than hide them," she affirms; "it's just healthier that way" (178). Nevertheless, her husband, Rudy, sees her not as a concrete, uncomplicated person but rather as a "woman whose face and attitudes are known to something over half of the measurable population of the United States, whose name is on lips and covers and screens. And whose heart's heart is invisible, and unapproachably hidden" (175). Edilyn's central conflict, then, is to reconcile her real self and the content of her "heart's heart" with her fabricated identity as a celebrity. This conflict comes to a head the night she appears, as both a "celebrity" and a "real person," on David Letterman's famously slippery and self-mocking program, which Wallace insightfully depicts as a diabolical funhouse of mirrors and self-reflexive irony—an "anti-show," in the words of one character, in which nothing is really the way it appears.

Wallace's depiction of David Letterman's show, and the complex matrix of irony and absurdity that made it, in its early days on CBS, so innovative, functions in the story as an emblem of what postmodernism has become. For Wallace, "Metafiction's real end has always been Armageddon," by which me means that the original purpose behind metafiction's preoccupation with self-reflexivity, irony, parody, and absurdism was to explode naive notions of art as a window to reality. "The great thing about irony," he goes on to say, "is that it splits things apart, gets us up above them so we can see the flaws and hypocrisies and duplicities." Nevertheless, over time irony can become "the song of the prisoner who's come to love his cage."[10]

Even more important, these same tools can become positively toxic when they are appropriated by the very institutions that are their target—which is exactly what Wallace feels Letterman has done. In the story, Letterman appears onstage with a tiny label affixed to his cheek that reads "MAKEUP." When the audience applauds, the camera focuses on the APPLAUSE sign. When Letterman tells Edilyn, "*Terribly* nice to see you," he is essentially parodying the unctuous flattery that television talk show hosts *like himself* generally bestow upon their guests. In short, *Late Night with David Letterman* is a late-night television talk show that generates humor by parodying the conventions of the light-night television talk show, the same way John Barth writes "novels which imitate the form of the Novel, by an author who imitates the role of the Author." And for Wallace, Letterman's strategy, in addition to representing a natural cultural development, also has unexpectedly serious implications. "Even though . . . self-consciousness and irony and anarchism served valuable purposes, were indispensable for their times," he says, "their aesthetic's absorption by U.S.

commercial culture has had appalling consequences for writers and everyone else."[11]

To get a sense how "appalling" these "consequences" are, witness the hair-clutching anxiety Edilyn, her husband, and their friend Ron experience when they try to prepare her for her appearance on the program. Rudy warns Edilyn that the show's frank "hokeyness" is hardly "benign." "The whole thing feeds off *everybody's* ridiculousness," Rudy argues. "It's the way the audience can tell he *chooses* to ridicule himself that exempts the clever bastard from real ridicule" (181). In other words, Letterman ridicules—through irony and parody—everything in the show, including the show itself, in order to demonstrate that "everything is clichéd and hyped and absurd, and that's *just* where the fun is" (183). The key is never to be sincere, since the "joke is now *on* people who are sincere" (182). They advise Edilyn to be "seen as being *aware*" that she is in on the big joke, to be "seen as making fun of yourself, but in a self-aware and ironic way," and to be not so much insincere as "*not*-sincere" (185).

Edilyn forcefully protests, both to her husband and, in an indirect way, to Letterman himself. Over and over again she insists that she is a woman gifted with un-ironic self-understanding, and she also refuses to accept the "dark fearful thing you seem to see in David Letterman" (179), that is, this layered and sinister matrix of self-mocking, and therefore self-protective, irony. Nevertheless, while on the show, Edilyn stares Letterman in the face and says, "You're looking at a woman with no illusions, David" (194), a line Letterman gently deflates by responding, "I'm an illusion with no *woman*" (194), which gets a relieved laugh from the audience. Typical of Wallace's art and his characteristic technique, Edilyn's declaration emerges from within a complex structure of doubled self-reflexivity, for the story is a self-conscious story about a woman who is an actress who appears as "herself" on a program in which nothing is sincere or genuine. The declaration has force precisely because it is placed amid Wallace's elaborate ironic deflation of deflating irony, somewhat the same way a double-negative expression becomes, by definition, an affirmation.

The story concludes, like all the stories in *Girl with Curious Hair*, with a deferred ending, that is, a conclusion that somehow points to the world outside the text, beyond the enclosed space of the page. Edilyn insists that, while "inside" the program, she could see Letterman clearly, completely—"I *saw* him," she cries —whereas Rudy maintains, "He *can't* be seen. That's what the whole thing's about, now. That no one is really the way they have to be seen" (199). Edilyn then asks her husband "what way he thought he and [she] really were, then" which, she declares in the story's final line, "turned out to be a mistake" (201). The Letterman appearance has therefore opened a fatal fissure in their marriage: it has disclosed the fact that Edilyn and her husband are on irreconcilably opposite ends of the irony spectrum, and that this chasm can have "appalling consequences" for the way two people interact with each other. Edilyn's heart's heart is invisible and unapproachably hidden from her husband precisely because he has contracted Letterman's disease and has hidden his *own* heart's heart from his wife. He, like the broader culture he in some sense represents, is trapped in irony's cage, while Edilyn, in her effort to climb out, is as alone outside as she would be inside.

## "Say Never"

One of the slighter pieces in the collection, "Say Never" nevertheless works well as a homage to and parody of Philip Roth's lighter work. The story lacks a central narrator, assigning this task instead to a trio of voices that speak independently of one another and thereby create a kaleidoscopic narrative that culminates in what one character calls a "unified moment's revelation of separateness" (221). At the story's center is Leonard Shlomith Tagus, a married college professor who becomes sexually obsessed, and then sexually involved, with his brother Mickey's luscious Spanish girlfriend, Carlina Rentaria-Cruz, whom Lenny refers to as the "cinnamon girl." Lenny publicizes his affair in the form of an affidavit-like letter sent to "that community of [his] family and intimate friends," and the subsequent piece traces the impact of this news on Lenny's widower mother and his brother Mickey, who spends most of the piece plotting his revenge.

Mrs. Tagus's neighbor, Labov, opens and closes the piece, narrating in a voice reminiscent of Bernard Malamud's and Saul Bellow's poetic Jewish immigrants, with their lyrical Yiddish-inflected American English. Wallace does a nice job of inhabiting this voice, and his affection and respect for Labov's Old World pragmatism and fount of family feeling serves as the story's moral center. As in Roth's work, Labov's values clash against the contemporary values of the overintellectual and hyper-self-conscious Lenny, who, like Alexander Portnoy, Peter Tarnopol, and Nathan Zuckerman before him, cannot seem to resist the "urge . . . to explain" (220). The pathetic rationalizations he offers, as well as his realization of their failure to explain, function as an indictment of Roth's work, even as Labov's stoic decency undermines Roth's Old World straw men.

In his letter, Lenny asks his readers to compare Carlina with Bonnie. Carlina is "full-lipped, candy-skinned, brandy-haired. . . . a girl the color of dirty white, eyes a well-boiled white and hair like liquor, scintillant and smoky; precisely pointed breasts that shimmy when her chest caves in" and so on (213). Conversely, Bonnie is "a wide-bottomed, solid, pale-as-all-indoors woman of thirty-four" whom Lenny knows "in milliscopic detail" (213). In addition to these physical differences, Lenny contrasts Carlina's air of careless "merriment" with Bonnie's air of careful, plodding, domestic responsibility. As he succinctly puts the case, "A unit of cinnamon milk, on fire with love for no one ever, vs. exhaustively tested loyalty, hard-headed realism, compassion, momentum, a woman the color and odor of Noxzema for all time" (222).

Much of this reads like a pastiche of *Portnoy's Complaint* or those unforgettable early chapters of *The Counterlife,* and yet what's missing—deliberately—is Roth's fierce anger, his anarchic humor. Whereas Roth's characters know they are not winning but that they nevertheless have a case, Lenny's letter convinces neither himself nor his readers. He even calls the missive "a doomed exercise in disinformation" (219). Wallace also helps along Lenny's defeat by giving the first and last words of the story to the indomitable Labov, who not only shares Bonnie's compassion but also possesses a writer's eye for detail that ultimately undoes Lenny's "wish to be willful." The story's crucial paragraph arrives just past the midpoint and consists of Labov's moving and almost offhand memories of Lenny's life-before-Carlina: "Josh Tagus and Saul Tagus and little Becky Tagus [Lenny and Bonnie's children] in pajamas with pajama-feet attached, yawning over milk in plastic mugs with cartoons on their sides. Lenny smoothing their fine thin child's hair and reading to them Gibran or Novalis under a soft lamp. You know from warmth? There is warmth in the home of Mr. and Mrs. Leonard Tagus" (218). Nothing Lenny says can overcome this fleeting yet unforgettable vision of familial bliss, one not played for laughs, as in *Portnoy's Complaint* (itself not lacking in lovely and unforgettable portraits of family feeling) but rather placed here unobtrusively as a stinging indictment of Lenny's selfishness. And, indeed, though Lenny is not privy to Labov's narrative, he nevertheless concludes his narrative by admitting, "Though even the novice alone can see quickly that a life conducted, temporarily or no, as a simple renunciation of value becomes at best something occluded and at worst something empty: a life of waiting for the will-be-never" (223). The title, then, is an imperative and a warning. Lenny trapped in family responsibility and the repetition of marriage, chooses, like one of Kierkegaard's doomed aesthetes, to "will" himself into the unknown, into the moment, where desire will forever chase a thing that recedes. To say "yes" to the libido, in other words, is to "say never."

## "Everything Is Green"

The narrator of this sketchlike story—the shortest piece in the book, more a breather before the following novella than a story in its own right—is a young man named Mitch who, like a great many characters of 1980s minimalist fiction, lives in a double-wide trailer, cannot fully articulate what he is feeling, and finds himself at loggerheads with his lover, in his case a woman named Mayfly. Though the primary function of the piece is to recapitulate the book's ongoing exploration of interiority and exteriority, Wallace also uses this wisp of a story to enact his final critique of the minimalist mode, employing the style one more time not as indictment but rather as a vehicle for lyrical transformation.

At forty-eight, Mitch is considerably older than his elusive young lover Mayfly. Unfortunately, he has made her "the reason

I got for what I always do" (229). He tells her, "Every thing that is inside me I have gave you," then complains that "there is needs which you can not even see any more, because there is too many needs in you that are in the way" (229). In this latter regard, Mitch is Bruce's cousin in confusion, a male lover who has once again tried to make his lover a "receptacle for one's organs, fluids, and emotion" (156) and who is bewildered by the fact that this lover remains a self-contained person, impervious to his effort to penetrate and inhabit her interiority. As Mitch puts it, "But now I am feeling like there is all of me going in to you and nothing of you coming back anymore" (230).

Significantly, Mayfly, throughout the story, sits beneath a window streaked clean by a heavy rainstorm from the night before. Rather than respond to Mitch's pleas for access and his professions of love, Mayfly turns her attention to the world outside the window, where "everything is green" (230). Mitch sees something different: he sees the "other trailers" that "are not green and [his] card table out with puddles in lines and beer cans and butts floating in the ashtrays" (230). When she repeats her assertion, Mitch realizes "the whisper is not to me no more I know" (230). The story ends with Mayfly looking out the window—at the world beyond the self in contemplation of what T. Rex Minogue called in "John Billy" "meadowphysics"—and Mitch looking at Mayfly, who, he finally admits in a concluding moment of clarity, "has a body," that is, an impervious sheath that keeps her always and forever separate from him. He concludes, "And she is my morning," thereby equating her with the vibrant living world to which Mayfly has been trying to direct him. She is, in other words, outside him, alive and beyond his touch. Now he is ready to be her lover.

"Westward the Course of Empire Takes Its Way"

Clocking in at 150 pages, "Westward the Course of Empire Takes Its Way," the concluding piece from *Girl with Curious Hair,* has the page bulk of a short novel and the dramatic compression of a short story that goes on too long. Taken on its own as a freestanding work, the novella is an engaging piece of pretentious juvenilia; read as a precursor to *Infinite Jest,* it stands as a fascinating programmatic declaration of intent. As the title clearly suggests, the work seeks to chart, if not to arrive at, a new direction for narrative art, one that will move fiction past John Barth's literature of exhaustion and the new realism of the 1980s. Mark Nechtr, the novella's clumsily named hero/artist, desires "to write something that stabs you in the heart. That pierces you, makes you think you're going to die" (333). Though neither Nechtr nor the work's narrator can pinpoint what this new, heart-stabbing brand of fiction will be called— "Maybe it's called metalife. Or metafiction. Or realism. Or gfhrytytu. . . . Maybe it's not called anything"—both affirm that it will "use metafiction as a bright smiling disguise, a harmless floppy-shoed costume" to lure the reader into its dangerous interior, where Mark's arrow/pen will find its target. "Westward" is *not* that piece of fiction, a fact both Wallace and his narrator surrogate are at pains to declare up front; *Infinite Jest,* by way of contrast, emphatically *is.* The novella, then, for all its faults, stands as one of the most important texts in Wallace's oeuvre, an astonishingly confident preface to a masterpiece he had not even written yet.

Wallace first opens himself up to criticism by setting the piece in a graduate-school fiction workshop. Like everything else in the story, this choice of setting is a deliberate provocation as well as a central component of the novella's purpose. The piece is quite literally a piece of "workshop fiction," that is, a story about creative-writing workshops that also seeks to "workshop" some of Wallace's own ideas about how to move past the institutionalization of postmodernism and minimalism and return fiction to those readers who want to be "stabbed in the heart." It is also a work of criticism whose primary target is the meta-fiction of Wallace's strongest artistic influence, John Barth. As Wallace points out in his acknowledgements, the piece is unapologetically "written in the margins" of American literature's most famous piece of metafiction, John Barth's "Lost in the Funhouse," a story that was also, not accidentally, perhaps the first work of American fiction to reflect the pernicious influence on authorial creativity of creative writing workshops. "Criticism is response," one character affirms early in the story, "which is good," since an idea worthy of criticism is an idea that "engages imaginations" and spurs on the creation of new work. Likewise, Wallace's story openly criticizes Barth in the hope that such a critique will generate something new.

Ultimately, Wallace treats Barth's achievement as the oedipal father of his own artistic enterprise, in deliberate accordance with Harold Bloom's famous theory of artistic influence as outlined in *The Anxiety of Influence*. In Bloom's formulation, "Westward" enacts a *clinamen*, or a "poetic misreading or misprision" of Barth's famous story, in that it offers itself as "a corrective" to "Lost in the Funhouse," a text that, Wallace might say, borrowing Bloom's language, "went accurately up to a certain point, but then should have swerved, precisely in the direction" that "Westward" proposes.[12] Far from being precursors to or inadvertent influences on the story, Barth and Bloom serve as foregrounded "objects" of the text itself, thereby making the

novella as a whole a self-conscious act of patricide. More specifically, "Westward" should be read as a metafictional critique of
metafiction that seeks to demolish even metafiction's own claim
to imperious self-consciousness in the hopes that, "out of the
rubble," Wallace can go on to "reaffirm the idea of art being a
living transaction between humans."[13]

Barth's hero in "Lost in the Funhouse" is a thirteen-year-old
boy named Ambrose Mensch, a vaguely autobiographical figure
for Barth himself. The story, set in Maryland during World War
II, concerns a family trip to Ocean City Amusement Park, during which young Ambrose literally gets lost in the park's funhouse attraction. The experience marks a double awakening,
figured in the story as Ambrose's fall from innocence. Alone and
separated from his brother, not to mention the object of his
desire, a neighbor girl named Magda, Ambrose figures out both
that funhouses are "for lovers" and that he is doomed to be a
writer. This sexual and vocational awakening results in a form
of self-consciousness that Barth dramatizes as debilitating self-
alienation. Likewise, the writer of the story—possibly the adult
Ambrose remembering this event—experiences difficulty telling
his story, so self-conscious is he about the nature of his task. The
text therefore becomes a self-referencing hall of mirrors, refer-
ring back to itself, exposing its levers, and leading the reader
down a confusing labyrinth of false starts and double turns. The
opening passage signals the author's intention: "For whom is
the funhouse fun? Perhaps for lovers. For Ambrose it is *a place
of fear and confusion.*" The concluding paragraph completes
this idea: "[Ambrose] wishes he had never entered the funhouse.
But he has. Then he wishes he were dead. But he's not. Therefore he will construct funhouses for others and be their secret
operator—though he would rather be among the lovers for

whom funhouses are designed."[14] Here, the numerous layers of the story converge: Ambrose the boy lost inside the funhouse wishing he could return to his presexual innocence merges with Ambrose the adult postmodern writer who wishes he could return to a time when writing stories was not so fraught with self-consciousness. But Barth also expresses here a fundamental lament for all writers, who must toil in creative anxiety to make funhouses/texts that others get to experience freely, as lovers and readers. What is more, the two Ambroses at work here are both, Barth suggests, lost inside the story in that they have become constructs of language and therefore subjects of their own fictions. Hence the text becomes a funhouse of self-reflecting mirrors with no exit, no way back into the world of the real.

The hero of Wallace's story is, in more ways than one, Ambrose's offspring. His name, Mark Nechtr, references Ambrose's name in two ways: the first name evokes an earlier Ambrose story from Barth's collection, "Ambrose his Mark," in which Ambrose first acquires his name (and therefore enters the prison house of language), while the second name, "Nechtr," with its missing final vowel, calls attention to the fact that "Ambrose" essentially falls two letters short of the word "ambrosia," food of the gods. Wallace's Mark Nechtr, then, is the nectar of Barth's ambrosia. Mark Nechtr is also a writing student in the workshop of a one "Professor Ambrose," the star of the East Chesapeake Tradeschool Writing Program and the author of a famous short story titled "Lost in the Funhouse." Wallace's strategy here is multilayered and pointed: whereas Ambrose is Barth's constructed version of his own self-alienated identity as a writer, Wallace makes the fictional construct the object of his patricide, thereby getting back at Barth from inside the very structure in which Barth "lost his way." As Ambrose tells Nechtr, he, Ambrose, "*is* a character in and the object of the seminal *Lost in the Funhouse;* but he is not the main character, or hero or subject, since fictionists who tell the truth aren't able to use real names" (261). Ambrose is also an object inside Wallace's funhouse, but he is also the "subject," since he is a fictionalized version of Wallace's target, John Barth himself.

The novella's narrator—apparently another member of the workshop—tells us that Mark "doesn't trust" Ambrose's influence on him but that he "listens to him" all the same. "Even when he doesn't listen to him, he's consciously reacting against the option of listening, and listens for what not to listen to" (293). Mark, then, is *Wallace*'s own Ambrose, that is, his a fictionalized version of his own writerly identity. Late in the novella, we even learn that Mark will one day write a somewhat autobiographical story about his own writerly anxieties in which his fictional alter ego will be named Dave. Unlike the nervous, physically inept Ambrose, Mark is "one of those late-adolescent chosen who radiate the kind of careless health so complete it's sickening" (233). If Ambrose is Barth's figure for the writer of exhaustion, then Mark Nechtr is Wallace's projection of the writer of literature's resuscitation. Mark is also an archery prodigy, perhaps a nod to Wallace's own career as a near-great juniors tennis player and surely a metaphor for Mark's authorial identity, wherein the arrow and its target become rich, layered symbols for the pen and the reader, respectively. Whereas the funhouse, with its mirrors reflecting mirrors, serves as Barth's symbol for the postmodern text, archery becomes Wallace's symbol for the new relationship between writer and reader that he is proposing. In a passage that deftly justifies the presence within the text of the "author" figure, Barth's narrator observes, "In a funhouse mirror-room you can't see yourself go on forever, because no matter how you stand, your head gets in the way."[15] Conversely, Wallace's narrator, in a clearly related passage, explains,

> As you . . . draw your 12–strand string to the tip of your nose, the point of your arrow, at full draw, is somewhere between three and nine centimeters to the left of the true straight line to the bull's-eye, even though the arrow's nock, fucked by the string, is *on* that line. The bow gets in the way, you see. So logically it seems like if your sight and aim are truly true, the arrow should always land just to the left of target-center, since it's angled off in the wrong direction right from the beginning. But the straight-aimed and so off-angled target arrow will stab the center, right in the heart, every time. It is an archer's law that makes no sense. (293–94)

It is also, in Wallace's conception, an authorial law that makes no sense. The arrow, regarded as Wallace's pen, hits the "heart" only when it is "off-angled" from the start, that is, aimed not "realistically" toward its subject but rather obliquely, fabulously, perhaps self-reflexively. Whereas Barth sees the mediating writer as an impediment to clear vision, Wallace sees that same writer as the mediator who, though in the way, also allows for the text to "stab the center, right in the heart." What matters is not the point of departure—the artist, with his hangups and self-consciousness—but rather "what happens *while it's traveling* to the waiting target" (294).

Wallace takes his most devastating shot at Barth via the novella's central plot device, in which Mark accompanies his wife, Drew-Lynn Eberhardt, a former child actor, to Collision, Illinois, where she will attend the Reunion of Everyone Who

Has Ever Appeared in a McDonald's Commercial, an event created by J. D. Steelritter, an advertising and marketing genius who is also engaged in turning Professor Ambrose's short story, "Lost in the Funhouse," into a national franchise of Funhouse discothèques that promise "New and *Improved* Fun" (242). Here Wallace makes his most overt argument that Barth's postmodernist techniques have not only been appropriated by popular culture but in fact have been turned into a "franchise" of sorts. Wallace's narrator argues that metafiction is not only "safe to read, familiar as syndication" (333), but also similar, in some ways, to advertising and popular culture. Popular culture, we learn, "is the *symbolic representation of what people already believe*" (271), whereas the techniques employed by the advertising profession, in Steelritter's conception, bear more than a passing resemblance to the impulses driving Barth's metafictional project. "Stories are basically like ads," Steelritter explains, since both are "like getting laid," that is, both are seductions that feed on the fears and desires of the seduced. Steelritter is the John Barth of advertising, for he, too, wants to push advertising to its "end," its exhaustion, and the reunion in Collision is his means of doing so. Once everyone who has ever appeared in a McDonald's commercial is gathered together, he will shower them all with "U.S.D.A. Grade A blood" and watch "thirty years' consumers, *succumbing*, as *one*" (310). In this way he hopes to disclose—as Barth does with his metafictional techniques—"What They Want," and in this moment of recapitulation and self-reflexivity, "advertising will have finally arrived at the death that's been it's object all along. And in that Death will of course become Life" (310). Here Wallace alludes to Barth's famous pronouncement, in "The Literature of Exhaustion," that the postmodern writer should "paradoxically turn the felt ultimacies of our time into material and means for his work—*paradoxically*, because by doing so he transcends what appeared to be his refutation."[16] Similarly, the public, confronted with a demonstration of the "end" of all advertising, will "doubt what they fear, believe what they wish" and "fact will become fiction will be fact. Ambrose and his academic heirs will rule, without rules. *Meatfiction*" (310).

Typically, Mark finds Steelritter's theories both disturbing and "apposite," for they zero in on what has always troubled him about Ambrose's story, as well as his teacher's "willingness to franchise his art into a new third dimension—to build 'real' Funhouses" (331). For him, Ambrose is constructing "a Funhouse for lovers out of a story that does not love" (332). Like an ad—and particularly sophisticated contemporary ads in which the product being advertised is largely secondary to the seductive world created by the ad itself—a metafictional story is always "untrue, as a lover" because "Itself is its only object. It's the act of a lonely solipsist's self-love" (332). Metafiction fails because it does not invite us inside but rather makes us stand back and watch the author look at his own reflection; the reader is left *outside,* alone, and the one thing Mark hates more than anything in the world is "to believe he is alone. Solipsism affects him like Ambrosian metafiction affects him. It's the high siren's song of the wrist's big razor" (303). Once again linking metafiction and advertising, Wallace has Steelritter echo Mark's language when he affirms that all advertising feeds on the "solipsistic delusion" that each of us feels like he or she is "the only person in the world who feels like he's the only person in the world" (305). "Solipsism binds us together, J.D. knows. . . . It's Steelritter's meat" (309). Wallace's work, conversely, seeks not to depict solipsism but rather to overcome it.

Not surprisingly, Mark's lover, D.L., is a self-proclaimed postmodernist whose first story for workshop opens with the line, "Nouns verbed by, adverbially adjectival" (234). Perhaps even more so than Ambrose and Steelritter, she represents everything about postmodern literature that Wallace longs to demolish. Paradoxically, she struck her childhood admirer Tom Sternberg as "*developed*" at an early age yet seems to him now, in her adult guise, as not only "*under*developed" but also "undesirable" and "*unlovable*" (281). Elsewhere Wallace describes her as "greedy and self-serving, and not near naïve enough to get away with the way she seemed"; what's more, there is "little to love" since she cannot "see past her infatuation with her own cleverness to separate posture from pose, desire from supplication" (234). In another nod toward Barth's *Lost in the Funhouse,* which opens with a dramatic monologue told by a self-conscious and metaphysically preoccupied sperm as he works his way toward an awaiting egg, Wallace has Mark marry her because she has apparently gotten pregnant from a one-night stand during which Mark used protection. When we later learn that she has faked the pregnancy, we understand that Wallace is indicating not only that D.L. cannot "produce" as a lover but also that his new art will "marry" D.L.'s cynical postmodernism with Mark's naïve openness.

This will be a tense marriage, to say the least. In the paraphrase sketch of Mark's breakthrough story that occupies the novella's final movement, his alter ego Dave is involved with an appealing but "self-obsessed" lover named "L—," clearly a reference to D.L. but also, perhaps, a nod to *Girl with Curious Hair*'s dedicatee, also called L—. Inasmuch as this L— might refer to an actual person in Wallace's life, the novella also makes clear that L— could also stand for "Literature," which in turn would make D.L. stand for "Death Literature" or the literature of exhaustion. In the story, Dave returns from a successful archery tournament, gets into a fight with L—, and watches as she stabs herself with his pen/arrow. Though the coroner declares the cause of L—'s death to be "old age" and Dave is innocent of the murder—really a suicide—Dave nevertheless realizes his fingerprints are all over the shaft and so goes to prison for a crime he did not commit but for which he accepts complicity. He is "Not Guilty, yet is at the same time *guilty* of being Not Guilty: his adult fear of the community's interpretation of his prints and shaft has caused him to abandon his arrow, to betray a lover, to violate his own primal instinct toward honor" (360). Like Wallace, then, Dave ignores the coroner's analysis of L—'s "natural exhaustion" but also takes credit for his complicity in helping to "kill" L— with his pen/arrow. In short, the story is "interpreted by the workshop as about a whole new generation's feelings of amorphous but deserved guilt, confinement, fear, confusion, and yes, the place of honor in the general postmodern American scheme of things" (364).

While in prison, Dave is set upon by a vicious "counterfeiter" named Mark, who, one night, affects an escape. Mark here represents a recursive link back to the outer frame of the story and to Nechtr himself, but he also feeds back into the way the novella "counterfeits" Barth's "Lost in the Funhouse." Dave is "guilty" of the same crime as Mark; what's more, the way these two figures reverse the reality/fiction dichotomy parallels Wallace's own use of "Ambrose" as the novella's version of the real John Barth. In all four cases, the names create a closed circuit that allows the world outside the text to maintain its integrity. Tellingly, when Dave is offered the chance to "rat out"

Mark and thus get rewarded with "solitary confinement," a clear improvement on his status within the prison as everyone's rape victim, Dave refuses the offer, declaring instead, "I'm going to be sentenced to Life" (365). The puns here are rich and suggestive: Dave is going to made into "sentences" that will return him to "Life," and he will accomplish this by not giving over to the prison—which we now understand has been from the beginning a reference to the famed "prison house of language" erected by poststructuralist thought—"the one thing" that he cannot lose: his honor. As Ambrose himself remarks, during the story's workshop session, "The argument here is that [Dave's refusal] keeps safe in its ghastly silent center the green kernel that is the true self" (368).

Herein lies the heart—literally and figuratively—of Wallace's method and the primary rationale for the vast recursive structure that he will employ in *Infinite Jest*. Like Mark's Dave, Wallace will in fact enter the prison house of postmodern self-reflexivity and experience all the cruelty that such enclosure might involve, but he will also "keep[] safe in its ghastly silent center" the world of the real, the world outside the text, that is, the text's transcendent referent. Directly quoting a Cynthia Ozick story entitled "Usurpation (Other People's Stories)," the narrator describes the novella's originating "story" as existing *outside* the text itself: "The tale is . . . menacingly alive, self-sufficient, organic, sounding the distant groan of growth, trading chemicals briskly with the air, but still outside the creature who desires to take it inside and make a little miracle" (294).[17] The edible roses that Ambrose gives Mark as a gift also feed into this theme of outside/inside. The roses, D.L. understands, marry "desire and fear into a kind of passionate virtuosity"—the latter phrase, of course, drawn, once again, from Barth's essays—

and yet they represent for her "Aesthetic Murder-One" in the way they represent the (literal) eating of beauty. "D.L.'s got some desires, but says no thanks to eating what stands outside you, red and eternal" (320). Barth's work insists that there is no escaping the funhouse of the text; Wallace's work, conversely, insists that there must remain *something* outside the text, something "red and eternal" and "menacingly alive, self-sufficient, organic, sounding the distant groan of growth, trading chemicals briskly with the air."

This latter assertion perhaps accounts for why "Westward," like so much of Wallace's work, fails to reach a satisfying conclusion. Again anticipating the structure and design of *Infinite Jest,* the whole final movement of the novella is a protracted tease, as Steelritter, his son DeHaven, Mark, D.L., Sternberg, and "Magda"—who, in another case of elaborate textual recursivity, either represents the "actual" Magda of Barth's short story or is Ambrose in disguise—all move slowly toward "Collision" and the orgiastic "end of advertising" staged by Steelritter. But they never get there. They head north, rather than west, only to watch DeHaven's "pastiche" car conk out. Westward toward completion the story does in fact move, but, as in the story-within-the-story that actually "concludes" the novella, Wallace withholds the actual collision in favor of a deeper recursivity that serves to put off final arrival and keep something safe and integral outside the text. The structure is a play on Zeno's paradox, whereby one can approach but never finally reach X, where the gap between the two coordinate points—X and Y, Wallace's Mark and You the reader—represents the place where the novella finally gets "sentenced to Life."

The novella thereby fulfills Mark's (and Wallace's) desire to build a text that treats its reader like a lover and that has been constructed by an "architect who could hate enough to feel enough to love enough to perpetrate the kind of special cruelty only real lovers can inflict" (332). In this sort of story, the writer will "shove" the reader inside the text, where everything is "wildly disordered, but creepily so, hard and cold as windshield glass; each possible sensory angle is used, every carefully-taught technique in [the writer's] quiver expended, since each 'technique' is really just a reflective surface that betrays what it pretends to reveal" (331). The reader/lover will move through the text and experience "the motion of travel, except no travel," with the "Exit and Egress and End in full view the whole time" (332). Meanwhile, the architect will "get back out before the happy jaws meet tight" (331). Finally, in a late reprise of the novella's ongoing archery metaphor, Wallace describes the narrative movement as similar to the way a "whistling arrow zigzags, moving . . . alternately left and right, though in *ever diminishing amounts* . . . , until at a certain point the arrow, aimed with all sincerity just West of the lover, is on line with his heart" (333). When DeHaven's car stalls just shy of Collision, the novella itself has paradoxically aligned itself with the reader's heart.

Not surprisingly, the story ends somewhat where it begins, with a quotation from Barth's "Lost in the Funhouse." One of the novella's two epigraphs is the first line of Barth's story: "For whom is the Funhouse fun?" The answer, of course, is, "For lovers." Since Wallace's lover is his reader, whom his text "loves" in a way that Barth's does not, he aptly concludes his story with a direct appeal to the reader, who is still inside the text with the Exit finally in view. There has been no "conclusion" or "collision," but this "cruelty" is offset by the text's final concern for the reader's well being. The text promises that "no salesman will call" and that it "wants nothing" from the reader any longer. The reader is simply asked to "listen to the silence behind the engines' noise," that is, to the secure world outside the text, which the text has not placed inside. That silence is a "love song," for it is an indicator of the novella's respect for the real world to which all worthwhile literature must finally return us. The song is sung for the lover because, the text affirms in its final line, "You are loved" (373). No longer lost inside the funhouse, that place of "fear and confusion," and insured of his integrity through the recursive creation of both Mark and Dave —not to mention Ambrose and Magda and even Ronald McDonald himself, played here by Steelritter's son DeHaven— Wallace essentially declares himself ready to build a genuine funhouse that will rival that of his predecessors and assuage, rather than re-present, loneliness. And that funhouse will be the novel *Infinite Jest*.

---

# CHAPTER 4

## *Infinite Jest*

### Too Much Fun for Anyone Mortal
### to Hope to Endure

With his first two books, *The Broom of the System* and *Girl with Curious Hair,* David Foster Wallace firmly established himself as a precocious new talent with ambition, originality, and energy to burn. Clearly Wallace deserved all the attention and praise he had garnered. Nevertheless, these books were still formative: inasmuch as they sought to chart a new direction for postmodern fiction, they were perhaps even more concerned with establishing a blueprint for Wallace's subsequent career. The young author—still in his twenties at the time—could not have been any clearer about the literary tradition into which he wanted to be placed, or any more direct and audacious about the claims he made for his possible, but still imminent, importance. As his narrator declared in "Westward the Course of Empire Takes Its Way," Wallace, right from the beginning, saw himself as "a boy hotly cocky enough to think he might someday inherit [John Barth's] bald crown and ballpoint scepter, to wish to try to sing to the *next* generation."[1] From the bold black arrows that preceded the individual chapters in *The Broom of the System* to the title of his programmatic novella, these books announced at every turn that more was to come.

Seven years would pass before readers had an opportunity to see if Wallace was as good as his word. In the meantime, the literary landscape had changed considerably, somewhat due to Wallace's own influence. In the wake of Wallace's bold revival of—to use John Barth's phrase—postmodern "maximalism," a number of new writers—chiefly William Vollmann, Jonathan Franzen, and Richard Powers—had emerged to stake a claim to the same throne that Wallace had declared as his own. Between 1989 and 1996, the literary community saw the publication of Vollmann's *Fathers and Crows,* Franzen's *Strong Motion,* and Powers's *The Gold-Bug Variations,* all of them important novels that, in their size, thematic scope, and formal ambition, revisited the same tradition of postmodern self-reflexivity and encyclopedic breadth that Wallace had tapped into with his first two books. Almost overnight the game had changed, and the stakes had gotten higher.

Even among heightened competition, *Infinite Jest,* the 1,079-page novel Wallace unleashed on the world in early spring of 1996, more than fulfilled the immense promise he had hinted at in his earlier work. It also established him as perhaps the foremost writer of a remarkable generation of ambitious new novelists—a generation that, as Wallace himself had predicted in his second book, he would someday lead. Once again proving that "cynicism and naïveté" are not mutually exclusive, Wallace produced a book that works as both a labyrinthine work of Pynchonesque complexity as well as a tender and comic coming-of-age story. Like *The Broom of the System, Infinite Jest* is set in a slightly cockeyed near future; also like its predecessor, the book yokes together a vast, heterogeneous collection of themes and concerns. Wallace continues to link issues of language, signification, solipsism, and objectification, as he did in *The Broom of the System,* while at the same time expanding *Girl with Curious Hair*'s preoccupation with pop-culture, irony, and self-reflexivity. To these abiding concerns he adds a number of new preoccupations, such as drug addiction, terrorism, politics, and tennis. The result is a book that functions as both the culmination of his earlier work and a remarkable expansion of his reach and ambition. Whereas the earlier books are frankly anxious about the various debts they owe to the preceding generation of postmodern writers, *Infinite Jest,* perhaps more so than anything else Wallace has thus far published, stands on its own as a work of tireless invention and lasting importance, standing shoulder to shoulder with such works as Pynchon's *Gravity's Rainbow,* Gaddis's *The Recognitions,* and Barth's *Giles Goat-Boy* without for a moment seeming derivative or ancillary.

What every reviewer and reader of *Infinite Jest* must first contend with is the book's sheer bulk, its massive size. The length is at once a challenge, a threat, and an enticement. But the book is not only incredibly long; it is also, in many ways, deliberately difficult, the way so much of the century's great fiction has been. The book features an enormous cast of characters numbering in the hundreds, employs an intricate and insular mock argot of coined terms and made-up slang, engages directly and learnedly with such arcane subjects as theoretical math and lens technology and computer science, and concludes with a hundred pages of endnotes. To read the book a reader needs two bookmarks, one to mark her progress through the body text and the other to track her progress through the endnotes. And because of the book's supersophisticated vocabulary and its complex syntax, this same reader should also keep handy an *OED* and perhaps even a *Pharmaceutical Encyclopedia.*

For all of this, almost all of the book's initial reviewers were also amazed its warmth and accessibility. One reviewer called it "surprisingly readable," while novelist David Gates, in *Newsweek,* described the reading experience as "weird fun," which phrase pretty much captures what Wallace is up to with this novel. The book itself is an "infinite jest"—a seemingly endless source of readerly pleasure—yet it is also, paradoxically, both a diagnosis and a critique of the culture's addiction to pleasure. Frank Louis Cioffi, in a perceptive reader-response essay recently published in *Narrative,* succinctly articulates the nature of this paradoxical agenda when he writes, "The novel's impact derives in part from how it is at once an easy, pleasurable novel to read— full of narrative action, excitement, local delights—and at the same time a trying, annoying, difficult novel that is constantly interrupting itself, breaking comfortable routines it has set up, and, in many cases, syntactically reinventing the English language." *Infinite Jest* embodies the seductive pleasure-agenda of television and pop culture and at the same time embeds this pleasure-agenda in a demanding and imposing fictional structure in order, as Wallace puts it, "to force you to work hard to access its pleasures, the same way that in real life true pleasure is usually a by-product of hard work and discomfort."[2]

In these and other ways, *Infinite Jest* fulfills Wallace's ambition, as laid out in "Westward the Course of Empire Takes Its Way," to create a story that loves enough to be cruel. Like the projected work outlined in that novella, *Infinite Jest,* with its mesmerizing prose and its freewheeling comedy, is itself a funhouse into which the reader is seductively invited. The novel's tremendous length, its numerous syntactical and structural difficulties, its metafictional devices, its circular plot structure, and even its anticlimactic conclusion create a funhouse in which there is "the illusion (sic) of both the dreamer's unmoving sprint and the disco-moonwalker's backward glide." This sense of a "dreamer's unmoving spring" resides in the way the novel's plot advances and retreats at the same time, in the way the reading itself moves from the body text to the endnotes and back again, and in the way the "action" grinds to an actual halt for the last 170 pages, most of which are cast from the perspective of paralyzed and immobile Don Gately. Wallace understands that "it would take one cold son of a bitch to write such a place erect," yet he also understands—affirms, rather—that this sort of funhouse is a "whole different breed from the basically benign and cheery metafiction" of his forbears. This kind of funhouse, he declares, takes "an architect who could hate enough to feel enough to love enough to perpetrate the kind of special cruelty only real lovers can inflict."[3] Or, to put Wallace's argument another way, the book is cruel to its readers, but for the readers' own good.

To get a sense of how this two-part strategy actually operates, one need only look at Wallace's now famous—possibly infamous—use of endnotes. At the most basic level, the endnotes disrupt the narrative; simultaneously, they call attention to the fact that the book we are reading is a construct, that the world of the book is a mediated world. The endnotes are at once the novel's most overtly metafictional device, the most visible emblem of its enormous difficulty, and one of its most inexhaustible sources of fun. Readers of the book quickly learn that the notes can provide useless information, essential information, extra but nonessential narrative, or even, at times, narrative that is more important to the ongoing novel than the passage to which the note is attached. Readers can, and even must, devise some way to read through the book that allows them to keep their focus on the story while also mining the notes for all their information, comedy, and readerly pleasure. Paradoxically, the notes enhance the reader's intimacy with the text even as they highlight the story's artificiality. Wallace, speaking of another work of his, explains his intentions in this way: "It's trying to prohibit the reader from forgetting that she's receiving heavily mediated data, that this process is a relationship between the writer's consciousness and her own, and that in order for it to be anything like a real full human relationship, she's going to have to put in her share of the linguistic work." In doing that "linguistic work," Wallace and his reader become a community where meaning is made, in Wittgenstein's sense. At the same time, the metafictional elements of the endnotes do double duty as indicators of the story's mediation and a means by which Wallace can "reaffirm the idea of art being a living transaction between humans."[4]

Such a multivalent, circular novel presents special problems for the critic, who must decide where to start unpacking the plot, particularly since that plot achieves meaning through layering rather than through traditional cause and effect. As critic Katherine Hayles remarks, "For such a novel any starting point would be to some extent arbitrary, for no matter where one starts, everything eventually cycles together with everything else." Hayles is surely right, as the following pages will show. Still, most readers have discerned at least two primary plot lines, both of which are linked by a third strand. Cioffi speculates that the work is really "three novels in one," each "novel" cast in a more or less traditional form that is undercut and complicated by the unorthodox subplots that spiral off and create bewildering connections reminiscent of Thomas Pynchon's method in *Gravity's Rainbow.*[5]

The plot line of central importance involves Hal Incandenza, a seventeen-year-old "lexical prodigy" and aspiring tennis pro who studies, trains, and experiences deep-rooted dread at the Enfield Tennis Academy, run and owned by his brilliant but also troubled parents, Avril and Jim, the latter of whom committed suicide five years prior to the novel's historical present. This plot, as many have noted, constitutes a more or less traditional bildungsroman, that is, a novel of development and education, a reading that is particularly apt in view of the many similarities between Hal and Wallace. The Hal story, with its concentration on boarding-school life, its cast of precocious teenagers and grotesque cripples, and its numerous moments of high comedy, also invokes such past works as John Irving's *The Hotel New Hampshire* and even Charles Dickens's *David Copperfield*. The plot of second importance—a "metamorphosis" story, according to Cioffi—focuses on Don Gately, a massive twenty-eight-year-old oral-narcotics addict who is recovering from his addiction at the Ennet House Drug and Alcohol Recovery House, located just down the hill from the Enfield Tennis Academy. The "linking plot" is a quest narrative involving the search for the master copy of a lethally entertaining film called *Infinite Jest* that renders anyone who sees it a catatonic infant capable of nothing more than repeated viewing. This narrative strand links the previous two stories, which otherwise barely interact, chiefly through the figure of the lethal film's "auteur," none other than Hal's dead father, James Incandenza. Meanwhile, one of the stars of the film, radio actor Joelle van Dyne (stage name "Madame Psychosis"), is both a former girlfriend of Hal's older brother, Orin, and a new resident of Ennet House—not to mention Don Gately's potential future lover. Certainly, this third plot invokes the paranoid quest narratives of Pynchon's *V., The Crying of Lot 49,* and *Gravity's Rainbow,* yet at the same time it is also more overt (and funny) than Pynchon in the way it parodies the quest narratives of popular entertainment, whose archetypal conventions both Pynchon and Wallace playfully employ. In Wallace's case, these source narratives include the traditional detective story, Hollywood thrillers, and even J. R. R. Tolkien's *The Lord of the Rings*.

In addition to all the narrative genres listed above, Wallace's encyclopedic novel also takes on the conventions of science fiction, specifically in its use of a futuristic setting. *The Broom of the System* was also set in the "future," but only in an imagined 1990, a mere three years after the date of the book's publication; aside from the invention of the Great Ohio Desert, very little about the world of that novel seems different from our own. Conversely, *Infinite Jest* is a world all to itself, a virtual reality in the most literal sense of that term. Broadcast television has been replaced by a complex system of rentable "cartridges" manufactured and distributed by a monolithic Microsoftlike company called InterLace, with additional programming provided through "spontaneous transmissions" via a vast "grid" that seems modeled on our own Internet. The InterLace system therefore allows viewers the opportunity to "more or less *100% choose what's on at any given time.*"[6] Since this new system eliminates commercial advertising, the government, sometime early in the new millennium, devises Subsidized Time, whereby calendar years are no longer designated by numbers—1998, say—but rather by commercial products. Hence one year is renamed the Year of the Whopper, followed a year later by the Year of the Tucks Medicated Pad, and so on. The bulk of the novel takes place during the Year of the Depend Adult Undergarment, which appears to correspond to the actual calendar year 2009.[7]

But there is much more. Late in the preceding millennium, one Johnny Gentle, former Las Vegas crooner turned politician, is elected to the U.S. presidency as leader of the "Clean U.S.

Party," a strange amalgam of "ultra-right jingoist hunt-deer-with-automatic-weapons types and far-left macrobiotic . . . ponytailed granola-crunchers" whose chief campaign slogan is "A Tighter, Tidier Nation" (382) and whose second most pressing objective, amid the void left by the end of the Cold War, is to unite the country in opposition to "some cohesion-renewing Other" (384). Gentle's remarkable joint solution to these two problems is, first, to transform a huge swath of New England into a massive glass-walled toxic waste dump called "The Great Concavity," the northeastern tip of which borders Quebec; and second, in response to the sudden dissolution of NATO, to collapse the United States, Canada, and Mexico into a single continental power called the Organization of North American Nations—O.N.A.N. for short. Thus does he dispose of the country's mounting waste, toxic and otherwise, while also creating a brand new "cohesion-renewing Other," namely angry Quebecois separatists and, by extension, disenfranchised Canadians in general. A decade or so after their original conception, Johnny Gentle's giant Concavity and InterLace's at-home entertainment network have yielded a population of lonely, solipsistic voyeurs, an entire nation—continent, rather—overdosing on nonstop entertainment and information, all transmitted instantly by way of the InterLace Dissemination Grid and viewed via high-resolution Teleputers, or TPs, all within the coddled comfort of their increasingly cagelike homes. The streets are meanwhile overrun with bewildered drug addicts and "feral hamsters" bloated to monstrous size, thanks to the toxic and radioactive waste of the Great Concavity. What's more, Quebecois separatist terrorist groups of every sort haunt the public's collective unconscious.

From these basic building blocks Wallace creates densely imagined world that is less a prophetic vision of our future than a slightly askew parallel universe. It is almost as if U.S. history, sometime around the date of the book's publication, branched off into one of those countless "many worlds" hypothesized by quantum physicists. According to this theory, whenever a quantum physicist makes a determination whether or not an observed proton is a particle or a wave, the universe splits so that in one universe, the one in which the observation takes place, the proton is, say, a wave, while in an almost identical universe that same proton is a particle. The two universes now run parallel to one another, each one shaped by the outcome of the respective observation.[8] The world of *Infinite Jest* is just such a parallel world, one that, in its complex and thorough imaginative self-containment, manages paradoxically to call increased attention to the world *outside* the novel, that is, the world of the reader, the observer, since the book refuses to allow the reader passively to accept the world within as seamless with the world inside. Wallace has remarked that, for him, the "valence" of fictional meaning is equally distributive: the fiction is changed by the reader as much as the reader is changed by the fiction. What he means by this strange idea is that his books are, in effect, "simply language, and language lives not just in but *through* the reader."[9] The futuristic setting, then, disentangles the world of the novel from the world of the novel's reception, thereby emphasizing the fact that the book is merely language; at the same time, this parallel world, like a "new" universe in a quantum phenomenon, assumes meaning only virtue of the observer/reader who brings the world to life.

For all its artificiality, the world of the novel is still very "real" to Wallace's characters, who inhabit Johnny Gentle's postmillennium O.N.A.N. as naturally as Tolkien's hobbits and orcs maneuver their way through Middle Earth. As suggested above, *The Lord of the Rings* is also a possible analogue for the novel's quest narrative, whereby the film itself, referred to throughout the novel as "the Entertainment," becomes Wallace's stand-in for Tolkien's famous Ring. Whereas in Tolkien's trilogy the magical Ring is pursued by ring wraiths, black-hooded riders who tirelessly pursue the questing hobbits at every turn, in Wallace's novel the role of ring wraiths is taken over by a group of Quebecois terrorists in wheelchairs—the dreaded *Assassins des Fauteuils Rollents*—who hope to disseminate the film through the InterLace grid in the interest of furthering the cause of Quebecois separatism. For them the Entertainment is a *samizdat* text—*samizdat* being a Russian word defined by Hal as "any sort of politically underground or beyond-the-pale press or the stuff published thereby" (1011n)—while for others it is an outwardly benign pleasure device that turns deadly and debilitating.

Though the film sits firmly at the core of the story, Wallace deliberately shrouds it in tantalizing mystery. We get glimpses of people watching the film, as well as a number of sometimes conflicting accounts of the film's content, yet we never get to see the film directly: the book's primary symbol is in fact an absent center. Still, a number of the *samizdat's* features can be outlined with some certainty. James Incandenza allegedly produced the movie in the Year of the Trial-Sized Dove Bar, three months before he committed a grisly suicide by exploding his head in a microwave oven. In an elaborate mock bibliography of Incandenza's complete works, Wallace's narrator declares that the film is listed as "unfinished, unseen" (993n). The only listed star is "Madame Psychosis," more properly Joelle Van Dyne, whom Orin once nicknamed "the P.G.O.A.T.," an acronym for the Prettiest Girl Of All Time. Orin gave her this name because she "induced in heterosexual males . . . the Acteon Complex, which is a kind of deep phylogenic fear of transhuman beauty" (290). The mock-Freudian term refers to Ovid's account in *The Metamorphosis* of Acteon, a hunter who is turned into a stag after watching the chaste goddess Diana bathe. In one account of the film's content—supplied by a character named Molly Notkin, whose reliability, for various reasons, remains questionable— Joelle is alleged to portray "some kind of maternal instantiation of the archetypal figure of Death, sitting naked, corporeally gorgeous, ravishing, hugely pregnant, . . . explaining in very simple childlike language to whomever the film's camera represents that Death is always female, and that the female is always maternal. I.e. that the woman who kills you is always your next life's mother" (788). In Joelle's own account—also somewhat suspect, since she admits she never saw the completed film—this same main character wears an "incredible white-floor-length gown of some sort of flowing material" and spends the film bent over a crib saying "I'm sorry. I'm so terribly sorry. I am so, so sorry" (939). Both accounts agree that the vantage point of the film is a "crib's-eye view," and that this driving scene utilizes a special lens attached to some sort of turret that Incandenza termed "an auto-wobble" or "ocular wobble" (939). Apparently this lens, with its wobble effect, is designed to reproduce "neonatal nystagmus," a reference to the "wobbled and weird" quality of a newborn's primitive powers of vision (939).

Although this is all we know about the content of the Entertainment, it is surely enough, for even these scant particulars comprise a concise outline of the novel's major themes. Symbolically, the film conflates two of the book's principal concerns: the mounting centrality of pop culture and our culture's increasing susceptibility to addictive drugs. With its preoccupation with mothers, infantile desire, and pleasure, the film also serves as Wallace's response to the work of French psychoanalytic theorist Jacques Lacan, whose complex rereading of Freud corresponds, in some ways, to Derrida's rereading of Continental philosophy. Just as *The Broom of the System* addresses the alienating trap of Derridean deconstruction, *Infinite Jest* takes on Lacan's bewilderingly difficult theories about desire, pleasure, subjectivity, and infantile preoccupations with mothers. Although the film, which is the novel's central metaphor, seems to be the primary weapon of Wallace's critique—the above description of its contents reads like a direct transcription of Lacan's ideas—Lacanian concepts permeate the entire novel. Therefore, in the same way that a coherent reading of *The Broom of the System* first demands a familiarity with Wittgenstein's *Philosophical Investigations,* a cogent interpretation of *Infinite Jest* first entails a brief encounter with Lacanian theory.[10] Ultimately, *Infinite Jest* demonstrates that Lacan's model of the psychological subject is a seductive but ultimately alienating and harmful idea that can and should be overcome.

Lacan's fundamental innovation was to declare that "in the unconscious is the whole structure of language," which in turn means that "the notion that the unconscious is merely the seat of the instincts will have to be rethought." For Lacan, a poststructuralist deeply influenced by the work of linguist Ferdinand de Saussure, that "language" consists of signifiers that stand for some always deferred signified. Therefore, even at the most presumably irreducible psychic core of our interiors, our unconscious, Lacan discovers an unbreachable gap, that between a signifier and a signified. "The S [Signifier] and the s [signified] of the Saussurian algorithm are not on the same level," Lacan tells us, "and man only deludes himself when he believes his true place is at their axis, which is nowhere."[11]

His concept of the "mirror stage" best articulates the implications of this formative idea, for the mirror stage in Lacan's chronology of psychological development marks the moment when a child first acquires an individual subjectivity, or, more specifically, first recognizes that she is a discrete self, separate from others. In his brief but formative essay, "The Mirror Stage As Formative of the Function of the I As Revealed in Psychoanalytic Experience," Lacan speculates about what exactly is happening in the mind of a child who, although "outdone by the chimpanzee in instrumental intelligence, can nevertheless already recognize as such his own image in the mirror." Prior to this moment, the child imagines a complete identification with all that is outside her, variously cited in Lacan as the "other" and the "(m)other," the latter being the primary source for the satisfaction of desire. Lacan argues that when the child recognizes her reflected image in a mirror, she comes to recognize herself *as* a self, but only in the form of that objective, and inverted, image. In other words, in order for the child to realize she is a distinct being, irreparably separated from others and, in a typically Lacanian pun, (m)others, she must recognize "herself" in the form of an image. She acquires a subjectivity but only by becoming alienated from herself. Or, as Lacan puts it, this image "symbolizes the mental permanence of the *I,* at the same time as it prefigures its alienation."[12] The word *I* has an antecedent for the user that is always prior to that *I* and ultimately inaccessible, in accordance with Lacan's Saussurian *Signifier/signified* equation. The place where they might join—their "axis"—is, for Lacan, "nowhere."

This dialectic of the child and its own image then serves as a springboard for Lacan's larger conception of subjectivity, which, typically, is inextricable from the world of language. The subject, in Lacan, is constituted through language—the *I* with its elusive, always deferred signified—and is therefore also always already deferred, always an "other" totally separate from the self that would presumably be identical with it. To be a subject is to be a "split subject," internally divided between a "self" and an "other," and the omnipresent fact of language is the agent of that alienation. This split subject then spends the rest of her life desiring a return to that early wholeness, that lost one-to-one connection with the (m)other, and this desire takes the form of a series of endless substitutions—material goods, other people, drugs, you name it. This never-to-be-placated desire serves as Lacan's own version of the Freudian id, yet it differs from Freud in that it is not a coherent "engine" within us but rather the product of a lack. Of course, none of these substitute objects gives the subject the "wholeness" she seeks: the desire is endless, insofar as it continues to operate as a substitute for that infantile longing for maternal plenitude.[13]

Wallace is at once sympathetic to and contemptuous of this desire for a return to maternal plenitude. On the one hand, he appreciates the ingenuity with which Lacan accounts for the peculiar unhappiness that permeates our culture of *material* plenitude, for not only does the Lacanian model diagnose why we seem to be getting *more* depressed the more drugs, entertainment, and pleasure we access, but it also builds its diagnoses atop the bulwark of poststructuralist thought, also the frame for Wallace's beloved postmodern metafiction. On the other hand, Wallace sees Lacan's model as a trap, one that can be embraced for good reasons that nevertheless turn out to create more problems than they solve. The film itself is Wallace's most visible emblem of his Lacanian program, for it both embodies and parodies Lacan's ideas. For instance, the fundamental source of the

Entertainment's lethal appeal is its ability to give viewers what they think they have wanted all their lives: namely, a return to some state of maternal plenitude. The viewer is that child staring into a mirror that sends back a vision of the mother *apologizing*—and for what, exactly? Perhaps for not being there, always, as the provider of pleasure and wholeness. Now she *is* there for the viewer, providing the very pleasure the viewer has been seeking elsewhere all along. That viewer therefore is done with desire, and done with desiring.

Yet this complex symbol of the film is buttressed by a number of viciously funny set pieces that attack Lacan right at the jugular, the most prominent of which comes late in the novel, in the form of a support group geared toward helping one access one's "Inner Infant." Participants in this group gather in a room, clutch teddy bears, and tap into their feelings of infantile abandonment. "I'm feeling my Inner Infant standing holding the bars of his crib and looking out of the bars," whines one participant, "and crying for his Mommy and Daddy to come hold him and nurture him" (802). A breakthrough in this form of therapy comes when a participant acquires the "courage and love and commitment to [his] Inner Infant to take the risk and go actively over to somebody that might give [him] what [his] Infant needs," with the other participants chanting "*Needs. Needs. Needs. Needs. Needs*" (808). Wallace's point here couldn't be any clearer: nearly everyone in the significantly designated Year of the Depend Adult Undergarment is a grownup baby in diapers, crawling on all fours in search of something to fill that need for maternal plenitude, for wholeness, or, at the very least, someone or something to blame for his or her own unhappiness. Hal, the novel's hero, admits that "he rather envies a man who feels he has something to explain his being fucked up, parents to blame it on," (805), yet Wallace also understands that this leveling of blame, like Lacan's model, is a fiction, a trap, and a cage.

Madame Psychosis herself is perhaps the richest, most overdetermined focal point for this intricate critique of poststructuralist psychology. Her name can be scanned as "metempsychosis," that is, the transmigration of souls, an interpretation that certainly applies to the effect her beauty has on the film's viewers. As the P.G.O.A.T. and the source of the so-called Acteon complex, she is also a Medusa figure, a woman so lethally beautiful that she transforms anyone in her field of vision into an inanimate object. Incandenza is even reported to have made, early in his career, an experimental postmodern film titled *The Medusa v. The Odalisque,* described at one point as a self-reflexive exercise in mirrors and exhaustion in which all the members of an audience-within-the-film slowly turn, one by one, into stone or ruby statues (396–97).

In her guise as the film's mother-symbol, she also functions as the primary emblem of Incandenza's complex "mother-death-cosmology," itself another pointed critique of Lacan. As the popular radio talk-show host of the strange, formless program, *Sixty Minutes More or Less with Madame Psychosis,* broadcast weekly on the student-run FM station of the Massachusetts Institute of Technology, she provides listeners with something close to maternal security. The primary allure of the show lies in the quality of her voice, which, according to one character, "seems low-depth familiar . . . the way certain childhood smells will strike you as familiar and oddly sad" (189–90). Fittingly, in the role of the apologizing mother in *Infinite Jest,* she represents none other than Death herself, "as in the figure of Death, Death incarnate" (850). As such, she dramatizes Incandenza's central point, namely that "Death happens over and over, you have many lives, and at the end of each one (meaning life) is a woman who kills you and releases you into the next life" (850). That woman is always, he concludes, your next life's mother.

For the novel's multitude of desperate drug addicts, that seductive, murderous woman is the Substance that controls their lives. Once these characters succumb to their addiction, their preaddiction selves are murdered, never to rise again, while the woman-murderer, here the drug that has enslaved them, becomes the mother-creator of their new addictive lives, now little more than "womb[s] of solipsism" and forms of "death in life." The film's debilitating effect on its viewer therefore recapitulates the addictive experience. Not accidentally, Madame Psychosis is also the street name for a particularly lethal "organo-synthesized hallucinogen" named DMZ, which Hal Incandenza may or may not have ingested near the end of the novel. Hence, whether playing the ravishingly beautiful maternal nude or the endlessly apologizing celestial mother, Madame Psychosis presents to the film's lonely viewers an irresistible vision of wishes fulfilled, a pornographic object of masturbatory desire (this all takes place in O.N.A.N., after all), one that provides viewers with the fulfilling desire they have been seeking all their lives. At the same time, the thing you desire most—Lacan's (m)other—is the thing that will kill you. Such desiring will also lead you to death-in-life, a catatonic state of pure desiring, one that involves a form of self-annihilation similar to the process of metempsychosis.

Here again the film calls to mind Tolkien's Ring myth, particularly by way of Tom Shippey's recent analysis of the Middle Earth cycle, *J. R. R. Tolkien: Author of the Century.* Early in his consideration of *The Lord of the Rings,* Shippey addresses various objections raised through the years regarding Tolkien's inconsistent handling of his own Ring symbolism. As Shippey points out, "The Ring has bad effects on some people, but no effect at all on others."[14] To account for this problem, Shippey suggests that the Ring's effect might best be understood as "addictive." As he puts it, "One use [of the Ring] need not be disastrous on its own, but each use tends to strengthen the urge for another. The addiction can be shaken off in early stages . . . but once it has taken hold, it cannot be broken by will-power alone."[15] Like Tolkien's Ring, Wallace's mysterious Entertainment can be figured as an addiction, a product that we freely choose to embrace but which has the paradoxical end effect of robbing us of our wills.

Remy Marathe and Hugh Steeply, two spies in the ongoing terrorist war between O.N.A.N. and the Quebecois separatists, conduct a number of philosophical dialogues that explore this conflation of choice and addiction. For Marathe—a Quebecois triple agent and uneasy member of the *Assassins des Fauteuils Rollents*—the mere existence of such a film, made by "an American man in the U.S.A.," indicates the tragic extent to which U.S. citizens have lost their way. Even more damning is the fact that the Bureau of Unspecified Services—O.N.A.N.'s version of the CIA—is frightened of the film, for this fear indicates to Marathe an awareness on the part of the B.U.S. that the U.S.A. "would die—and let its children die, each one—for the so-called perfect Entertainment" (318). The film itself functions for the Quebecois separatists as a mythological Tree of the Knowledge of Good and Evil: the success of their plan to disseminate the film is predicated on the willingness, indeed the eagerness, of U.S. citizens to view it, despite what they might have heard about its debilitating effect on the viewer. Were the population simply to refuse to watch the film, the plot would fail, and yet Marathe knows this outcome is unlikely, for he realizes that the U.S. is a country of people who "choose nothing over themselves to love," and who "would die for this chance to be fed this death of pleasure with spoons, in their warm homes, alone, unmoving" (318). The film reverses the Genesis archetype in that choosing to eat of the fruit—that is, to watch the film—consigns one to infantilism, whereas refusing the temptation grants one adultlike control over one's will and affirms one's obligation to something other than one's own pleasure. Despite his many misgivings about the Quebecois terrorists that he is betraying, Marathe acknowledges that at least they "still know what it is to choose," which for him means being willing to "die for something larger" than one's own pleasure. "You are what you love," he argues. "You are, completely and only, what you would die for without, as you say, the *thinking twice*" (107).

Hugh Steeply, Marathe's American counterpart, plays William James to Marathe's self-sacrificing nationalist. Echoing James's formulation in "The Moral Philosopher and the Moral Life" that "the essence of good is simply to satisfy demand,"[16] Steeply argues that "our whole system is founded on your individual's freedom to pursue his own individual desires" (423). The anarchic possibilities of this ethical system are balanced by "a certain basic amount of respect for the wishes of other people," so that one's "total and overall happiness is maximized by respecting your individual sanctity," thereby producing a "community where [one's] own wishes and interests are respected" (426). Marathe, correctly reading Steeply's Jamesian model as a form of utilitarianism, explains, "Maximize pleasure, minimize displeasure: result: what is good. This is the U.S.A."

(423). In the postmodern world of Wallace's novel, however—and Wallace's world is still, for all its inventiveness, our world—this bloodless utilitarianism is a recipe for disaster. If, in fact, the essence of the good is simply to satisfy demand—and James, with his language of "cash-value" and "practicality," hardly shied away from the capitalistic implications of his ideas—what happens to "goodness" when one lives in a culture that has achieved the ability to satisfy every demand, instantaneously? After all, the final triumph of InterLace hinged upon its collusion with something called the American Council of Disseminators of Cable, which, early in the millennium, attacked the Big Four networks "right at the ideological root" of this American vision of freedom, "the psychic matrix where viewers had been conditioned (conditioned, rather deliciously, by the Big Four Networks and their advertisers themselves . . .) to associate the Freedom to Choose and the Right to Be Entertained with all that was U.S. and true" (412).

As Steeply admits, the only thing that might forestall a descent into pure chaotic self-gratification on a national scale is the old utilitarian catchall of "enlightened self-interest" (428). Unfortunately, enlightened self-interest in Wallace's novel generally takes the form of cynical self-reflexivity, a form of meta-self-awareness that corresponds in many ways to the self-conscious metafictional strategies of Barth's literature of exhaustion. In both cases, the end result is a form of entropic death. As in *Girl with Curious Hair*, where Wallace argues that Barth's strategies have been co-opted, and thereby diffused of their radical power, by pop culture, *Infinite Jest* portrays a culture trapped in a terrible cage of pop irony and narcissism, where the cage is one's own thinking, that is, one's own self-reflexive, and therefore falsifying, belief in enlightened self-interest. Wallace's characters are "all jonesing and head-gaming and mokus and grieving and basically whacked out and producing nonstopping output 24-7-365" (273). They "identify their whole selves with their head," creating narratives of self-control and sophisticated, aesthetic constructions of their identities that seek to assuage the dread of being, of self-responsibility. In a bit of vicious irony, this same attempt at psychic self-control actually breeds addiction, for, in the words of one of the novel's most heroic characters, Don Gately, himself a recovering drug addict, "the Disease [of addiction] makes its command headquarters in the head" (272). Drugs and entertainment—in and of themselves innocent objects of desire, in the Jamesian sense—offer a release from that insistently craving interior, a release from the cage of self-consciousness that often results, paradoxically, in the construction of an even more confining cage, such that "what looks like the cage's exit is actually the bars of the cage" (222). As Joelle asks of the film *Infinite Jest,* "Was the fatally entertaining and scopophiliac thing Jim alleges he made out of her unveiled face . . . a cage or really a door?" (230). The answer, unfortunately, is that it is a door to another cage.

Yet the "disease that makes its command headquarters in the head" is not just addiction to substances but also hyper-self-consciousness in general. The narrator tells us that "veteran Boston AAs" will often "divide and hyphenate" the word "DIS-EASE" "so that it becomes *DIS-EASE*" (203). This dis-ease is best understood as *despair,* a concept central to Søren Kierkegaard's psychological phenomonology, particularly as outlined in *The Sickness unto Death,* where he identifies one form of despair as that of "not wanting to be oneself; or on an even lower level: not wanting in despair to be a self; or lowest of all: wanting a new self."[17] Nearly all of Wallace's characters suffer from this despair of not wanting to be themselves, or, more pointedly, a self at all. Drugs are a particularly alluring means of escape from self, for without them Wallace's characters often find themselves "unable to withstand the psychic pressures that [have] pushed them over the edge into . . . 'self-erasure'" (791). Self-consciousness and irony also provide an illusion of escape and self-erasure—an illusion, moreover, that breeds more despair. Wallace's desperate drug addicts are essentially "aesthetes" in Kierkegaard's famous formulation. An aesthete is someone who lives for pleasure and who—as Kierkegaard explains in the great *Concluding Unscientific Postscript to "Philosophical Fragments"*—"holds existence at bay by the most subtle of all deceptions, by thinking. He has thought everything possible, and yet he has not existed at all." As such, aesthetic existence, essentially "is depression," while "at its maximum, it is despair."[18]

Wallace associates aesthetic existence with a particular brand of postmodern sophistication that treats reality, so-called—here equated with Kierkegaard's "existence"—as text or simulacrum, or as a pastiche of various phony conventions. Behind that ironic sophistication, however, lurks despair, the sort of despair that leads, say, to drug addiction. Inasmuch as postmodern self-consciousness teaches us to be wary of clichés and to detect and decode ideologically interested metanarratives that pass themselves off as essentially present, it also blinds us to the positive and simple truths that often lie behind those clichés and metanarratives, however constructed and contingent they may be. "How do trite things get to be trite?" asks one of the novel's desperate AA members. "Why is the truth usually not just un- but *anti*-interesting?" (358). Wallace's method again and again is to embrace that cynicism—for it is the very air we breathe—and turn it on itself in order to recover those naïve yet solid truths that are worth preserving, "not just un- but *anti*-interesting" though they may be.

Wallace clues us into his Kierkegaardian theme as early as the novel's third episode, in which Hal Incandenza, unable to communicate due to his having either ingested the lethal drug DMZ ("Madame Psychosis") or accidentally viewed the Entertainment, tries unsuccessfully to convince a group of college administrators that, though he is both a tennis and an intellectual prodigy, he is also a human and "not a machine." He then asserts (silently, since his ability to communicate has been irreparably damaged), "I feel and believe. I have opinions. . . . I believe the influence of Kierkegaard on Camus is underestimated." (12). Like all of Wallace's despairing drug addicts, Hal, a chronic marijuana addict, bears the stamp of Kierkegaardian aesthetic despair. Hal, like "most Substance-addicted people," is "also addicted to thinking, meaning [he has] a compulsive and unhealthy relationship with [his] own thinking" (203). Wallace's prose is particularly adept at conveying the layered and compulsive nature of this sort of incessant intellectual "jonesing." Hal sometimes terms this brand of intellectual analysis "'marijuana thinking,'" really a layered form of hyper-self-consciousness, as illustrated in this random example from the great sea of interior monologues that characterize the novel's primary site of activity: "Hal wonders, not for the first time, whether he might deep down be a secret snob about collar color issues . . . then whether the fact that he's capable of wondering whether he's a snob attenuates the possibility that he's really a snob" (335). Hal not only thinks obsessively about himself but also about the *way* he thinks about himself; he sometimes even thinks about the way he thinks about the way he thinks about himself, such that his thoughts double back on themselves into "a paralytic thought-helix." Self-consciousness thus becomes a nightmarish hall of mirrors, a Barthian funhouse that has ceased to be any fun at all.

Even more importantly, Hal possesses a quality that Kierkegaard would call "hiddenness" and that most intensely identifies the aesthete. In Kierkegaard's analysis, aesthetes use self-conscious thinking in order to hide from themselves.[19] Likewise, Hal, in hiding his marijuana smoking from his friends and family, also in a sense hides it from himself. As the narrator explains, "Hal likes to get high in secret, but a bigger secret is that he's as attached to the secrecy as he is to getting high" (49). This realization, which Hal acknowledges, becomes not a clue to his problem but rather one more thing to think about: "He broods on it abstractly sometimes, when high: this No-One-Must-Know thing. It's not fear per se, fear of discovery. Beyond that it gets too abstract and twined up to lead to anything, Hal's brooding" (54). What such thinking *should* lead to, of course, is self-discovery, yet the very style of Hal's brooding, like much of Wallace's inimitable prose, is designed to obfuscate what it is actually determined to reveal. And in any case, as Hal himself seems to recognize, "It's a lot easier to fix something if you can see it" (55).

Hal's brother, Orin, declares that "he'd grown up . . . dividing the human world into those who were open, readable, trustworthy v. those so closed and hidden that you had no clue what they though of you but could pretty well imagine it couldn't be anything all that marvelous or else why hide it?" (738). Similarly, all the characters in *Infinite Jest* are divided into those who are open and those who are closed and hidden. Unfortunately, most of them fall into the closed and hidden category. Joelle Van Dyne, who is addicted to freebase cocaine, most dramatically embodies the latter, for she wears a veil over her face at all times, a visible emblem of her membership to something called the Union of the Hideously and Improbably Deformed (533). The narrative is unclear—or perhaps deliberately ambiguous—as to why Joelle wears the veil. In one account, given again by the unreliable Molly Notkin, Joelle is said to have had corrosive acid poured onto her face by her mother, thereby making her, literally, hideously and improbably deformed.[20] Conversely, Joelle, speaking to a group of Quebecois terrorists, explains that she "used to go around saying the veil was to disguise lethal perfection, that [she] was too lethally beautiful for people to stand. It was a kind of joke" (940). Finally, she tells Don Gately, whom she admires and might in fact love, "Don, I'm perfect. I'm so beautiful I drive anybody with a nervous system out of their fucking mind. Once they've seen me they can't think of anything else and don't want to look at anything else . . . Like I'm the solution to their deep slavering need to be jowl to cheek with perfection" (538). Whatever the reason, Joelle and the Union of the Hideously and Improbably Deformed represent the novel's most visible instance of Kierkegaardian hiddenness. As Joelle explains to Don Gately, members of the group—that is, a community devoted to *hiding*—are not just hiding their deformity but also their shame about their wish to hide: "What you do is you *hide* your deep need to hide, and you do this out of the need to *appear* to other people as if you have the strength not to care how you *appear* to others. . . . You take your desire to hide and conceal it under a mask of acceptance" (535). Once again, Wallace has managed to turn the strategies of postmodern metafiction back on themselves in such a way as to demonstrate that "what looks like the cage's exit is actually the bars of the cage" (222). Self-reflexivity, far from being the solution to Barthian exhaustion, is now, a generation later, the primary cause of that same brand of exhaustion.

Gately—who, aside from Hal's seriously deformed older brother Mario, is the novel's least "hidden" character—connects Joelle's "paralytic thought-helix" about the meaning of her veil to the demise, early in the new millennium, of videophony, in which telephone callers interfaced directly with each other's televised image. In one of the more inspired comic set pieces in the novel, Wallace traces the rise and fall of this new technology, the commercial viability of which was eventually demolished by callers' horror at "how their own faces appeared on the TP screen": "Even with high-end TPs' high-def viewer screens, consumers perceived something essentially blurred and moist-looking about their phone-faces, a shiny pallid *indefiniteness* that struck them as not just unflattering but somehow evasive, untrustworthy, *unlikable*" (147). Callers eventually assuaged their unease by replacing their own video-transmitted faces with High-Definition Photographic Imaging—"i.e., taking the most flattering elements of a variety of flattering multi-angle photos of a given phone-consumer and . . . combining them into a wildly attractive high-def broadcastable composite of a face" (148). This new technology in turn gave rise to a new form of "pyschosocial stress" borne from phone-users' sudden reluctance "to leave home and interface personally with people who . . . were now habituated to seeing their far-better-looking masked selves on the phone" (149). In the end, "only callers utterly lacking in self-awareness continued to use videophony" until, eventually, the industry collapsed entirely (151). Once again, openness leads to self-consciousness, which then leads to despair and hence to an even more insidious form of hiddenness.

Alcoholics Anonymous, a program devoted to "sharing" and group therapy, serves as Wallace's tentative antidote to all this paralyzing psychological concealment, the paradoxical product of hyper-self-consciousness. Quite unexpectedly, AA gets transformed from a too easily parodied form of pop psychology to a genuine and viable Kierkegaardian religion, one that attempts to solve the problems of irony, aesthetic self-consciousness, and the dread of being. Boston Alcoholics Anonymous even has its own name for the type of layered self-consciousness that functions as a means of self-concealment: "Analysis-Paralysis." The term clearly recalls Hal's "paralytic thought-helix" and also describes the peculiar effect of Wallace's prose. "Analysis-Paralysis" refers not only to the double-helix nature of the drug addict's aesthetic, that is, intellectual, attempts to rationalize away the truth of his own addiction, but also to the way drug addicts might dismiss AA slogans as banal, clichéd, or vapid—which, in many respects, they are. Their vapidity, however, is the source of their truth. And to accept them without irony, without intellectual disdain, is to take the first gesture toward genuine openness, which Kierkegaard identifies as the primary feature of ethical existence, the antidote to aesthetic despair: "The ethicist *has despaired*. . . . In despair, he *has chosen himself*. . . . Through this choice and in this choice he becomes *open*."[21] The ethicist owns up to his own despair, accepts it and claims it as his: this is, in part (but by no means in full!) what Kierkegaard means when he affirms that "subjectivity is the truth." The ethicist is then prepared to open himself to the outside world again.

Don Gately seems (unconsciously) to echo Kierkegaard's language when he describes AA as a place in which people "say they'll love you till you can like love yourself and accept yourself, so you don't care what people see or think anymore, and you can finally step out of the cage and quit hiding" (534). The banality of AA's numerous slogans acts as a test of sorts, as a way to gauge one's willingness to give up aesthetic sophistication, useful in and of itself but only insofar as it is not the door to another cage, to another means of self-concealment. As Kierkegaard remarks in *Either/Or,* "It is by no means my intention to deny that to live aesthetically when such a life is at its highest may call for a multiplicity of intellectual gifts, yea, even that these must be intensively developed to an uncommon degree; but nevertheless, they are enslaved, and transparency is lacking to them."[22] Conversely, AA slogans like Ask For Help and Turn It Over and Keep Coming and Surrender to Win —"simple advice" that seems even to Gately "like a lot of clichés"—nevertheless have pure transparency if they can actually be followed, since, as Gately says, "the clichéd directives are a lot more deep and hard to actually *do*. To try to live by instead of just say" (273). Hence when Geoffrey Day, one of Gately's charges, having just been offered up the slogan Analysis-Paralysis, sneers, "Oh lovely. . . . By all means don't *think* about the validity of what they're claiming your life hinges on . . . Simply open wide for the spoon," Gately replies, "For me, the slogan means there's no set way to argue intellectual-type stuff about the Program" (1002n). Day's characterization of the Program as infantile is only partly correct: open wide, yes, but do not imagine you are being fed with a spoon. Dependence on the spoon is what the AA person is overcoming. Characteristically, AA even has a slogan for overcoming the urge to "argue intellectual-type stuff about the Program": the slogan reads "My Best Thinking Got Me Here" (1026).

The crucial difference between Kierkegaard and AA—and this might serve as Wallace's critique of Kierkegaardian thought—is that AA is a community, whereas Kierkegaard focuses always on subjectivity in isolation—or, at any rate, in private contact with God. AA refigures Kierkegaard's dialectic of subjectivity and objectivity as a contrast between being "In the Program" and being "Out There, where the Disease is" (1002n). As the veteran Boston AAs are wont to say, "Nobody ever Comes In because things were going really well" (349). Of course, the Disease also "makes its headquarters in the head," perhaps the book's ultimate "cage," so the paradox of AA is that to be Out in the World is to be trapped In the Cage, whereas to be In the Program is, effectively, to be Out, because, although the community of AA is a refuge, it is also a place where one can open oneself to the truth. Moreover, the principal message of AA is, "You are not unique . . . : this initial hopelessness unites every soul in this broad cold salad-bar'd hall. . . . Every meeting is a reunion, once you've been in for a while" (349).

Wallace is also much more comfortable with AA's nondenominational idea of a "Higher Power" than with Kierkegaard's dogmatic Christian God. The AA God of Wallace's novel is Kierkegaardian in the sense that it is conceived as a "sort of benign anarchy of subjective spirit" (366). Yet it is also undogmatic, unspecific, and the useful product of a community of sufferers. The AA concept of a vague, unspecified Higher Power perfectly suits Wallace's cynically naive purposes, for he is not proposing in this novel a conventional spiritual answer to our malaise but rather a postpostmodern diagnosis of same. Higher Power is yet another banal AA cliché that becomes, in Wallace's hands, an unexpectedly powerful idea with surprising implications both for the book's readers as well as for the novel's ongoing attempt to advance beyond postmodernism. As in AA, Wallace approaches the concept of God, or rather of gods in general, pragmatically, for gods in all their guises are possibly fictional creations important, as poet Wallace Stevens has put it, "not alone from an aesthetic point of view, but for what they reveal, for that they validate and invalidate, for the support that they give."[23]

The above passage, from Stevens's great *Adagia,* resonates directly with Wallace's "AA God," the primary God in *Infinite Jest,* for the "AA God" is not any one thing but rather a fluid concept that is more a "necessary fiction," in Stevens's sense, than an, if not the, transcendental signified. As the narrator explains, "One of AA's major selling points [is] that you get to choose your own God. You get to make up your own understanding of God or a Higher Power or Whom-/Whatever" (443). Gately, for one, clearly understands God to be a fiction, for he doesn't even really "believe" in the God to which he prays. Rather, he admits that "when he kneels at other times and prays or meditates or tries to achieve a Big-Picture spiritual understanding of a God as he can understand Him, he feels Nothing—not nothing but *Nothing,* an edgeless blankness that somehow feels worse than the sort of unconsidered atheism he Came In with" (443). Yet each night, in accordance with AA doctrine, he performs the ritual of prayer, and this *ritual,* this aesthetic form, has helped remove the "Desire and Compulsion" of his addiction. Not surprisingly, the experience leaves him bewildered: "He couldn't believe it. He wasn't Grateful so much as kind of suspicious about it, the Removal. How could some kind of Higher Power he didn't even believe in magically let him out of the cage when Gately had been a total hypocrite in even asking something he didn't believe in to let him out a cage he had like zero hope of ever being let out of?" (468). His AA sponsors have two typically gnomic and hard-nosed answers to Gately's question. First, whenever he asks "the scary old guys How AA Works . . . they smile their chilly smiles and say Just Fine. It just works, is all; end of story" (350). Second, they tell him "that maybe anything minor-league enough for Don Gately to understand probably wasn't going to be major-league enough to save Gately's addled ass" (468). So Gately continues with his ritual, praying to what he knows to be a fiction but which is meaningful and real primarily, to paraphrase Stevens, for what it reveals, for what it validates and invalidates, for the support that it gives.

Elsewhere in the *Adagia* Stevens affirms, "It is the belief and not the god that counts," and that "the final belief is to believe in a fiction, which you know to be a fiction, there being nothing else. The exquisite truth is to know that it is a fiction and that you believe in it willingly." Stevens outlines here his concept of "necessary fictions," beliefs understood to be aesthetic creations but affirmed nevertheless. Stevens is important to Wallace's concept of God and the AA Higher Power because Stevens' conception of poetry as the supreme fiction stands as a direct antecedent to the literature of exhaustion that Wallace is seeking to overcome. Modern literature in Stevens' seminal argument is the literature that emerged after Nietzsche's Death of God, where God himself, or gods in general, are regarded finally as fictions, necessary though they may be. It is a short step, therefore, to affirm, as Stevens does, that poetry is the supreme fiction, for, as he writes in *Opus Posthumous*, "In an age of disbelief, or, what is the same thing, in a time that is largely humanistic, in one sense or another, it is for the poet to supply the satisfactions of belief." One of the "satisfactions" modern poetry must supply is "the revelation of something 'wholly other' by which the inexpressible loneliness of thinking is broken and enriched." Wallace's work, too, seeks to break and enrich the inexpressible loneliness of thinking, yet it must do so *after* the exhaustion of Stevens' own modernist project. If modern literature for Stevens ascends to the paradoxical status of the secular-sacred, postmodernism marks, for Wallace, the loss of even that bracketed form of the sacred. As Wallace puts it, "It's almost like postmodernism is fiction's fall from biblical grace. Fiction became *conscious* of itself in a way it never had been."[24]

It is therefore no accident that Gately arrives at AA with "0 in the way of denominational background or preconceptions" (443). He is, in this sense, postmodernism's baby: he must begin his spiritual journey at postmodernism's zero point, where even modernism's secular sacred has been exhausted. Equally significant is the fact that Gately's zero-point "Nothing . . . feels worse than the sort of unconsidered atheism he Came In with," because this Nothingness is the void of self-consciousness, of knowingness, of Wallace's "cynicism." Yet Gately's Higher Power, deconstructed and dismantled though it is, still works, for reasons he cannot cynically describe. Similarly, in the same way traditional metafiction seeks to demystify literature by disclosing "how" it works, by revealing all its mechanisms and declaring them to be conventions, interested devices, Wallace's post-metafiction seeks to exhaust the question of "how does it work?" in such a way that the cynical reader is placed in the same condition as the novel's desperate AA addicts, who must finally accept that the answer is "Just fine."

For Hal Incandenza, Gately's primary counterpart in the novel, this search for God or a Higher Power is figured as a search for genuine feelings and emotions, particularly those involving his reaction to his father's suicide. Whereas Gately, a nonintellectual, begins with an "edgeless blankness" that is itself a kind of void waiting for creation, Hal, a linguistic genius who can recite from photographic memory complete pages of the *OED*, is postmodernism's paralyzed prodigy, a Kierkegaardian aesthete trapped in a cage that Tony Tanner has called the City of Words. "I consume libraries," he explains at one point. "I wear out spines and ROM-drives. I do things like get in a taxi and say, 'The library, and step on it'"; at the same time he insists, "I am not a machine. I feel and believe" (12). Hal's problem is that everything he "feels" and "believes" is mediated somehow, compromised by words, by what deconstructionists call "textuality." The grief he "feels" over his father's suicide is one of many emotions he longs to access directly but cannot, while the decisive fact of his father's suicide and his own muted and self-conscious reaction to it constitute the primary synapses of his particular psychic ache. Hal, like Gately, wants to "feel" and "believe," even though he is trained to regard most things worthy of belief as fictions, as texts. Hal wants to be consciousness of his Self even though he is blocked from that experience by his intense self-consciousness.

His experience with "grief" is a perfect case in point. In his own account of his state of mind during the "funeral period," he says, "I seemed to have been evincing shock and trauma" (251). Seemed to whom? To everyone, presumably—his mother, his friends, and, in a vague way, himself. Even his assigned "grief-therapist" exacerbates his problems with self-consciousness and self-alienation, for the therapist asks him not only "how did it feel" and "how does if feel," but also "how do you feel when I ask how it feels" (252). Hal *does* feel something, of course, but he also worries that were he to voice those feelings he would therefore tear them from the prelinguistic Real that is his interior and transport them into the alienated world of textuality. Specifically, the discourse that would lay claim to his feelings is the discourse of "grief therapy," so Hal attempts to deflect attention from his own feelings, which he wants to preserve, by mastering that selfsame banal discourse. As he reports to his brother Orin, he reads straight through the entire "Copley Square library's grief section" and returns to his therapy sessions fully armed: "I went in and presented with textbook-perfect symptoms of denial, bargaining, anger, still more denial, depression" (253). When this stratagem fails to appease the unironic grief therapist, Hal begins to experience "fear that [he] was somehow going to flunk grief-therapy," a fear that is so strong that his family members incorrectly interpret his anxiety as visible evidence of the grief that he is trying to preserve. His solution to this layered problem is to begin empathizing with the therapist, to imagine what the therapist wanted from him and so try to deliver it. In other words, he seeks to solve his problems with self-consciousness and self-reflexivity—that is, his worry that his real feelings are simply linguistic constructions—by becoming self-conscious and self-reflexive *about* that same self-consciousness and self-reflexivity. And it works. By projecting not "grief" as it is explained in grief-therapy discourse but rather a "textbook" breakdown that is geared toward giving the therapist what he wants, Hal manages to access "genuine affect and trauma and guilt and textbook earsplitting grief, then absolution," all while maintaining the inviolate integrity of his actual feelings (256).

Hal therefore never speaks his feelings directly, but rather hides those feelings behind a wall of cynical, hip irony. The hidden feelings in turn remain caged inside him until they become the walls of his own solipsistic cage. Hal argues that, for young people of his generation, "Sentiment equals naïveté on this continent (at least since Reconfiguration)" (694). So the young will "wear any mask, to fit, to be part-of, not be Alone" (694). The problem is that in wearing these masks, Hal and his peers end up alienated from themselves. Although they are now part of a "group," they are at the same time lonely for "this hideous interior self, incontinent of sentiment and need, that pulses and writes just under the hip empty mask, anhedonia" (695). In an endnote to that last passage, the narrator explains that this feeling of loneliness is really a vague sense that Hal "misses somebody he's never even met" (1053). The "somebody" is, of course, himself. Not uncoincidentally, Hal's father is given the moniker "Himself," a means by which Wallace can connect the unknowable Other (in this case Hal's elusive father) with Hal's own interior self, his own subjectivity. Not only are the interiors of others hidden from us but our own interiors are hidden as well. Hal knows neither himself nor Himself.

Obviously, then, Hal's story serves as the second half of Wallace's elaborate and ingenious critique of Lacan. One could even say that Hal's problems stem, in part anyway, from his amorphous yet poignant recognition of the Lacanian problem. Hal's interior is founded, he feels, on an absence, a lack, and his sense of self is compromised in all cases by the tyranny of language, that alienating yet also defining means of self-actualization. While speculating on the elusive cause of his father's suicide, Hal comes to realize that, possibly like his father, he, Hal, "hasn't had a bona fide intensity-of-interior-life-type emotion since he was tiny; he finds terms like *joie* [*de vivre*] and *value* to be like so many variables in rarefied equations, and he can manipulate them well enough to satisfy everyone but himself that he's in there, inside his own hull, as a human being—but in fact he's more robotic than [tennis rival] John Wayne" (694). In short, Hal's status as a fully present human being with an "intense interior life" has been undermined by his world-weary understanding that "intensity-of-interior-life-type emotions" like happiness and fundamental ethical concepts like "value" are really just constructs, "so many empty variable in rarefied equations"—that is, *words*. That is why he feels that "inside [him] there's pretty much nothing at all" (694).

Orin Incandenza, Hal's womanizing older brother, has also internalized Lacan, so much so that he uses Lacan's ideas to justify his pathological need to seduce woman after woman, all of whom he ironically refers to as "Subjects." Hal captures this irony when he tells Orin, "It's poignant somehow that you always use the word *Subject* when you mean the exact obverse" (1008n). The Subject position in Lacan is always, in a sense, an Object position, since the Subject is always already a signifier of a deferred signified. Likewise Orin, whose name begs us to read it (also ironically) as "origin," seems to accept the Object-like nature of Subjectivity. Yet his name is also a hole, a lack: he is often referred to, simply, as "O," Lacan's shorthand notation for "the Other." The period in her name is important, too, for it places a grammatical seal on this hole, a visible emblem of Orin's attempt to achieve complete psychic containment. His Subjects are, in this sense, objective manifestations of his own horribly displaced Subjectivity, with its absent signifier. His first agenda is to *win* the Subject from "something other than he"; once he has achieved this aim, he then surrenders himself fully to her so that "he is both offense and defense and she neither, nothing but this one second's love of her, *of*-her," until there is "inside her a vividness vacuumed of all but his name: O., O. That he is the One" (566). The result, of course, is that he hates his subjects, "a hatred that comes out disguised as a contempt he disguises as . . . tender attention," for his sense of self depends upon these Subjects on which he feeds. And he hates them because the satisfying "oneness" he seeks can never be achieved. Because the desire for oneness is grounded in his longing for a reconnection with an interior core that has been replaced/displaced by the linguistic structure of his subjectivity, Orin suffers from what Lacan calls "the indestructibility of unconscious desire—in the absence of a need which, when forbidden satisfaction, does not sicken and die."[25] Indeed, that strange hyphenated word, "*of*-her," in the earlier passage, seems to be a parodic nod to the stylistic idiosyncrasies of deconstruction, with its love of hyphenations and parenthetical bracketing of words-within-words, a fitting tic to place in the mind of Orin Incandenza who regards "the truth as *constructed* instead of *reported*," an idea he came upon "educationally" (1048n). Well versed in the absence-presence language of deconstruction and Lacanian psychoanalytic theory, he undertakes seduction as a way to make himself "One," rather than an interiorly divided play of *différance*, and ends up tied to a "chain of signifiers" that never ends. He is, in many ways, the fulfillment of Lacan's characteristic dictum, "Le desir de l'Homme, c'est le desire de l'Autre," which is often translated to read, "Man's desire is for the Other to desire him."[26]

Orin's seduction technique also plays with the tropes of metafiction and self-consciousness. His childhood friend Marlon Bain describes Orin as "*the least open man* I know," and yet, typically, he achieves this "hiddenness" through a pose of complete openness. In fact, a feigned openness lies at the heart of all his various, and numbered, seduction strategies. For instance, according to Bain, Orin sometimes approaches his potential subjects with the line, "Tell me what sort of man you prefer and I'll affect the demeanor of that man" (1048n). This strategy works, Bain, affirms, because it allows Orin to portray himself as someone who "Transcend[s]-The-Common-Disingenuity-In-A-Bar-Herd-In-A-Particularly-Hip-And-Witty-Self-Aware-Way" and who also can help the Subject enter "Into-This-World-Of-Social-Falsehood-Transcendence" (1048). Bain calls this strategy "a pose of poselessness," and one can detect, once again, Wallace taking a stab at the metafictionalists of the past. Orin uses self-consciousness and irony to transcend various social falsehoods, much as Wallace's artistic forebears did. The result, however, is not increased openness but in fact another kind of falsehood, perhaps an even worse sort of falsehood than the one it was intended to blast away. In seeking to cut through false sentiment, Orin ends up with a terrifying, debilitating loneliness that he passes onto the Subjects he paradoxically objectifies so wittily, so openly.

Here is where Wallace levels his most concrete attack on the Lacanian model. In a parenthetical passage placed in close proximity to the passage outlined above describing Orin's lovemaking technique, the narrator murmurs, "(This is why, maybe, one Subject is never enough. . . . For were there for him just one, now, special and only, the One would be not he or she but what was between them, the obliterating trinity of You and I into We. Orin felt that once and has never recovered, and will never again)" (566–67). What was between them: that is the One. Once again Wallace here affirms Wittgenstein's communitarian model of signification as the solution to Orin's relativistic nightmare of perpetual displacement and interior absence. Orin's sense of emptiness is an ontological error—perhaps it is Wallace's assessment of Lacan's error—for our subjectivity, while still possibly grounded in language, actually achieves meaning and connection through the recursive dynamic that sits at the heart of Wittgenstein's concept of meaning as *use*. The meaning of Orin's interior can be located not in others or in himself but in the "the obliterating trinity of You and I into We." Or, in Lacan's terms, the fulfillment he seeks can be found in the reconnection of the signifier and the signified by virtue of the communitarian model of meaning proposed in the *Philosophical Investigations.*

Wallace also seems to have Lacan in his sights when he characterizes "the internal self" as a "not-quite-right-looking infant dragging itself anaclitically around the map, with big wet eyes and froggy-soft skin, huge skull, gooey drool" (695). That strange word "anaclitically" derives from the term "anaclitic," which *Webster's Ninth* (not a favorite of dictionary-memorizing Hal) defines as "characterized by dependence of libido on a nonsexual instinct." This metaphorical infant is Wallace's image for the pre–mirror stage human, the *Kern unseres Wesen* ("nucleus of our being") of Freudian psychology. The infant is also Hal's model for someone who is "really human, since to be really human (at least as he conceptualizes it) is probably to be unavoidably sentimental and naïve and goo-prone and generally pathetic, is to be in some basic interior way forever infantile" (695). The key phrase above is the narrator's parenthetical disclaimer, "(at least as he conceptualizes it)." Hal can only conceive of genuine, straightforward emotion as issuing from an "infant," since only pre–mirror-stage infants still believe their feelings are somehow *theirs*, rather than products of an unconscious founded on an absence. Typically, Hal and Orin (and just about everyone else in the novel) are lonely for "this hideous interior self, incontinent of sentiment and need, that pules and writhes just under the hip empty mask, anhedonia" (695). This passage clearly identifies Lacan's theory not as an irrefutable truth but rather as a "hip empty mask" and the cause of anhedonia, a particularly debilitating form of melancholy that he describes as a condition borne from seeing "full and fleshy" concepts like *happiness* and *love* as stripped to their skeletons and reduced to abstract ideas. They have, as it were, denotation but not connotation. "The anhedonic can still speak about happiness and meaning et al.," Wallace explains, "but she has become incapable of feeling anything in them, of understanding anything about them, of hoping anything about them, or of believing them to exist as anything more than concepts. Everything becomes an outline of the thing. Objects become schemata. The world becomes a map of the world. An adhedonic can navigate, but has no location. I.e., the anhedonic becomes, in the lingo of Boston AA, Unable To Identify" (693). Lacanian thinking, then, in Orin's own terms, is not a truth reported but a truth constructed, and what these sophisticated, poststructuralist depressives have really "constructed" are their own cages, cages in which they hide the "hideous interior self" where un-hip truth and sentiment reside. Moreover, that infantile "interior self" has not been displaced: it has been *suppressed*.

Wallace contrasts Orin's pathological hiddenness with the benign, heroic openness of the Incandenza middle child, Mario. Mario is, quite literally, a "not-quite-right-looking infant . . . with big wet eyes and froggy-soft skin, huge skull, gooey drool." Mario was born two months early in a state of "incomplete gestation," his paternity unclear. By the age of twelve he had grown no bigger than a toddler, while by nineteen, his age during the main action of the novel (April–November, the Year of the Depends Adult Undergarment), his size is "in a range somewhere between elf and jockey" (313). His arms are "magiscule S's" that curl out from his thorax, his feet are "not only flat but perfectly square," and his skin is "an odd dead gray-green." One of his eyelids hangs lower than the other over perpetually open eyes, while his face is pinched forever in an "involuntarily constant smile" (314). To stand upright he must rely on "a .7–meter steel pole that extends from a special Velcroed vest and angles about 40° down and out to a slotted piece of lead blocking" (315). What's more, and perhaps most significantly, Mario suffers from "Familial Dysautonomia, a neurological deficit whereby he can't feel physical pain very well" (589).

For all this, Mario is completely free of subterfuge, of anger or resentment. For Hal, the impossibly damaged and sunny and open Mario is "a (semi-)walking miracle. People who're somehow burned at birth, withered or ablated way past anything like what might be fair, they either curl up in their fire, or else they rise. Withered saurian homodontic Mario floats" (316). For Hal's mother, Avril, Mario is "the family's real prodigy, an inbent savant-type genius of no classifiable type, a very rare and shining thing, even if his intuition—slow and silent—scares her, his academic poverty breaks her heart, the smile he puts on each A.M. without fail since the suicide of their father makes her wish she could cry" (317). To all others, he is the world's listener, an invitation to openness, this due to the way "bullshit often tends to drop away around damaged listeners, deep beliefs revealed, diary-type private reveries indulged out loud; and listening, the beaming and brady-kinetic boy gets to forge an interpersonal connection he knows only he can truly feel, here" (80). Mario even wonders why "everyone at E.T.A. over the age of about Kent Blott finds stuff that's really real uncomfortable and they get embarrassed. It's like there's some rule that real stuff can only get mentioned if everybody rolls their eyes or laughs in a way that isn't happy" (592). Finally, when a representative from the Union of the Hideously and Improbably Deformed approaches Mario with his spiel about "the openness of concealment," Hal tells the "guy to go peddle his linen somewhere else" (317).

Mario, then, is the one truly human figure in the novel, the one character who is not only in "some basic interior way forever infantile" but also unembarrassed about representing all that is "unavoidably sentimental and naïve and goo-prone and generally pathetic." A horrible grotesque exaggeration of some sentimental Dickensian cripple—Tiny Tim turned into a toxic nightmare—Mario is one more instance of Wallace parodying what he is embarrassed about, but still committed to, loving and affirming.

It is no accident, moreover, that Wallace's most visible figure for the truly human is a horribly deformed boy. Apparently, pure sentiment and naïveté are, in his world, so rare, so much a "miracle," that they represent a deformation of the norm. Yet— contrary to Lacan's theory of interior displacement—everyone in the novel is carrying this deformed, stillborn infant inside them; even worse, they are smothering this infant with hip irony, narcotics, and denial of self-responsibility. About midway through the novel, a young woman explains to an AA group that her addiction is the result of her growing up as the adopted daughter of a crazy foster mother who also had a catatonic, horribly retarded biological daughter about whom she, the mother, "was in total Denial." The girl goes on to relate how she was forced to share a bedroom with the stepdaughter, whom she refers to as "It," and how she was forced to take the retarded sibling with her on dates. As she tries to explain, "The nightmarishness of Its continual pale soggy ubiquitousness in her young life would alone be more than sufficient to cause and explain [her] later drug addiction" (371). The vegetable-like stepsister, here "It," represents the speaker's denial of self-responsibility, really of her true interior self, that she is not owning up to. Similarly, James Incandenza, himself a terminal alcoholic, keeps the horribly deformed Mario around him all the time, largely out of comfort but also because it is Mario, a visible emblem of Incandenza's own denial, who keeps his father supplied with Wild Turkey (379).

In a related, and more grisly, digression, a "round pink girl with no eyelashes at all and a 'base-head's ruined teeth'" retells her unforgettable story to a group of AA members, a story in which she gives birth to a stillborn infant while "compulsively loading up the glass pipe" (376). She finishes the rest of her drugs, still "umbilically linked to the dead infant," falls asleep, and awakes to encounter not only the dead fetus but also "the real business-end of the arrow of responsibility" (377). Instead of owning up to her deed, however, she erects "a fortification of complete and black Denial" and begins carrying the dead infant around as if it were alive. The infant is not deferred, as Lacan would have it, but rather denied, suffocated. Nevertheless, it remains forever attached to us, umbilically, stillborn but still inescapably ours. With openness, self-responsibility, and empathy, however, we can resuscitate the infant, as happens when the woman described above finishes telling her story and finally confronts the correct end of that arrow of responsibility: "The speaker is truly new, ready: all defenses have been burned away. Smooth skinned and steadily pinker, at the podium, her eyes squeezed tight, she looks like she's the one that's the infant" (379).

Here Wallace finally clues us into the positive component of James Incandenza's Death Mother cosmology, as well as to the positive obverse of the book's devastating critique of Lacan and the infantile culture of Johnny Gentle's Postconfiguration O.N.A.N. This positive narrative is inextricably bound up with the novel's critical discourse, and both strands are linked through the work of the book's primary "auteur," James O. Incandenza, a figure who functions ingeniously as the oedipal patriarch within the novel whom Wallace is killing off in order to recover his own positive Inner Infant. Incandenza's film *Infinite Jest* is a dangerous piece of art that perpetuates the culture's desire for self-forgetting, a desire to be returned to the catatonic state of the womb, where needs are met and fed perpetually, endlessly. At the same time the film was undertaken, as Incandenza's "wraith" says, to "reverse thrust on a young self's fall into the womb of solipsism, anhedonia, death in life. A magically entertaining toy to dangle at the infant still somewhere alive in the boy . . . To bring him 'out of himself'" (839). The infant "still somewhere alive in the boy" is the "real human" of sentiment and pure feeling, stripped of defenses and totally open—in other words, the human being inside Hal's cage of irony and emotional displacement. Incandenza's art, unfortunately, panders to the other infant, the dead infant of Denial that remains attached to us, "umbilically," no matter how we try to smother it or sever it with irony or drugs. Incandenza's intentions are sound; it's his methods that are the problem. The result is a body of work that, like so much postmodern fiction in Wallace's view, exacerbates the very problems it seeks to overcome.

Orin admits that he agreed with a film critic who "kept saying that [his father's] films were like the planet's most psychotic
psyche working out its shit right there on the screen and asking
you to pay to watch him" (1038n). Incandenza's "shit" is typically oedipal in nature, or at least paternal, for Wallace inserts
into the novel two illuminating flashback sequences detailing
Incandenza's relationship with his father, sequences that actually
tell us quite a bit about why Incandenza makes the kinds of
films he does in fact make. In the first sequence, told in third-
person limited perspective, Incandenza's father, a failed actor
who ends up making his living as the Man from Glad for "the
Glad Flaccid Plastic Receptacle Company," instructs ten-year-
old James that he is a body, first and foremost. "You're a
machine a body an object, Jim, no less than this rutilant Mont-
clair, this coil of hose here or that rake there" (159). In the second sequence, told in the first person by James himself and
originally published in an anthology titled *The Child of Inspiration: Spontaneous Reminiscences by Seventeen Pioneers of De-
Cycle Lithumized Annular Fusion,* Incandenza describes a day
in winter 1963 during which he and his drunk and enraged
father try to fix a "squeak" in the master bedroom bedframe. In
the Year of the Depend Adult Undergarment, the sound of a
"squeaking" wheelchair axle is associated with the vicious
Wheelchair Assassins, and is in fact their warning call; as the
narrator explains, "'To hear the squeak' is itself the very dark-
est of contemporary Canada's euphemisms for sudden and vio-
lent de-mapping [i.e., death]" (1034n). Hence this scene is laced
with imminent death. Sure enough, as the "flaccid and floppy"
mattress continues to cause problems and the bed continues
ominously to "squeak," the father suddenly and unexpectedly

vomits blood and keels over, unconscious. Rather than rush to his aid, Incandenza walks slowly to his own room, jumps on his bed, and knocks over a floor lamp that, in the course of its fall, shears off the closet door doorknob, which falls to the floor and rolls around in a curious circular motion that Incandenza technically identifies as a "cycloid, L'Hopital's solution to Bernoulli's famous Brachistrochrone Problem, the curve traced by a fixed point on the circumference of a circle rolling along a continuous plane" (502). The sight of his father's failure and collapse functions not as a decisive moment in Incandenza's emotional development but rather as the instant he "first became interested in the possibilities of annulation" (503). ("Annulation" refers to a ringlike anatomical structure.)

James Incandenza, then, is a cold, closed figure with serious paternal resentment, a man who has been trained to hide his emotions behind cold logic and surface objectivity. Not surprisingly, his films seamlessly reflect these psychological defenses. They are, to a piece, self-reflexive and postmodern, so much so that the lengthy "filmography" included among the book's endnotes reads like an extended parody of the postmodern canon. A number of films are named *Cage,* a clear reference to John Cage's music. One of these films is described as a "soliloquized parody of broadcast-television advertisement for shampoo, utilizing four convex mirrors, two planar mirrors, and one actress," a clear invocation of poet John Ashbery's postmodern poem of self-examination and self-reflexivity, "Self-Portrait in a Convex Mirror," a major source text for Wallace's short story "Little Expressionless Animals." Other films parody Thomas Mann (*Death in Scarsdale*), John Updike and Sam Peckinpah (*Fun with Teeth*), William Blake (*Pre-Nuptial Agreement of Heaven and Hell*), and John Barth and Thomas Pynchon

(*Möbius Strip*), the latter of which is described as a "pornogra-phy-parody, possible parodic homage to Fosse's *All That Jazz,* in which a theoretical physicist ('[Hugh G.] Rection'), who can only achieve creative mathematical insight during coitus, con-ceives of Death as a lethally beautiful woman" (990n). A foot-note to the endnote cites a scholarly article titled "Has James O. Incandenza Ever Even Once Produced One Genuinely Original or Unappropriated or Nonderivative Thing?" (990nn), the answer being, "No."

Joelle, one of the novel's real heroes and often a mouthpiece for Wallace, offers the most complete and damning assessment of Incandenza's work, one that is pointed and significant enough to quote at length:

> The man's Work was amateurish, she'd seen. . . . More like the work of a brilliant optician and technician who was an amateur at any kind of real communication. Technically gorgeous, the Work, with lighting and angles planned out to the frame. But oddly hollow, empty, no sense of dramatic *towardness*—no narrative movement toward a real story; no emotional movement toward an audience. Like conversing with a prisoner through that plastic screen using phones . . . like a very smart person conversing with himself. . . . mor-dant, sophisticated, campy, hip, cynical, technically mind-bending; but cold, amateurish, hidden: no risk of empathy. (740)

All of Wallace's characteristic complaints about the postmod-ernists of the previous generation are lined up here: sophisti-cated but cold, hip but hidden, technically mind-bending but nonempathetic. Joelle concludes that the work's feeling for its audience is "one of contempt," its insistent use of parody makes Incandenza "no better than a camp follower[] in [an] ironic mask," and its use of satire provides clear evidence that he has "nothing new . . . to say" (740).

Hal's suicidal father also acts as Wallace's own postmodern father. Incandenza is Pynchon, Barth, and Nabokov all rolled into one. He creates the film *Infinite Jest,* the lethally closed entertainment that makes catatonic infants of its viewers, while Wallace creates the novel *Infinite Jest,* which contains the film. The book, contrary to Incandenza's film, loves its audience because, as explored earlier, it is willing to be cruel. Metafiction of the sort Incandenza produces is "untrue, as a lover," because it "cannot betray. It can only reveal. Itself is its only object."[27] What is more, in revealing itself solely, Incandenza's work helps him escape from *himself,* since he remains hidden behind its mirrors and self-reflecting surfaces. "Freedom from one's own head, one's inescapable P.O.V." (742): that is the point of Incandenza's art, an insight made even more poignant in light of Incandenza's suicide, itself an attempt to secure freedom from his own head.

Contrast this with the manic density of Wallace's novel, the prose of which provides not an escape from "annular" self-consciousness, from "thought-helixes" and "analysis-paralysis" but rather extended immersion in these modes of thought. Steeply speculates that perhaps the Entertainment's lethal appeal has "something to do with density. The visual compulsion. Theory's that with a really sophisticated piece of holography you'd get the neural density of an actual stage play without losing the selective realism of the viewer screen. That the density plus the realism might be too much to take" (490–91). Wallace's novel also operates on verbal density, which in turn creates in the reader an addictive compulsion. Cioffi has even argued that the reader becomes a sort of "addict" of Wallace's prose, one more instance of the novel mimicking the work of art that gives it its title. At the same time, Cioffi explains, "By making the novel a kind of addiction. . . , Wallace creates a work that . . . not only presses the reader into service, as a character in the novel's world, but . . . [also] forces the reader to recognize the kind of behavior she is engaged in. To read *Infinite Jest* is, in some way, to become the pathologically ambitious tennis player, the desperate show-off, the helpless addict—and to know it."[28] Unlike the film, then, the novel *Infinite Jest* keeps us supine on the couch, as it were, reading compulsively, trapped for long stretches of time, and yet the end result is not escape from consciousness but a disconcerting self-consciousness of one's own despair, of one's own cowardly desire for escape from self.

Wallace makes overt this complex theme of artistic patricide through the novel's intricate allusions to two primary texts of patrimonial anxiety, Shakespeare's *Hamlet* and Dostoevsky's *The Brothers Karamazov*. The *Hamlet* references are ubiquitous, beginning with the novel's (and the film's) title, which is culled from that play's famous graveyard sequence, while the Dostoevsky references are a bit more muted and hence less important. In the crucial passage from *Hamlet* the tragic hero, surrounded by Horatio and a pair of clownish gravediggers, stares at a skull and proclaims, "Alas, poor Yorick. I knew him, Horatio, a fellow of infinite jest, of most excellent fancy. He hath bore me on his back a thousand times, and now—how abhorred in my imagination it is" (5.i.169–72). Not uncoincidentally, "Poor Yorick Entertainment" is the name of Incandenza's production company. In this configuration, Hal is Hamlet, a brooding and self-conscious antihero who is forced to deal with the death of his father as well as his knowledge of his mother's flagrant infidelity with her own half-brother, Charles Tavis (C.T.), the current headmaster of the Enfield Tennis Academy and hence Incandenza's successor. Avril, then, is Gertrude, while C.T. is the novel's Claudius. Hal clues us into his own Hamlet role through a seventh-grade paper he writes on the emergence of the "post-postmodern" hero of "*non*-action, the catatonic hero, the one beyond calm, divorced from all stimulus, carried here and there across sets by burly extras whose blood sings with retrograde amines" (142).

Late in the novel, Hal also speculates that it has "always seemed a little preposterous that Hamlet, for all his paralyzing doubt about everything, never once doubts the reality of the ghost [of his father]. Never questions whether his own madness might not in fact be unfeigned. . . . That is, whether Hamlet might only be *feigning* feigning" (900). Likewise, the ghost of Incandenza appears to be everywhere: Himself's ghost seems to be responsible for moving around the objects in Ortho Stice's room (942), while the ghost of Incandenza speaks to the comatose Don Gately in the novel's long coda. Furthermore, Incandenza's postmortem appearances seem to be motivated by a desire to warn those still alive of Avril Incandenza's possible involvement with the Quebecois terrorists. Avril herself is Quebecois, and she is clearly (and comically) involved with Hal's primary tennis rival, John "The Darkness" Wayne, also a Quebec native. Before his demise, Incandenza also tries, in the guise of a "Professional Conversationalist," to warn Hal of the family's "sordid liaison with the pan-Canadian Resistance" as well as the mother's "cavorting with not two but over *thirty* Near-Eastern medical attachés" (30). Incidentally, a nameless "Near-Eastern medical attaché" is the first person in the novel to view the dreaded Entertainment: he does so, significantly, on the first of April (the French for which is "Avril").

Finally, this same John Wayne is present, in a mask, while Hal and Don Gately, in the most overt allusion to Hamlet (and the scene from which the novel gets its title), dig up the exploded head of James Incandenza, in which head perhaps resides the Master Copy of the Entertainment (16–17). Incandenza alludes to the former possibility in his "Professional Conversation" with Hal, in which he remarks that the "quote-unquote 'complimentary' Dunlop widebody tennis racquet's supersecret formulaic composition materials of high modulus-graphite-reinforced polycarbonate polybutylene resin are organochemically identical . . . to the gyroscopic balance sensor and *mise-en-scène* appropriation card and priapistic-entertainment cartridge implanted in your very own towering father's anaplastic cerebrum" (30–31). Gately, too, confirms the latter when he "dreams" the critical "grave-digging" scene, this dream being, perhaps, prophetic, since the actual event, narrated by Hal, seems to have taken place after Gately emerges from the hospital. The narrator explains, "He dreams he's with this very sad kid and they're in a graveyard digging some dead guy's head up and it's really important, like Continental Emergency important" (934). The sad kid is, obviously, Hal/Hamlet, while the "Continental Emergency" is clearly the result of the Quebecois terrorists having finally secured a copy (possibly even the Master) of the Entertainment. Gately's dream continues: "The sad kid is trying to scream . . . that the important thing was buried in the guy's head and to divert the Continental Emergency to start digging the guy's head up before it gets too late." Finally, Hal grabs the head, holds it up by its hair, "and makes the face of somebody shouting in panic: *Too Late*" (934).

The references to *The Brothers Karamazov* adhere primarily to the subplot involving Orin's jealousy over his father's possible sexual liaison with Joelle Van Dyne. Orin is the novel's angry, nihilistic Dmitry, with Hal taking on the Ivan role, particularly in his ongoing late-night discussions with Mario over his nonbelief in God. Mario, in his role as the novel's saintly figure of openness and empathy, assumes the ascetic cloak of Alyosha, most directly in a sequence placed late in the novel involving E.T.A.'s head trainer Barry Loach and his brother, a Jesuit priest who suffered "at the age of twenty-five a sudden and spiritual decline in which his basic faith in the innate indwelling goodness of men like spontaneously combusted and disappeared—and for no apparent reason" (967–68). The two brothers argue back and forth over this question of "God's supposed mimetic and divine creation," a series of "rather heated and high-level debates on spirituality and the soul's potential, not that much unlike Alyosha and Ivan's conversations in the good old *Brothers K*." (969). Loach eventually asks his brother to allow him to "prove somehow . . . that the basic human character wasn't as unempathetic and necrotic as the brother's present depressed condition was leading him to think," and the brother agrees, namely by challenging Loach to don the costume of a homeless person and stand outside the Park Street T station and hold out his hand. Loach does so, and is ignored by all passersby save one: Mario Incandenza, who "had no one worldly or adult along with him there to explain to him why the request of men with outstretched hands for a simple handshake or High Five shouldn't automatically be honored and granted" (971). Alyosha/Mario triumphs. Empathy wins.

These echoes all support a reading of the final section of the novel as an enactment of Wallace's conflicted attempt both to honor the heritage of his artistic forefathers and to kill them off at the same time. This narrative strand reaches its culmination when the "wraith" of James Incandenza appears inside the consciousness of Don Gately, who is paralyzed in a hospital bed. The wraith, in effect the ghost of Incandenza/King Hamlet, speaks at length about his art and specifically the film *Infinite Jest,* yet he is also trying to enlist Gately in his effort to save both the country from the film and Hal from his own brooding solipsism. Ironically, the art Incandenza's wraith describes, and which he affirms he never managed to produce, sounds much less like his own work and more like the work that contains him. The wraith speaks, for instance, about his desire to give voice to what he calls "figurants," those silent background figures who constitute the "realistic" *mise-en-scène* of the barroom restaurant in the 1980s television program *Cheers,* a show, not uncoincidentally, whose star character, Sam, is a recovering alcoholic. In his films, the wraith continues, he made sure that "you could bloody well hear every single performer's voice, no matter how far out on the cinematic or narrative periphery they were" (835). His films also sought to capture "the dramatic pathos of a figurant," who is "completely *trapped* and *encaged* . . . in his mute peripheral status" (835). This aspect of his art constitutes his attempt to redeem his failure to communicate with his son Hal. He tells Gately, "No horror on earth or elsewhere could equal watching your own offspring open his mouth and have nothing come out," a development he refers to as his "son's retreat to the periphery of life's frame" (837). So the Entertainment serves as his attempt to connect with Hal and bring the boy "out of himself" (839).

Yet the work is a failure in both regards, for it does not love, it is not open: it is self-alienated and so contributes to the alienation, anhedonia, and solipsism that it seeks to overcome. Conversely, Wallace's novel *does* succeed where Incandenza's art fails. As critic Tom LeClair has recently argued, the wraith's description of "figurants" reads like a description of Wallace's own novel, which follows "periphery" characters and storylines for pages on end and in which every character, no matter how "secondary," gets treated with lavish and dense attention: it's no wonder the novel is so long. Both LeClair and Catherine Nichols also connect the wraith's desire to foreground the periphery to the novel's extensive use of endnotes, which "blur the distinction between the foot and the head, errata and material central to the story."[29] Similarly, Wallace's novel, with its addictive prose and its restless, insistent empathy for all these crippled, deformed, despair-ridden characters, succeeds in drawing readers "out of themselves," effectively reversing thrust on our fall into "the womb of solipsism, anhedonia, death in life."

In effect, the "dead" Incandenza is "reborn" in the novel into a spokesman for Wallace himself, into Wallace's own "wraith." Whereas Incandenza remained aloof, hidden, from his own work, this wraith—as Wallace—appears inside the work as a Professional Conversationalist with Gately, who, in his own supine position in a bed, free of drugs and feeling extraordinary pain, becomes the book's "ideal reader." The wraith even tells Gately that "it couldn't ordinarily affect anybody or anything solid, and it could never speak right to anybody, a wraith had no out-loud voice of its own, and had to use somebody's like internal brain-voice if it wanted to try to communicate something, which was why thoughts and insights that were coming from some wraith always just sound like your own thoughts, from inside your own head, if a wraith's trying to interface with you" (831). This is also how Wallace hopes to enter into the communitarian language game between text and reader that is the book's primary site of play. Although his work is for the most part an informed critique Derridean poststructuralism, Wallace admits that he does affirm the poststructuralist argument for "the death of the author," for he insists, "Once I'm done with the thing, I'm basically dead, and probably the text's dead: it becomes simply language, and language lives not just in but *through* the reader." Once again, however, he amends his Derrida with a healthy dose of Wittgenstein: the text is not a chain but a "form of life" that exists *only* as an exchange between himself and a reader. The book does not refer back to itself solely to call attention to its artificiality but rather to create a free space in which the language can exist "simply [as] language." Yet it is language that "lives." And the reader's interior is the place where that text comes alive. Similarly, in an ultimately favorable review of H. L. Hix's 1992 critique of the "death-of-the-author" theory, *Morte D'Author: An Autopsy,* Wallace praises Hix for proposing a "solution" to the various theoretical problems that theory has inaugurated, a solution, he says, that "is a combination of a Derridean metaphysics that rejects assumptions of unified causal presence and a Wittgensteinian analytic method of treating actual habits of discourse as a touchstone for figuring out what certain terms really mean and do." In other words, Hix, like Wallace, amends Derrida by way of Wittgenstein. Wallace, in an oblique reference to his own methods, also speaks of "the wicked fun" of watching "how Hix uses the deconstructionists' own instruments against them."[30]

As with *The Broom of the System,* Wallace also once again figures this living interaction between the book's language and its reader as a Wittgensteinian "game." Wallace's intense mathematical and analytical interest in the game of tennis provides the best outlet for him to explore his Wittgensteinian theme. As outlined in the introduction, Wallace claims that he "discovered definite integrals and antiderivatives" at the same moment he abandoned his dream of becoming a professional tennis player; as a result, his approach to tennis, as he has amply illustrated both in *Infinite Jest* and in his extraordinary *Esquire* piece, "String Theory," is closer to that of a "math wienie" than a sports enthusiast.[31] In fact, he republished "String Theory" in *A Supposedly Fun Thing I'll Never Do Again* under the unwieldy title "Tennis Player Michael Joyce's Professional Artistry as a Paradigm of Certain Stuff about Choice, Freedom, Discipline, Grotesquerie, and Human Completeness," a catalogue of themes that reads, not accidentally, like an outline of *Infinite Jest*.

His stand-in for this component of his theme is a character named Gerhardt Schtitt, head coach and athletic director at Enfield. Schtitt "approached competitive tennis more like a pure mathematician than a technician" (81). For him, the game is about "the places where things broke down, fragmented into beauty" (81), a blend of "*not*-order" and "limits" that is best understood in terms of something called "Extra-Linear Dynamics," which an endnote describes as an offshoot of "the pure branch of math that deals with systems and phenomena whose chaos is beyond even Mandelbrotian math's Strange Equations and Random Attractants" (994n). These (largely parodic) technicalities aside, Schtitt's mathematical analysis of tennis functions as yet another self-reflexive description of the novel's Wittgensteinian method, in which communication with the reader is a game. Tennis, like Wallace's novel, is geared toward "expansion, the aleatory flutter of uncontrolled, metastatic growth," while any given match—much like the novel's circular, nonlinear plot, as well as its incessant probing of both its characters' and its readers' interiors—is a process of "*in*foliating," producing an "infinity of infinities of choice and execution, mathematically uncontrolled but humanly *contained,* bounded by the talent and imagination of self and opponent, bent in on itself by the containing boundaries of skill and imagination that . . . kept both [players] from winning, that made it, finally, a game, these boundaries of self" (82). Schtitt's language of "skill and imagination" makes all of this sound more aesthetic than mathematical, which is Wallace's intention. A bit later in this section, Wallace invites us to read Schtitt's linked unit of "self and opponent" as a metaphor for the reader and the book, or rather the book's language, conceived here as a manifestation of Wallace himself. For instance, Schtitt argues that the "true opponent, the enfolding boundary, is the player himself," while "the competing boy" on the other side of the net is "not the foe: he is more the partner in the dance" (84). The book is the reader's partner, then, and its self-reflexive strategies correspond to Schtitt's description of "Tennis's beauty's infinite roots" as "self-competitive." His final description of the player's role in this self-competition reads like a direct statement of Wallace's narrative strategies: "You compete with your own limits to transcend the self in imagination and execution. Disappear inside the game: break through its limits: transcend: improve: win. Which is why tennis is an essentially tragic enterprise. . . . You seek to vanquish and transcend the limited self whose limits make the game possible in the first place. It is tragic and sad and chaotic and lovely. All life is the same, as citizens of the human State: the animating limits are within, to be killed and mourned, over and over again" (84). Again, for "game" here, read "this book." The point is clear: Wallace is engaged in a "self-competitive," that is, self-reflexive, game with his reader, yet the two are not to be conceived as a self and an opponent but rather as "partners in a dance," a dance whose aim is both to transcend the self, via the reader's prolonged immersion in the interior of all its desperate "figurants," and also to confront directly the inner limits that make up the reader's unavoidable self.

Because of this "infoliating" agenda, the novel deliberately withholds a linear conclusion to its "infinite" plot strands. The classic term for narrative resolution, "denouement," is a French word that means, literally, "untying." The conclusion of *Infinite Jest*'s plot, by way of contrast, does not "untie," that is "resolve," its tensions but rather leaves them tangled, densely unresolved. In fact, the first section of the novel constitutes the conclusion, or at least the most "recent" event, which means the novel is circular, beginning with its ending and ending with its beginning. Between that final sequence and the opening scenes, however, there is a significant gap, a void, into which all the novel's unanswered questions fall endlessly, like coins down a well with no bottom. As the novel grinds slowly, excruciatingly, towards its anticlimax, Hal is seen wandering around the Enfield dorms with a hilarious smile adhered to his face; his friend Mike Pemulis, who had earlier scored a dose of DMX, seems distraught about something; Don Gately is paralyzed in a hospital bed and trying valiantly to withstand the hospital's attempt to give him painkillers; a group of Quebecois tennis players is descending on Enfield for a tournament; the Wheelchair Assassins seem to have secured a copy of the film (or not) and are also converging on Enfield; and Orin Incandenza is left, like the cockroaches he most fears, trapped beneath an enormous glass cage, speechless and helpless. We never conclusively learn whether the Entertainment gets disseminated, if Gately survives, or what has happened to Hal—has he accidentally watched the film, or has he accidentally ingested the DMZ? Wallace's legion of obsessive fans have combed through these issues and posted possible answers on various web sites, and these potential solutions are both intriguing and maddening in their inconclusiveness.

Wallace's point seems to be that these issues are not the issue. According to Joelle van Dyne, James Incandenza himself "had a thing about entertainment, being criticized about entertainment v. nonentertainment and stasis," and Wallace, too, wants to raise this same conflict in the minds of his readers. Entertainment is soothing, entertainment concludes, solves problems, offers self-forgetting; nonentertainment unsettles, remains incomplete, remains static. Recall Wallace's description in "Westward the Course of Empire Takes Its Way" of his new kind of "cruel" funhouse novel, in which "there is the motion of travel, except no travel." Likewise Wallace clearly has elected to take that risk—that is, to drag his reader through 1,100-odd pages of dense fiction only to withhold a satisfying conclusion. He even has Hal remember a grisly film of his father's entitled *Accomplice!* whose last five hundred seconds consist of an old man repeating "Murderer" over and over again. He then wonders, "Is the puzzlement and then boredom and then impatience . . . and then near-rage aroused in the film's audience by the static repetitive 1/3 of the film aroused for some theoretical end, or is Himself simply an amazingly shitty editor of his own stuff?" (947).

Wallace may or may not be a "shitty editor of his own stuff," but he does have a "theoretical end" to his madness, one that again contrasts his novel with Incandenza's film. Hal dismisses the film as "abstract and self-reflexive: we end up feeling and thinking not about the characters but about the cartridge itself" (946). Conversely, Wallace's novel, by resisting conventional closure, leaves the reader trapped inside the novel and its protagonists' interiors. There is no conventional "release" from the book, just as there is no final "release" from the self into which we are trapped. Instead, there is only the possibility of empathy with the interior of others. The false escapes offered by entertainment and drugs only create more cages, whereas this novel confronts the inescapability of the interior by leaving all the major characters still trapped inside themselves without any exit, without even the ability to *speak*. Hal, as the beginning of the novel shows us, has grown mute: he opens his mouth only to emit "subanimalistic noise and sounds" (14), while Gately, strapped in his hospital bed and intravenously fed nourishment, can do nothing but listen. Both are, in a sense, infants again. Hal declares that in his current state he has "become an infantophile," while Gately's condition is in every way that of the fetus in the womb, even down to his strange sense of the hospital ceiling bulging and deflating, "shiny as a lung" (809).

The final condition of both characters is linked to their decision to give up narcotics: Hal has foregone marijuana as a result of a surprise urine test that almost disqualifies him from an upcoming tennis match, while Gately is determined not to accept painkillers despite the grotesque horror of his condition. Catherine Nichols, speaking of Hal's eventual condition, argues that the "degree to which this transformation poses a threat to the values of *Infinite Jest*'s dominant culture is underscored by the terror his spoken sentiments incur."[32] Like the horribly deformed Mario, Hal has become a "*sub*animalistic" freak purely by refusing to hide from himself anymore. Indeed, no one else can even understand him any longer. By no longer killing, or at least hiding from, their "inner infants" of pure sentiment and feeling with drugs and entertainment, both characters have essentially *become* those inner infants. Each has become his own "hideous interior self, incontinent of sentiment and need," the same interior self that once "pulse[d] and writhe[d] just under the hip empty mask, anhedonia" (695). The book refuses to offer its reader a soothing "conclusion" for the same reason that Gately refuses his painkiller. In effect, the ending of the novel forces the reader to play the role of one of those unfortunate viewers of the dreaded Entertainment—trapped, catatonic, with no escape in sight. The difference is of course that viewers of the film stay where they are because they have found release from their selves and from self-responsibility ("I'm sorry. I'm so terribly sorry. I am so, so sorry"), whereas the reader of Wallace's similarly titled novel is trapped inside the infantilized and *therefore* unimaginably brave, feverish, and naked interior of Don Gately. Nothing soothing about this at all.

Still, if, as Schtitt says, the book's "animating limits are within," then he also says that these limits are "to be killed and mourned, over and over again." Similarly, Incandenza's "death mother cosmology" argues that "you have many lives, and at the end of each one (meaning life) is a woman who kills you and releases you into the next life" (850). These ideas inform, and perhaps even explain, why Wallace concludes the novel with a detailed account of the last time Gately ever did heroin, a sequence presented as a recollection or possibly an hallucination Gately has while still in his hospital bed refusing drugs. The novel provides hints that Gately has this hallucination/recollection because of delirium brought on by his intense pain; it is also possible that he "reexperiences" this episode *because* he has been given the painkillers after all. In any case, Gately, in the memory, comes to in the middle of a Dilaudid binge to find himself surrounded by a group of thugs, who have arrived to exact their revenge for a drug deal that has gone wrong. They then pump the already high Gately with a particularly lethal brand of heroin called "Sunshine," which an endnote describes as "Metro Boston's third-hardest thing to street cop after raw Vietnamese opium and the incredibly potent DMZ" (1079). The drug makes him "feel less high than disembodied" (981), and his penultimate memory, which is also the novel's, is of one of the thugs bearing down on him with a giant mirror, into which Gately looks and sees "clearly a reflection of his own big square pale head with its eyes closing as the floor finally pounced" (981). He then comes to "flat on his back on the beach in the freezing sand, and it was raining out of a low sky, and the tide was way out" (981). Thus the book ends.

Those final two images are rich and also richly ambiguous. Incandenza, in his role as the wraith, explains to Gately that "the woman who knowingly or involuntarily kills you is always someone you love" (850). That final dose of Sunshine could be read as the "death mother" who finally kills off his addictive self, for after this episode Gately begins his drug rehabilitation. At the same time, the present-tense Gately might have just been injected with Dilaudid, which means the whole "memory" is in fact a drug-induced hallucination. After all, Incandenza also says that those death mothers "are trying to make amends for a murder neither of you quite remember, except maybe in dreams" (850). In either case, the concluding image of Gately "flat on his back on the beach" is one of rebirth—the ocean as another womb—which means we end with Gately either at the remembered beginning of his sobriety, or at the beginning of his recovery from his wounds. The point is that he has been reborn from the womb of his addiction, and the woman who killed him—heroin, Dilaudid—has also given him birth, has saved his life. The ending is therefore both a death and a birth, an exhaustion and a replenishment.

# CHAPTER 5

# *Brief Interviews with Hideous Men*

## Interrogations and Consolidations

Wisely, Wallace did not rest on his laurels following the thunderous impact of *Infinite Jest.* Had he done so, he might have experienced the same sort of postmasterpiece paralysis that afflicted Ralph Ellison following *Invisible Man* or Thomas Pynchon following *Gravity's Rainbow.* Instead, Wallace consolidated his gains by issuing, back to back, two much more accessible works, the essay collection *A Supposedly Fun Thing I'll Never Do Again* (1997) and the story cycle *Brief Interviews with Hideous Men* (1999). Both books succeeded in broadening his audience and, more importantly, confirming—for good or ill, depending on the critic—what was most distinctive and significant about his art.

In fact, *A Supposedly Fun Thing* has since become one of Wallace's most beloved and widely read works, and for a very good reason as the essays in this collection display all the hallmarks of Wallace's inimitable style without the forbidding structural devices that make his fiction so challenging. Wallace has developed over the years a journalistic persona that expertly combines his emblematic cynicism and naïveté, with a surprising emphasis on the latter. The erudite and loquacious reporter who appears in these essays is a wide-eyed word-freak who fluctuates between Wordsworthian wonder and neurotic self-doubt. The combination is surprisingly effective, for it allows him to report on events with all the force of his formidable intellect while at the same securing an amiable, self-effacing relationship with his readers.

In addition, Wallace's unimpeachable eye for detail has never been sharper or more engagingly put to use than in the book's two most popular essays, both of them originally published in *Harper's:* "Getting Away from Already Being Pretty Much Away from It All," a lengthy account of Wallace's visit to the Illinois State Fair, and "A Supposedly Fun Thing I'll Never Do Again," his now-famous novella-length tale of misery and misadventure aboard a Celebrity cruise. The collection also includes a suitably unconventional treatment of David Lynch, a (typically) lengthy and breathless examination of semiprofessional tennis, and the essay "E Unibus Pluram: Television and U.S. Fiction," which has already been quoted at length throughout the present book. In his introduction to a special issue of the *Review of Contemporary Fiction* titled "The Future of Fiction," an issue he edited, Wallace declines to analyze the chosen essays because, he writes, "The pieces themselves are mostly pretty discursive, and I don't feel like anybody wants to hear me discursing about discursion."[1] The same thing should be said about the essays in *A Supposedly Fun Thing I'll Never Do Again* and about this writer's relation to them. Nevertheless, newcomers to Wallace's art are urged to begin with the essays for a lucid introduction to the peculiar pleasures and provocations that mark the fiction.

Somewhat in the same vein, *Brief Interviews with Hideous Men* functions as a more accessible and yet also less satisfying treatment of many of the central concerns at work in *Infinite Jest*. It is the one book in Wallace's corpus that, for all its charms, challenges, and singular achievements, does not significantly advance its author's art. It does, however, work as a decisive and articulate recapitulation of Wallace's by now characteristic themes, including depression, solipsism, community, self-consciousness—both textual and psychological—and the impact on our collective consciousness of therapeutic discourse writ large. The book also, in one memorable instance, revisits *Infinite Jest*'s linking of visual entertainment and various mythic archetypes, including those of Medusa and Narcissus. More a clearinghouse of still vital ideas than a bold shift in direction, *Brief Interviews with Hideous Men* is possibly Wallace's most "characteristic" book.

Even more so than its predecessor story collection, *Brief Interviews* has been carefully constructed so that it works better as a story cycle than a mere collection of short pieces. Wallace once again employs his contrapuntal method of alternating longer stories with short sketches and of placing thematically related pieces next to each other, to create a dialectical pattern of thesis, antithesis, and synthesis. The collection is also intricately bound together through its sustained theme of the "interview" and of interrogation in general. The title story is actually a four-part extended work of more than a hundred pages that consists of sixteen "interviews," presented here as a random sampling of some seventy-five such documents. (Though each interview is numbered and dated, no particular importance seems to be attached to these details.) Between and around the four "interview" sections, which are spread more or less evenly throughout the collection, are eighteen additional pieces, about a third of which constitute substantial stand-alone short stories, with the remainder consisting of short sketches. Three of the sketches bear the title, "Yet Another Example of the Porousness of Certain Borders," while two share the title, "The Devil Is a Busy Man." The longest extent piece, "The Depressed Person," runs to thirty-four pages; the shortest, hyperbolically billed as "A Radically Condensed History of Postindustrial Life," consists of seventy-nine words, not including the title.

Wallace has repeatedly said that the book is his attempt to address the subject of sex, which his work had hitherto shied away from addressing, and the statement is accurate so far as it goes. For although the book *does* address the subject more directly than do Wallace's other books, there is very little that is particularly *sexy* about the stories in *Brief Interviews with Hideous Men*. As longtime readers of Wallace's work might already expect, his characters are no better equipped to find release and solace in sex than in popular entertainment or drugs. Rather, sex becomes for Wallace's "hideous" men (and women) another means by which they can descend deeper and deeper into their self-made cages of self-consciousness and solipsistic dread. Like everything else in Wallace's world, not only has sexuality become hopelessly enmeshed in falsifying codes and conventions, but the people engaged in sexual activity are even *more* hopelessly enmeshed in their postmodern self-consciousness of these very same codes and conventions. They feel alienated not only from sexuality but also from their own response to their sexual alienation. As one character in the book explains, "Supposedly everybody now knows everything about what's really going on underneath all the semiotic codes and cultural conventions, and everybody supposedly knows what paradigms everybody is operating out of, and so we're all as individuals held to be far more responsible for our sexuality, since everything we do is now unprecedentedly conscious and informed."[2] What is striking about this relatively banal assessment of our current condition is that it operates in the story as part of a *pose*. The entire collection, in fact, like much of Wallace's best work, trains an ironic eye on the misuse of self-conscious irony.

The book positively brims with talk and more talk, much of it sophisticated and articulate and all of it geared toward an "honest" description of hideousness in the area of interpersonal relations. Over and over again Wallace demonstrates how self-professed "openness" can become an even more sinister form of deception. All the characters are in a sense metafictionalists of their own feelings, with the result that their openness leaves them even more lonely and despairing than they would have been had they simply remained dishonest. One character, for instance, wonders if "it's even possible that [his] honestly trying to head off the pattern of sending out mixed feelings and pulling away is just another type of way of pulling away" (99), and, in fact, he is absolutely correct, as his "honest" attempt to come clean to his lover turns out to be the first stage in his elaborately coded attempt to leave her. This pattern reappears throughout the book: characters declare their openness and their honesty in order to secure their lovers' trust, and even express concern that their openness about their own openness might be another ploy to deceive; and in every case, the point of such openness and honesty, however layered and meta-, is to deceive. In the words of one of the book's numerous therapist characters, these elaborate rhetorical devices are essentially "primitive emotional prophylaxes whose real function [is] to preclude intimacy" (49).

The book, then, continues with Wallace's ongoing attempt to ironize irony and to reverse thrust on postmodern self-reflexivity by performing a metafictional dismantling of metafiction. It contributes to Wallace's work in the way it shifts the emphasis away from the literary and toward the personal. In other words, whereas *Girl with Curious Hair* used its detailed analysis of postwar fiction and pop culture as a means by which to say something urgent about the state of then contemporary culture, *Brief Interviews with Hideous Men* directly dramatizes how completely the dis-ease of self-consciousness and irony has infiltrated the culture of the new millennium.

For all that, one cannot say that Wallace, in this book, has finally set aside his ongoing argument with his postmodern heroes and the pressure they exert on his freedom as a writer of fiction. The one piece in the collection that deals almost exclusively with literary (rather than sexual or inter-gender) themes, "Octet," also serves as the book's ironic meta-explanation of its own postmetafictional strategy. Borrowing its premise from John Updike's 1979 story "Problems," the piece consists of six short vignettes, or actually story premises, presented in the form of "pop quiz" questions, each of which ends with a question for the reader. The purpose, the story's narrator explains, is "to compose a certain sort of '*interrogation*' of the person reading them, somehow—i.e., palpations, feelers into the interstices of her sense of something, etc." (145). This narrator continually interrupts the piece to describe his own difficulties in putting the series together, a description of artistic anxiety that itself takes the form of a series of questions for the reader. The story is therefore self-conscious about its own self-consciousness, and, like many of the stories in *Brief Interviews,* threatens the reader with the prospect of an infinite regress of self-reflexivity.

Still, this narrator insists that the "formal exercism or pseudometabelletristic gamesmanship in the pieces' unconventional Pop Quiz–type structure" is "worth risking," given that the interrogation, so proposed, has an "urgency" that requires a fresh intervention into existing forms—including an intervention into old-school metafiction. The narrator's solution to his problem—that is, how to interrogate, or connect, with the reader both in spite of and as a result of the story's unavoidable self-consciousness and artificiality—is to make the story as "fundamentally lost and confused and frightened and unsure" as the reader (160). It achieves this aim by displaying its self-consciousness and anxiety not as "an innocuous formal belletristic device" but as a genuine instance of embarrassed (and embarrassing) uncertainty. It also uses its "postclever metaformal hooey" as a way to interrogate "the reader's initial inclination to dismiss the pieces as 'shallow formal exercises' . . . [thereby] forcing the reader to see that such a dismissal would be based on precisely the same sorts of shallow formalistic concerns she was (at least at first) inclined to accuse the octet of" (152).

Although the author of the story, since he has been turned into an "object" in the story, that is, a character, is still a mere device, the self-consciousness is designed paradoxically to seem real: the author-character even goes so far as to describe in detail sections of the story that were written and abandoned, sections that in turn become part of the overall "story" as well as components of the story's interrogative strategy. The narrator admits that "S[tandard] O[perating] P[rocedure] 'meta'-stuff" also displays a similar sort of "honesty" about its own artifice, and yet that brand of honesty, he insists, is a "sham-honesty that's designed to get you to like [the author] and approve of him," whereas the honesty this narrator employs parallels the desperate self-effacement of a person who goes to a party and actually "goes around at the party and goes up to strangers and *asks* them whether they like him or not" (158). The trick—and the source of the narrator's anxiety—lies in avoiding the trap of honesty as *ploy*, the latter of which he directly associates with "S.O.P. 'meta'-stuff," which, to him, seems to resemble the type of real-world person who tries to manipulate you into liking him by making a big deal of how open and honest and unmanipulative he's being all the time, a type who's even more irritating than the sort of person who tries to manipulate you by just flat-out lying to you, since at least the latter isn't constantly congratulating himself for not doing precisely what the self-congratulation itself ends up doing, viz. not interrogating you or have any sort of interchange or even really *talking* to you but rather just *performing* in some highly self-conscious and manipulative way. (147n)

This passage, found buried in a footnote, nevertheless provides the key to the entire book; significantly, it arrives at the halfway mark, that is, in the collection's "center." The passage overtly connects the metafictional conventions that were his target in "Westward the Course of Empire Takes Its Way" with the "real-world" sham-honesty that governs the bulk of *Brief Interviews*. In both cases, the charge is the same: meta-strategies of any sort are decadent when they are mere "performance" and self-consciously manipulative. The task here is to disclose the self-consciousness as manipulative and thereby enact an actual, two-way "interrogation" with the reader.

Wallace provides a number of additional clues that we are to read "Octet" as the descriptive core of the book. The story's title turns out to be an additional source of anxiety for the writer, since he began with the idea of creating eight "quizzes" and gets no further than writing six: four of the six appear in the published piece, while the long, concluding section in which the narrator takes the stage is numbered "Pop Quiz 9." Still, the narrator insists on calling it "Octet": he is, he admits, "intransigent on this point." The number eight is "organically unified," with its "two-times-two-times-two" structure, and creates "a Manichean duality raised to the triune power of a sort of Hegelian synthesis" (151). Careful readers of the book will note that Wallace provides *sixteen* "Brief Interviews with Hideous Men," that is, two-times-two-times-two-times-two, the whole of which not only achieves the interrogative structure proposed in the "Octet" but also constitutes, thematically, a Manichean duality resolved by a "Hegelian synthesis."

The "interviews" take a number of forms: some are dramatic monologues in which a male respondent answers a series of unspoken questions posed, one infers, by a therapist, sociologist, or some other "objective" researcher interested in male behavior; others are presented as "overheard" conversations between two male speakers in dialogue; still others read like transcriptions of arguments between a male and his female lover, the latter of whom assumes the role as the interview's silent questioner. In all three cases, the interviewer is silent, represented only by a "Q." wherein the question actually being posed must be deduced by the reader based on the nature of the answer. The structure therefore puts the reader "inside" the story as a character, making her a participant in the narrative's construction; in this way, Wallace succeeds, as he suggests in "Octet," in transforming the traditional self-conscious "author" figure of S.O.P. metafiction into a reader, who is "down here quivering in the mud of the trench with the rest of us" (160). Wallace is also, once again, invoking Wittgenstein's language game, since the pieces, in a sense, constitute a "game" in which meaning is a product of peculiar "rules" the pieces rely on for meaning, a "game," moreover, in which the reader must play a role. By playing this role and entering "into" the texts themselves, the reader breaks the "fourth wall" in reverse. Whereas the "author" of S.O.P metafiction breaks out of the story and speaks directly to the reader, here the reader breaks *into* the story and interacts directly with the characters, who are themselves hiding behind their own walls of self-conscious deception. In this way Wallace achieves what he sees as the primary aim of fiction, which is to "allow us imaginatively to identify with characters' pain" so that "we might then also more easily conceive of others identifying with our own. This is nourishing, redemptive; we become less alone inside."[3] The interviews employ a self-conscious literary device that provides the illusion of "true empathy," which Wallace, following Wittgenstein, realizes is impossible—that is, we cannot, literally, feel someone else's pain—while at the same time serves as a literal means of escaping the inevitable loneliness of our interior state, since our interiors, in the act of reading, becomes a site of voices in dialogue.

Wallace wants to test the boundaries of our willingness to "empathize," since the men we, as readers, interview are, as they are advertised to be, hideous. They are sexist, self-protective, self-absorbed, objectifying, and most of all, cruel. Many of them go one step further and try to absolve their cruelty by being "honest" and "open" about their own awareness of their cruelty. Moreover, they do not engage in dialogue, properly speaking, since Wallace presents only their answers to questions which are erased from the text. The reader assumes the position of someone who literally cannot get a word in edgewise. The reader's empathy, then, must be pure, since it cannot be returned by these characters. The stories force us to enter into the male characters' self-imposed cages of isolation and then silently stand by as these same men erect the bars of those same cages.

In the first significant interview, the reader takes on the role of a female lover whose male counterpart is attempting to leave her because, as he puts it, he can no longer live with her constant fear that he will some day leave her. "Maybe if I loved you a little less or cared about you less I could take it," he explains (21). Nevertheless, he declares that his leaving is "*not* the confirmation of all [her] fears" about his leaving but the *result* of those fears. What he worries about most, however, is not that he is going to hurt her but that she has been right about him all along. His leaving is really a plea for her sympathy, in essence a request that she realize how he "might be torn up about it too" (22). Surely he has not earned such sympathy, yet Wallace challenges us to empathize with his hideousness as an imaginative act of endurance, if you will, the reward for which is the comfort that "we might then also more easily conceive of others identifying with our own" pain.

This interview has its Hegelian partner in the form of another one-sided dialogue between a lover and her mate in which the male explains he is leaving in order to avoid hurting her down the road when, as he freely admits, he probably will leave her, based on his history. The male is self-conscious to a fault, admitting every contradiction in his method, including the possibility that his honesty in this matter is in fact a ruse designed to get her to pull away first: "Maybe deep down I'm such a cowardly shit that I don't even want to make the commitment of pulling way myself, that I want to somehow force you into doing it" (99). The situation is the exact obverse of its partner piece: whereas before the man leaves because, he says, he loves the woman so much that he cannot stand her suspicions, here the man leaves because he loves the woman so much that he cannot bear the thought of hurting her down the road.

In both cases, the lovers leave, and they manage to do so by feigning total openness. As Wallace says elsewhere about the "sham-honesty" of metafictional self-reflexivity, perhaps it would have been better for all involved if these figures had simply flat-out lied, rather than put on these self-congratulating performances which admit of no dialogue or reciprocity.

These "hideous men" are further linked to Wallace's traditional postmodern and poststructuralist targets in the way they all abdicate will or self-responsibility. The latter character declares, "I'm afraid maybe I'm just constitutionally incapable of doing anything other than pursuing and seducing and then running, plunging in and then reversing" (99). Other characters refer to their "history" or to the "patterns" that have governed their relationships with women up till then. They take comfort, even refuge, in regarding themselves as mere matrices of cultural forces, or products of dysfunctional upbringings, or victims of bad wiring, quite as they have been taught to do by contemporary therapeutic discourse and postmodern theory.

The most striking exemplar of this latter tactic is the man in Brief Interview #48 who explains, with great sophistication and erudition, how and why he goes about trying to convince his dates into letting him tie them up. Throughout his explanation he repeatedly flexes his fingers in the air to "signify tone quotes" around words or phrases whose meaning he wants to bracket or which have connotations from which he wants to distance himself. This tic, which, as even the interview's transcriber admits, gets increasingly more annoying, marks the speaker as more than an ironist; he is, in fact, a learned poststructuralist, so skilled in deconstructionist practice that he puts his own spoken language through the meat grinder of Derridean analysis. Invoking Foucault, he describes his proposal as "the heavily stylized formalism of {f[lexion of upraised] f[ingers]} *masochistic play*" (106). Similarly, to account for his motives, he blithely affirms, in accordance with Lacanian theory, "My mother's imago all but rules my adult psychological life, I am aware, forcing me again and again to propose and negotiate contracted rituals where power is freely given and taken and submission ritualized and control ceded and then returned of my own free will. {Laughter.} Of the subject's, rather. Will" (111). Even the "Lacanian slip" above he laughs off. Still, when he declares that this ritual of masochistic play ends with him breaking into tears and asking for his subject's "compassion," neither the reader nor, one feels, the speaker can determine whether the tears, when they come, are genuine: the speaker's tragedy resides in the fact that he experiences this uncertainty.

Similarly, the two graduate students in Brief Interview #28 look to Foucault and Lacan specifically to reaffirm the old patriarchal dynamic between men and women amid "today's postfeminist era" (229). With relish, they declare that contemporary women *must* be stuck in an irreconcilable bind between an old order and a new order and that they are not "strictly to blame for the terrible bind they've found themselves in" (232). Therefore, all this "talk about autonomy" is actually "an elaborate semiotic code, with the new postmodern semions of autonomy and responsibility replacing the old premodern semions of chivalry and courtship" (234). At the end of all this sophisticated theoretical analysis—with its appeals to "*history* . . . in a Foucaultvian sense" and the "Lacanian cry in the infantile unconscious"—the two theoreticians discover that women really "want to be rescued" by a powerful male. The hermeneutics of suspicion have therefore been cagily employed to reconstruct the deconstructed bourgeois social order, while Wallace's clever structure manages, with its ironic frame, to deconstruct *their* disingenuous reconstruction.

Wallace saves his most ingenious bit of sleight-of-hand for the final Brief Interview, a lengthy and audacious piece that also, for all intents and purposes, concludes the book. In keeping with the dialectical approach demonstrated above, this piece links up with an earlier Interview, both of them joined by the themes of suffering, empathy, and the power of storytelling. In the earlier Interview (#46), a young man engages in a dialogue with a young woman—the reader's "proxy" and silent voice—while both of them attend some sort of protest rally for violence against women. Early on in his long diatribe he asks why "getting incested or abused or violated or whatever or any of those things can't also have their positive aspects for a human being in the long run" (117). Citing Viktor Frankl's Holocaust memoir, *Man's Search for Meaning,* he tries to get his female listener to imagine a situation—in this case, a gang rape—in which she would be made to feel that she is not a person but rather a thing. Once someone is put in that position—as Frankl was during his Concentration Camp experience—that person would find learn that being a human being with "sacred rights" is in fact a *choice,* an assertion the person makes in the face of the world's attempt to affirm otherwise. This strange appropriation of Frankl's argument takes an even stranger turn when it is revealed that the gang rape the speaker has invoked might actually refer to something *he* experienced as a boy, which detail forces the woman, and the reader, to see his plea as an elaborate declaration of his own desperate attempt to survive his own experience. When, at the end of the Interview, the young man, perhaps in exasperated fury at the buried pain that he has just unearthed, turns on the woman and sneers, "What if I did it to you? Right here? Raped you with a bottle?"(124), the second person pronoun suddenly also refers to the reader inside the text, a reader who, as Wallace declares in "Octet," the text wants urgently to interrogate and whose powers of empathy it wants to challenge. Can the reader override her "knee-jerk politics about . . . victims," not to mention her sophisticated postmodern understanding of textual artificiality, and see the boy as a person and not a thing—that is, not as an "object" inside this clearly constructed text?

The bold challenges Wallace levels in this Interview get reprised in the spectacular final Interview, which also, ingeniously, serves as a culmination of all the devices and themes that have been operating in the interview format all along. The speaker is once again an intelligent and arrogant male speaking, once again, to a silent female who serves as the reader's proxy voice. Like the other speakers, he also uses his honesty and openness as a ploy. This interview is different, however, since it works on a dizzying number of levels, with narratives inside narratives and frames inside frames. The speaker is principally concerned with telling his silent auditor why he fell in love with his current girlfriend only after "she had related the story of the unbelievably horrifying incident in which she was brutally accosted and held captive and nearly killed" (287); the speaker therefore is trying persuade his listener via a narrative that has as its subject *his* being persuaded by someone else's narrative. Of course, the speaker is perfectly open and honest about everything that he felt while picking up the woman he is describing here, a "pickup" that, typically in this book, employed a sham honesty whose real purpose was deception. The whole piece, then, self-reflexively examines, explodes, and even reverses the traditional roles of speaker and listener, of subject and object.

The speaker's description of his pickup nicely exemplifies this self-reflexive strategy. He describes the woman as a "Cruncher," that, is a proponent of New Age religions and post-1980s hippie philosophy, whose "at-center-life-is-just-a-cute-pet-bunny" vision he dismisses as "smug-seeming naïveté." A friend of his also refers to people of this stripe as "the Inward Bound." The speaker picks up this naïve and "inward bound" person by telling her that, though he had originally intended to say he had "just been passing her blanket and . . . [had] felt a mysterious but overwhelming urge just to lean down and say Hi"—thereby using her own belief in cosmic oneness as a ploy—he actually wanted to be totally honest and thereby confess that he had *deliberately* approached her because he had felt a mysterious but overwhelming urge to do so. The speaker also tells his current auditor that he is "aware of how all this sounds" but that he has "no choice but to be brutally candid . . . about the way a reasonably experienced, educated man is going to view an extraordinarily good-looking girl whose life philosophy is fluffy and unconsidered and when one comes right down to it kind of contemptible" (289). The listener—and, by extension, the reader—is therefore put on notice that all this candid openness is potentially a trap.

This complex and layered frame—with its ironic take on ironic distance—contains at its center an account of a story that affirms the power of empathy in the face of unbelievable horror. In the woman's story, she goes hitchhiking and gets picked up by a "psychotic sex criminal," yet we only get this story as filtered through the speaker. For him, the incident she describes is unfortunately full of clichés that he cannot leave unexploded, as when, for instance, he explains that the "psychotic sex criminal" exits off to a secluded area, "which," he adds wearily, "seems to be what psychotic criminals always do" (293). He also can barely conceal his contempt at the woman's explanation that she felt, instantly upon entering the car, a sinister "energy field" that warned her of danger. Then, unexpectedly, the tone begins to shift. Declaring, with regret, "My Memory is more verbal than visual, I'm afraid," he goes on to describe, haltingly, the woman's fascinating and effective storytelling manner, which involved "an unexpected ability . . . to deflect attention from herself and displace maximum attention onto the anecdote itself" (296). The objectives of Wallace's elaborate game become instantly clear: by secreting the woman's story and her selfless, guileless, and straightforward telling of it at the center of a narrative that is brimming with its teller's layered self-consciousness, Wallace once again hopes to use self-reflexivity as a means of overcoming mere self-reflexivity.

This agenda is made even more explicit by the content of the woman's story itself, for, as she tells it—or as our speaker tells us she tells it—her method of avoiding death at the hand of the psychotic sex criminal is to "focus her way into the sort of profound soul-connection that would make it difficult for the fellow to murder her" (295). In short, she tries to empathize with him human-to-human, to enter his interior, however cosmically, and force *him* to see her not as a thing but as another human being. Whereas the young man in the earlier Interview insisted that each person much choose for himself or herself to assume the sacred right of being a human, the woman demonstrates, both in her narrative and in the telling of it, that in fact this process of human-making is a reciprocal arrangement: we acquire our sacred rights as humans only by *granting* those rights to others, however hideous. This process must also be selfless: it does not work if the intention is simply to acquire that status for oneself, for then the attempt becomes a ploy that eventually demeans both partners, the person making the appeal and the person to whom the appeal is made, as all the other hideous men in the book have inadvertently demonstrated. As the male speaker explains, the woman's narrative succeeds because its naïveté, while possibly "smug," is "nevertheless attractive" such that it helps *him* both focus on the anecdote itself and also *feel* "just what it must have *felt* like for her, for anyone, finding yourself through nothing but coincidence heading into a secluded area in the company of a dark man . . . who says he is your own death incarnate" (297). He then admits that her "odd affectless sincerity" allowed him to hear "expressions like *fear gripping her soul,* unquote, as less as televisual clichés or melodrama but as sincere if not particularly artful attempt simply to describe what it must have felt like" (297).

And at every juncture we are getting someone else's self-conscious description of a nonselfconscious narrative about direct empathy; the piece comes equipped with its own criticism, its own warnings, all of which clear the way for the mysterious act of empathy that lies at the center but which has also been protected from the text. As the speaker himself explains in another context, the frame makes the piece "divided and doubly complex" because it introduces "an element of self-consciousness" that is "itself an object of focus, like some sort of diffraction of regress of self-consciousness and consciousness of self-consciousness" (311). This refraction creates an empty space in the narrative, the space between two mirrors reflecting each other, and in this space resides the story's true heart, that act of empathy that is there as a product of the narrative because, paradoxically, it is not dramatized directly: it is not, in other words, an object of the text but rather its subject. In accordance with the dictum Wallace laid down in "Westward," the story "keeps safe in its ghastly silent center the green kernel that is the true self." What finally emerges is a story about storytelling, where storytelling itself can become a form of "focusing," as a way *into* that part of the reader's soul that is subject and not object. And, as always in the Interviews, the actual reader is right there inside the piece, as both "object" and "subject," as the person addressed directly and whose empathy becomes the work's silent and therefore living dynamic force.

The noninterview stories in the collection, both the lengthy freestanding pieces as well as the brief sketches, all, in various ways, amplify and re-explore the myriad themes and strategies at work in the extended title work. The two short works entitled "The Devil Is a Busy Man," for instance, both address the difficulty, if not impossibility, of pure and selfless giving, an idea that sits at the forefront of the final Interview. Likewise, the three short pieces titled "Yet Another Example of the Porousness of Certain Borders" all depict situations in which levels of consciousness and/or representation begin to bleed into one another. The final piece, by way of example, consists entirely of a young man's intense and obsessive description of a homemade haircut his mother once gave him, yet what concerns him most is the memory of his older brother mimicking his facial expressions in the crack between the two doors of the pantry. The mimicking gets progressively more cruel, as the younger brother even begins mimicking the narrator's distress at being mimicked, while all about him the spatial particulars of the situation suggest a closed energy system with openings to ward off entropy: rain outside beating on the windows, hot air in front of him (due to a burning stove) and cold air behind, an open utensil drawer and the cracked pantry doors. The piece ends with the narrator asserting that the younger brother's cruel mimicking represents what "lolly-smeared hand-held brats must see in the funhouse mirror—the gross and pitiless *sameness,* the distortion in which there is, tiny, at the center, something cruelly true about the we who leer" (320). The reference above to Barth's "funhouse mirror" confirms that this sketch, and the situation it sets up, should be read as "yet another" metaphor for Wallace's art, which uses distortions and funhouse mirrors to locate, "tiny, at the center," something cruel and true about the watcher/reader. The title, moreover, functions as a reminder that Wallace's work, as early as *The Broom of the System,* has always sought to stave off exhaustion by puncturing holes in its own structure, holes that lead back to the world outside the text.

Of the remaining full-length stories, four command our attention. Three stories from this group—"Forever Overhead," "Adult World" Parts I and II, and "The Depressed Person,"— engage in many of the same themes and strategies as "Octet" and the "Brief Interviews" cycle, while the remaining story, "Tri-Stan: I Sold Sissee Nar to Ecko," looks back to *Girl with Curious Hair* and *Infinite Jest.* Because it is the most anomalous story in *Brief Interviews,* it will be taken up first.

The story's ungainly title, when read aloud, puns rather obviously on two founding myths of the Western tradition: Tristan and Iseult, and Narcissus and Echo. The obviousness is intentional, of course, for in this story Wallace takes one more swipe at John Barth's postmodern mythic method, which, as discussed already in the chapter on *Girl with Curious Hair,* works as a corrective of sorts to the modernist use of myth principally associated with James Joyce's *Ulysses.* As Barth explains in *Chimera,* "Since myths themselves are among other things poetic distillations of our ordinary psychic experience and therefore point always to daily reality, to write fictions which point always to mythic archetypes is in my opinion to take the wrong end of the mythopoeic stick . . . Better to address the archetypes directly."[4] As he did in *Girl with Curious Hair,* Wallace goes one step further in this story, first, by parodying Barth's method, and two, by wresting myth from the literary tradition and inserting it into the popular culture, the new site of our collective consciousness. The piece tells the "mythic" story of a "wise and clever programming executive named Agon M. Nar" who turns his surgically enhanced daughter, Sissee Nar, into a television sensation and the object of national erotic obsession. Though the piece is ripe with Wallace's sharp wit and his at times tiresome imaginative energy, these stylistic pyrotechnics serve a serious purpose, for this story not only revises his old argument with John Barth but also uses this final act of artistic patricide as the springboard for a relatively serious inquiry into the role visual entertainment plays in our collective solipsism and aloneness, a theme he addressed as well in *Infinite Jest.*

In a passage that reads like a direct parody of Barth at the height of his self-indulgent cleverness, the story's narrator—the "fuzzy Henonian epiclete Ovid the Obtuse" (Ovid=David)—tells us that Agon M. Nar's success principally hinged on his ability to "shuffle & recombine proven formulae that allowed the muse of Familiarity to appear cross-dressed as Innovation" (235). Television sitcom genres have become, in Wallace's world, the new archetypes, while innovation in television works much the way innovation works in Barth's theory of storytelling—not as the arrival of newness but rather as the "reshuffling" of conventional forms. For Wallace, however, television's "Familiarity" serves to "soothe" audiences into a passive acceptance that opens the door to dangerous manipulation, so this story, with its overhanging deity "Stasis, God of Passive Reception & all-around Big Mythopoeic Cheese," interrogates how this form of manipulation actually works.

At the dawn of Cable, Agon M. Nar launches a new station called the Satyr-Nymph Network (S-NN) which plays nothing but reruns of old BBC dramatizations of Greek and Roman myths. Soon, the network begins filming its own retellings of the BBC dramatizations, in one of which, a piece called *Beach Blanket Endymion,* Agon M. Nar's daughter Sissee plays the title role. So gorgeous and surgically enhanced is she that, like her namesake Narcissus, she has never seen herself in the mirror; what's more, her beauty is so captivating that she has caught the eye of Stasis, which fact has raised the ire of his Hera-like wife, Codependae. (No comment.) As the story proceeds, Codependae hatches an elaborate plot to murder the gorgeous Sissee Nar, a narrative strand that also parodies the "star-stalking" stories that repeatedly clutter our already cluttered tabloid news media. In her role as Endymion, Sissee lies perfectly still in a state of rapturous nonmovement—"She was poetry in stasis"—leading Ovid the Obtuse to theorize that "Classic-minded viewers yearned for a maiden comatose, gloriously unconscious," this because "there seems to be something death-tending at the very heart of all Romance" (245). She represents, then, the erotic partner to the apologizing mother in Incandenza's film, *Infinite Jest,* and she also allows Wallace to make an only partially ironic comment on the power of television to create unreal ideals of beauty that, as this story illustrates through Sissee's tragic death, work to diminish us all.

"Forever Overhead," which was included in *Best American Short Stories* (1992), could not be any more different from the playful and self-indulgent "Tri-Stan": in many respects, it is the book's most straightforward and accessible piece. Cast in the reader-involving second-person point of view, the piece is essentially a coming of age story, one that, as is typical of Wallace's work, also cleverly updates the genre. As Barth shows in "Lost in the Funhouse," all coming-of-age stories are essentially dramatizations of the character's fall from innocence into a more fractious state of experienced self-consciousness. Self-consciousness, in turn, is inextricable from sexual consciousness. "Forever Overhead" plays freely with these archetypal ideas as it dramatizes a young boy's attempt, on his thirteenth birthday, to take a plunge (a fall) from a high dive.

"Crunchy animal hair" has lately sprouted around his privates, while two weeks prior his testicles dropped. Fittingly, he sees the "girl-women" at the pool differently now, their suit tops "delicate knots of fragile colored string against the pull of mysterious weights" and their hips containing "immoderate swells and swivels" (8). The boy also discovers, to his surprise, that on the morning of his thirteenth birthday he wants to go to the pool "alone." Like his budding sexuality, his desire for solitude is a new development, perhaps the product of his new self-consciousness, which has split him into a self and an entity conscious of that self: ergo the use of the second person. The pool below him he sees as a "system of movement," the tank "blue as energy," in which each splash in the water is regarded as a momentary "wound" that quickly "heals." Set against the dynamic energy of the pool and its symbolic status as a marker of time and onward movement is the boy's "overhead" perch on the high dive. Other divers crowd up behind him on the ladder, compelling him to leap, and yet he remains poised on the edge, in a paralysis of thinking and self-doubt that is perhaps the most characteristic state for a Wallace character. The boy even realizes that "being scared is caused mostly by thinking" (8), whereas the pool below him, as well as the fearlessness of the other divers, partakes of a "rhythm that excludes thinking" (12). The boy longs to stay "forever overhead" on that board, poised between stasis and movement, consciousness and self-consciousness, for he learns that "from overhead is it more real than anything" (14). Yet he also wonders if the "lie" is the world overhead. The story ends, as it must, with the boy plunging down into water/time, a lovely moment presented as an invitation: "Step into the skin and disappear" (16). In other words, enter the world below, the world of the real, and disappear there, inside your skin, where the true self resides, secret and safe from the self-consciousness that would displace it.

"Adult World" I and II, which originally appeared in *Esquire Magazine,* is also about sex and self-consciousness, only this time Wallace has assumed the point of view of a young woman, specifically a newlywed named Jeni who worries that her lovemaking technique with her new husband "was somehow hard on his thingie" (161). Much attention is paid to transcribing the winding thought-helix that constitutes Jeni's obsessive self-analysis, and we follow her through all her attempts to confront and overcome her problem, including a trip to an adult film and novelty shop called Adult World, where she buys a dildo. Eventually she calls a boyfriend to ascertain if he thought of other women while making love with her, much as she has begun to suspect her husband of doing. She imagines her husband's fantasizing issues from "a secret, impenetrable part to his character," a clear signal to us that this story is less about the woman's irrational anxieties and more about the way the sex act, for all its physical intimacy, cannot puncture the wall that separates one's own inviolate interiority from that of one's lover.

In the story's second half, Jeni learns that her ex-lover in fact still fantasizes about *her,* which revelation in turn leads to an "epiphany" in which she realizes "that true wellsprings of love, security, gratification must originate within self" (187). This realization compels her to return to Adult World to buy an additional dildo to aid her in her quest for "authentic responsibility for self," where she encounters her husband's car, clear evidence that his perceived distance from her was actually the product of his addiction to pornography. The story ends with her choosing to accept this problem, "bringing them now [in] that deep & unspoken complicity that in adult marriage is covenant/love" (188–89). Wallace emphasizes the vicious dramatic irony of this conclusion—namely, that the lovers are linked by the fact that they are both essentially solipsistic masturbators—by casting the story's second half in the form of the author's working notes. The narrative becomes a sketch of a sketch, a frame to a frame, one that leaves inviolate the woman and her husband as they descend deeper and deeper into their isolation and self-absorption.

"The Depressed Person," the story in the collection that most clearly parallels "Adult World," also takes as its main character a young woman, this one a wealthy, spoiled victim of punishing depression. In this story, Wallace takes to its formal and stylistic limit his by now familiar technique of dramatizing the self-reflexive nightmare of hyper-self-consciousness, while the prose, as well as the story's extensive use of footnotes, make it the book's final link back to the world of *Infinite Jest.* Here the footnotes serve a very specific purpose: they dramatize for the reader the layered nature of the woman's obsessive self-absorption, in which thoughts have tangents that themselves become winding thought helixes running parallel to the first-order line of self-consciousness. Both the Depressed Person and the young married woman in "Adult World" also function as the book's female counterparts to its cast of "hideous men." The Depressed Person is particularly unlikable, as she spends the entire story calling up friends from her "Support System" to talk through her depression issues, many of which involve her anxiety about how she is coming off to the friends she is calling every hour of the day and night. In short, whenever she seeks relief from her depression, she ends up feeling more depressed. Even her work with her therapist becomes another source of emotional pain, for she begins to realize that her reliance on the therapist amounts, basically, to her paying $1,080 a month "to purchase what was in many respects a kind of fantasy-friend who could fulfill her childishly narcissistic fantasies of getting her own emotional needs met by another without having to reciprocally meet or empathize with or even consider the other's own emotional needs, an other-directed empathy and consideration which the depressed person tearfully confessed she sometimes despaired of ever having it in her to give" (57n).

The story, the most controversial and problematic piece in the entire book, ultimately makes the point, repeatedly, that the true source of the woman's depression is not the various wounds she might have suffered at the hands of her parents or friends but rather her own voracious narcissism. Although the story was chosen for *Prize Stories: The O. Henry Awards 1999*, its original publication in *Harper's* was greeted with a flood of letters from readers, many of them expressing anger at what some regarded as Wallace's vicious portrait of the woman's psychological affliction, an affliction, many pointed out, that is now widely regarded as an illness. The story opens itself to such charges, to be sure, but only if it is read in isolation, apart from

Wallace's other work, and only if that reading fails to account for Wallace's complex ironic method. For the woman, more than anything else, is a victim of her own reliance on quick fixes for her narcissism, which she has mistakenly, and self-aggrandizingly, diagnosed as depression. She has been prescribed Parnate, Nardil, Xanax—drugs that clearly do work in relieving serious chemical depression. For her, however, "none had delivered significant relief from the pain and feelings of emotional isolation" (40). Meanwhile, when her therapist kills herself, the Depressed Person cannot manage to feel any sympathy, empathy or grief, but only a self-involved feeling of being abandoned. "What kind of person," she asks herself, "could seem to feel nothing—'*Nothing*,' she emphasized—for anyone but herself" (68). She is trapped in herself, in other words, incapable of "other-directed empathy," and *that* is her problem.

At one point she admits to her therapist "that what she felt *truly* starved for and really *truly* fantasized about was having the ability to somehow really truly literally '*share*' it (i.e. chronic depression's ceaseless torment)" (59n). Indeed, the feelings of pain and isolation are "central and inescapable to her identity" largely because they *are* her identity, they *are* her core, that lonely inviolate "true self" that Wallace's work both honors and paradoxically seeks to open up to communion with other selves. The story's vicious parody of therapy speak—Support Systems, the Blame Game, and so on—is actually a backhanded way of reconstituting those terms as positive components of Wallace's technique. An interiority that cannot empathize is essentially a void—a *Nothing*—whereas one that can move outside itself and imagine the pain of others is an interiority that not only can assuage its own isolation but also help assuage that of others. The Depressed Person's error is to wish, hopelessly, to "express the depression's terrible unceasing agony *itself*," whereas Wallace's work seeks to express pain and loneliness through an elaborate technique of distortion and indirection that leaves the core thing unexpressed and therefore alive, subject rather than object. "The Depressed Person," therefore, like much of *Brief Interviews with Hideous Men,* brings to a culmination the themes and techniques that have governed much of Wallace's work of the 1990s, and, as such, seems to close out this particular phase of his career.

At the height of the "minimalist" 1980s, David Foster Wallace almost single-handedly revived the then moribund tradition of postmodern "maximalism" inaugurated thirty years prior by William Gaddis, Thomas Pynchon and John Barth. In so doing, he opened up new space, and created new challenges, for young writers of intrepid ambition. His central innovation lies in the ingenious way his work enacts a metafictional critique of metafiction. Whereas the postmodern work of his forebears firmly grounds itself in a literary tradition whose grip it feels it cannot shake, Wallace's work demonstrates how the original postmodernists' reliance on self-consciousness, parody, and irony has now become a culture-wide phenomenon: not only is our pop culture equally self-reflexive and self-aware, but so are the people of Wallace's generation, for whom irony is a weapon and a badge of sophistication.

Irony is also a cage the doors of which his work wants to spring. He opens the cage of irony by *ironizing* it, the same way he uses self-reflexivity to disclose the subtle deceptions at work in literary self-reflexivity. The purpose behind this layered strategy is to create a space outside his work where direct, "single-entendre" principles can breathe and live. The

work paradoxically honors the postmodernists that it demol-
ishes, for it grants postmodern fiction its numerous metaphysical assumptions—about the inescapability of language and the
artificiality of fictional forms, specifically—and then uses its
own weapons against it to reaffirm the very things that so much
postmodern fiction was intent to explode. His work has therefore shown new writers a way to move beyond what John Barth
called "the Literature of Exhaustion," a way that does not reject
what has come before but rather uses those same achievements
as a way to create new and more vital work.

For all his playfulness and technical sophistication, then,
Wallace is a seriously committed writer whose work exerts an
urgent ethical pressure on its readers. In the end he is less concerned with "moving fiction beyond postmodernism" than he
is with addressing, and possibly alleviating, such real-world
problems as cruelty, solipsism, loneliness, and depression. In this
latter regard, his work most resembles that of Vladimir
Nabokov, a linguistic and artistic prodigy who, like Wallace,
uses self-reflexivity not as an end in and of itself but rather as an
ingenious way to expand and enrich the isolated interior of his
reader. Nabokov famously explained that his work seeks to create a state of "aesthetic bliss," a phrase many critics have taken
as evidence that Nabokov's work has no ethical import. On the
contrary, Nabokov describes "aesthetic bliss" as a state in which
"art (curiosity, tenderness, kindness, ecstasy) is the norm,"
which is tantamount to saying that his books invoke a realm
in which values like "curiosity, tenderness, kindness, [and]
ecstasy" hold sway above all others. Art that achieves aesthetic
bliss is "not concerned with pitying the underdog or cursing the
upperdog. It appeals to that secret depth of the human soul
where the shadows of other worlds pass like the shadows of

nameless and soundless ships."[5] This is hardly an aesthetics free of ethical ramifications. Likewise, Wallace's self-reflexive fictional structures, in the way they direct a damning mirror on our own defense strategies of irony and self-consciousness, invite us not only to transcend our own divided interiorities but also, through an act of empathy, literally an inhabiting of other shadow worlds, to reconnect with our hidden "true selves," the secret target of all of Wallace's work. Well versed though he is in post-structuralist thought, Wallace is ultimately a cagey and learned critic of poststructuralism, with its governing tropes of "decentering" and "deferral." Wallace's work "defers" its "true self," but in such a way that this deferred thing is affirmed as real, as vital.

As such, Wallace's work is, in effect, spiritual, even mystical. He has even affirmed that his approach to writing and thinking about fiction models the way he approaches religious issues. His work is verbal to a fault—copious, talkative, written and over-written, inexhaustible in its energy and its willingness to explain and explain and explain—and yet this endless outpouring of language serves a curiously negative purpose: it is an attempt to invoke indirectly the very things that it is *not* addressing. Similarly, he has remarked, "The stuff that's truly interesting about religion is inarticulatable." Whenever a person tries to explain her religious feelings, he goes on, what she's "really talking about is herself." Still, he declares that "though these heartfelt utterances present themselves as assuasive or argumentative, what they really are are—truly, deeply—*expressive*—expressive of a self's heart's special tangle, of a knowing and verbal self's particular tortured relation to what is unknow- and -sayable."[6] Similarly, Wallace's argumentative and self-reflexive work is ultimately, truly, deeply, expressive of what is unknowable and unsayable.

Still on the early end of forty, Wallace, perhaps the most influential writer of his generation, still has a long and rich career ahead of him. Having already published the career-making —and, one would assume, creativity exhausting—*Infinite Jest*, he has since proved his mettle by continuing to write and publish at a regular rate. And although recent stories like "Good Old Neon," "Mr. Squishy," and "Oblivion" tread by-now familiar stylistic and thematic ground, they also confirm Wallace's originality, creative energy, and commitment both to his craft and to the ongoing development of his career. If he can manage to avoid becoming trapped by his own stylistic innovations—the endnotes, the obsessive narrative voice, the egghead erudition crossed with pop-culture savvy—he should continue to lead the literary pack well into the new millennium.

# Notes

## 1. Cynicism and Naïveté: Modernism's Third Wave

1. David Foster Wallace, "Westward the Course of Empire Takes Its Way," in *Girl with Curious Hair* (New York: Norton, 1989), 242.

2. Wallace, "Derivative Sport in Tornado Alley," in *A Supposedly Fun Thing I'll Never Do Again: Essays and Arguments* (Boston: Little, Brown, 1987), 6.

3. Wallace, "Tense Present: Democracy, English, and the Wars over Usage," *Harper's,* April 2001, 41.

4. Wallace, "Derivative Sport," 3, 4, 13, 12, 9, 14.

5. Wallace, "An Interview with David Foster Wallace," interview by Larry McCaffery, *Review of Contemporary Fiction* 13 (summer 1993): 138–39.

6. Ibid., 142.

7. See George Steiner, *Real Presences* (Chicago: Univ. of Chicago Press, 1989), 93–96, but also 87–116.

8. Brian McHale, *Postmodernist Fiction* (New York: Methuen, 1987), 9–11.

9. Wallace, "An Interview," 134.

10. See Matei Calinescu, *Five Faces of Modernity: Modernism, Avant-Garde, Decadence, Kitsch, Postmodernism* (Durham, N.C.: Duke Univ. Press, 1987), 144–48.

11. See John Barth, "The Literature of Exhaustion," in *The Friday Book: Essays and Other Nonfiction* (New York: Putnam, 1984), 62–76.

12. Wallace, "An Interview," 150.

13. Wallace, "E Unibus Pluram: Television and U.S. Fiction," in *A Supposedly Fun Thing,* 66–67.

14. Wallace, "E Unibus Pluram: Television and U.S. Fiction," in *A Supposedly Fun Thing,* 65, 66, 61, 64, 49.

15. Ibid., 81.

16. A. O. Scott, "The Panic of Influence," in *New York Review of Books* 47, no.2 (February 10, 2000): 40.

17. Wallace, "E Unibus," 63; Wallace, "Westward," 304; Wallace, *Infinite Jest* (New York: Little, Brown, 1996), 694.

18. Wallace, *Infinite Jest,* 694–95; Wallace, "E Unibus," 65.

19. Wallace, "An Interview," 131.

20. Ibid., 144, 143. For a more sustained treatment of Wallace's approach to, and enthusiasm for, Wittgenstein's ideas, see his essay "The Empty Plenum: David Markson's *Wittgenstein's Mistress,*" *Review of Contemporary Fiction* 10 (summer 1990): 217–39.

## 2. *The Broom of the System:* Wittgenstein and the Rules of the Game

1. Ludwig Wittgenstein, *The Philosophical Investigations,* trans. G. E. M. Anscombe (New York: Macmillan, 1953), sec. 1 (p. 2$^e$).

2. David Foster Wallace, *The Broom of the System* (New York: Penguin Books, 1987), 73. Further references will be noted parenthetically.

3. See Justus Hartnack, *Wittgenstein and Modern Philosophy,* trans. Maurice Cranston (New York: Doubleday, 1965), 3–9. For more on his influence on logical positivism, see pp. 45–57.

4. Wittgenstein, *Philosophical Investigations,* sec. 67 (p. 32$^e$).

5. Wallace, "Tense Present: Democracy, English, and the Wars over Usage," *Harper's,* April 2001, 47n.

6. See, for instance, Charles Harris, *Passionate Virtuosity: The Fiction of John Barth* (Chicago: Univ. of Illinois Press, 1983); Christopher D. Morris, "Barth and Lacan: The World and the Moebius Strip," *Critique: Studies in Modern Fiction* 17, no. 1 (1975): 69–77; and Deborah Woolley, "Empty 'Text,' Fecund Voice:

Self-Reflexivity in Barth's *Lost in the Funhouse*," *Contemporary Literature* 26 (winter 1985), 460–81.

7. Jacques Derrida, "*Différance*," in *Critical Theory Since 1965*, ed. Hazard Adams and Leroy Searle (Tallahassee: Univ. Press of Florida, 1986), 125. As readers of Derrida already know, the gnomic term *différance* embodies a complex and multilayered concept a full accounting of which would be unnecessarily distracting in the present context.

8. John Barth, "The Literature of Exhaustion," 71.

9. Wittgenstein, *Philosophical Investigations*, sec. 25 (p. 12$^e$); Michael Weston, *Kierkegaard and Modern Continental Philosophy: An Introduction* (New York: Routledge, 1994), 126. Weston is only one of several prominent theorists who have tried to draw careful distinctions between Wittgenstein and Derrida. Perhaps the most thorough argument for Wittgenstein's "overturning" of Derrida belongs to Charles Altieri; see especially his book, *Act and Quality: A Theory of Literary Meaning and Humanistic Understanding* (Amherst: Univ. of Massachusetts Press, 1981). Altieri argues that once we introduce into our discussion Wittgenstein's concept of the "language-game," "Derrida's ontological skepticism is not so much refuted as revealed to be irrelevant for the rough grounds that sustain human communication. It may well be the case that we have no absolutely secure grounds for *truth*, but the more important question is whether we need these grounds for coherent discourse" (40). As if in response to Altieri's book, Henry Spaten has produced—with the express blessing of Derrida himself, who wrote a positive book jacket blurb—a counter-argument positing the inextricable similarities between Wittgenstein's theory and the practice of deconstruction. See Spaten, *Wittgenstein and Derrida* (Lincoln: Univ. of Nebraska Press, 1986).

10. See Lance Olsen, "Termite Art, or Wallace's Wittgenstein," *Review of Contemporary Fiction* 13 (summer 1993): 204.

11. See Wittgenstein, *Philosophical Investigations*, sec. 40 (p. 20$^e$).

12. See Olsen, "Termite Art," 202–3.

13. Marshall McLuhan, *The Gutenberg Galaxy: The Making of Typographic Man* (Toronto: Univ. of Toronto Press, 1962), 86. McLuhan is, in fact, citing Moses Hadas, *Ancilla to Classical Learning* (New York: Columbia Univ. Press, 1954), 51–52. For the relevant passage from Saint Augustine, see *Confessions,* trans. R. S. Pine-Coffin (New York: Viking Penguin, 1961), 114, where Augustine describes Saint Ambrose's reading method in the following terms: "When he read, his eyes scanned the page, and his heart explored the meaning, but his voice was silent and his tongue was still." Charles Morris also cites the McLuhan passage in his discussion of *Lost in the Funhouse* (see *Passionate Virtuosity,* p. 109). As shall be shown, Ambrose is not only the name of John Barth's fictional alter ego in his short story "Lost in the Funhouse" but also the name given to the Barth character in Wallace's "Westward the Course of Empire Takes Its Way."

14. See John Updike, *Rabbit, Run* (New York: Fawcett Crest Books, 1960), 159–61.

15. Wallace, "Rabbit Resurrected," *Harper's,* August 1992, 41; Wallace, "John Updike, Champion Literary Phallocrat, Drops One; Is This Finally the End for Magnificent Narcissists?" *New York Observer,* 13 October 1997.

16. Updike, 34, 92.

17. See Eve Kosofsky Sedgwick, *Between Men: English Literature and Male Homosocial Desire* (New York: Columbia Univ. Press, 1985), 21–27. Sedgwick's groundbreaking argument builds on Rene Girard's *Deceit, Desire, and the Novel.* As Sedgwick explains, "Girard seems to see the bond between rivals in an erotic triangle [involving two men and a woman] as being even stronger, more heavily determinant of actions and choices, than anything in the bond between either of the lovers and the beloved" (21). Sedgwick's contribution to this line of argument is to chart out the ways in which these bonds are in fact forms of suppressed "homosocial desire."

18. Thomas Pynchon, *The Crying of Lot 49* (New York: Harper and Row, 1966). Wallace has said that he read *The Crying of Lot 49* only *after* publishing *The Broom of the System,* largely in response to critics' repeated references to Pynchon's earlier novel. Though this is certainly possible, it seems somehow unlikely. Note, for instance, the striking similarities between Oedipa Mass's first "overhead" encounter with San Narciso, which she imagines as a circuit board (*Crying of Lot 49,* 24), and Wallace's overhead description of East Corinth, which turns out to be modeled after the profile of Jayne Mansfield (*Broom of the System,* 45).

19. For more on this, see Claude E. Shannon and Warren Weaver, *The Mathematical Theory of Communication* (Urbana: Univ. of Illinois Press, 1964). See especially pp. 8–16 of Warren Weaver's introductory essay, which lucidly lays out the grounds upon which Shannon adapts the concept of entropy to communication theory.

20. See Wittgenstein, *Tractatus Logico-Philosophicus,* trans. D. F. Pears and B. F. McGuinness (New York: Routledge and Kegan Paul, 1961), 4:211.

21. Wallace, *Girl with Curious Hair,* 269.

## 3. *Girl with Curious Hair:* Inside and Outside the Set

1. Wallace, "An Interview with David Foster Wallace," interview by Larry McCaffery, *Review of Contemporary Fiction* 13 (summer 1993): 130.

2. Wallace, *Girl with Curious Hair,* vi. Further references will be noted parenthetically.

3. T. S. Eliot, "*Ulysses,* Order, and Myth," from *The Selected Prose of T. S. Eliot,* ed. Frank Kermode (New York: Harcourt Brace Jovanovich, 1975), 177.

4. John Barth, *Chimera* (Greenwich, Conn.: Fawcett Crest Books, 1972), 208.

5. Lance Olsen, "Termite Art, or Wallace's Wittgenstein," *Review of Contemporary Fiction* 13 (summer 1993), 206; Wallace, "An Interview," 138; Wallace, "E Unibus Pluram: Television and U.S. Fiction," in *A Supposedly Fun Thing*, 22.

6. David Shapiro, *John Ashbery: An Introduction to the Poetry* (New York: Columbia Univ. Press, 1979), 1; John Ashbery, *Self-Portrait in a Convex Mirror* (New York: Viking, 1975), 69; Shapiro, *John Ashbery*, 7; Ashbery, *Self-Portrait*, 70, 73.

7. Wallace, "E Unibus," 56.

8. Wallace, *Infinite Jest*, 112.

9. Wallace, "An Interview," 131.

10. Ibid., 134, 147.

11. Barth, "The Literature of Exhaustion," in *The Friday Book: Essays and Other Nonfiction* (New York: Putnam, 1984) 72; Wallace, "An Interview," 146.

12. Harold Bloom, *The Anxiety of Influence: A Theory of Poetry* (New York: Oxford Univ. Press, 1973), 14.

13. Wallace, "An Interview," 142.

14. John Barth, "Lost in the Funhouse," *Lost in the Funhouse: Fiction for Print, Tape, Live Voice* (New York: Doubleday, 1967), 72, 97.

15. Ibid., 85.

16. Barth, "Literature of Exhaustion," 71.

17. For the specific quoted passage, see Cynthia Ozick, "Usurpation (Other People's Stories)," *Bloodshed and Three Novellas* (New York: Knopf, 1976), 131.

## 4. *Infinite Jest:* Too Much Fun for Anyone Mortal to Hope to Endure

1. Wallace, "Westward the Course of Empire Takes Its Way," in *Girl with Curious Hair*, 348.

2. Frank Louis Cioffi, "'An Anguish Become Thing': Narrative As Performance in David Foster Wallace's *Infinite Jest*," *Narrative* 8, no. 2 (May 2000): 162; Wallace, "An Interview," 127.

3. Wallace, "Westward," 331–32.

4. Ibid., 138; Wallace, "An Interview," 142.

5. Katherine Hayles, "The Illusion of Autonomy and the Fact of Recursivity: Virtual Ecologies, Entertainment, and *Infinite Jest*," *New Literary History* 30, no. 3 (summer 1999): 683–84; Cioffi, "An Anguish," 165.

6. Wallace, *Infinite Jest,* 416. Further references will be noted parenthetically.

7. Throughout the novel, Wallace keeps a running tab of the main characters' ages, and these clues provide the best evidence for internal dating. Yet even these clues do not always add up. Readers are told, for instance, that Don Gately, perhaps the novel's primary hero, is twenty-eight in November Y.D.A.U. Late in the book we learn that he smoked his first joint at the age of nine, while "watching broadcast televised niggers run amok in flaming L.A. Ca after some Finest [i.e., police] got home-movied crewing on a nigger in the worst way" (903), a clear reference to the Rodney King riots in April 1992. This would put Gately's date of birth at 1982 or 1983, depending on whether his birthday precedes or follows April. If he was born 1982, then he would be twenty-eight in 2010; if in 1983, the year would be 2011. Yet the month of November Y.D.A.U. corresponds to calendar year 2009, during which time November 8 will fall on a Sunday, as it does in the novel, and November 17 on a Tuesday, and so on. Clearly, there are two options to explain the ambiguity here: either Wallace accidentally misdated the Rodney King riots—confusing them perhaps with the date of the actual taping, which took place in March 1991—yet nevertheless intended Y.D.A.U. to correspond to the actual year 2009; or he has planted the inconsistency in order to frustrate such fruitless, but interesting, exercises as this.

8. See Timothy Ferris, *The Whole Shebang: A State-of-the-Universe(s) Report* (New York: Touchstone Books, 1977) 278–79. This theory also significantly informs John Updike's 1997 novel *Toward the End of Time,* which is also set in a near future and which was excoriated by Wallace in a review cited briefly in a previous chapter.

9. Wallace, "An Interview," 141.

10. In his essays and more recent fiction, Wallace has amply demonstrated his familiarity with not only Lacan but also Derrida, de Man, Barthes, and Foucault; what is more, his approach to Lacan's ideas parallels his approach to those of Derrida—that is, respect with a healthy dose of skepticism. See especially "Greatly Exaggerated" from *A Supposedly Fun Thing I'll Never Do Again,* in which Wallace outlines his argument against various theories proposed by Foucault and Derrida, and "Brief Interviews with Hideous Men (#48)" from the book of the same name, in which a sophisticated student of Lacan justifies why he desires to tie up the women he seduces. A full reading of this latter story can be found in the next chapter.

11. Jacques Lacan, "The Agency of the Letter in the Unconscious or Reason Since Freud," *Écrits: A Selection,* trans. Alan Sheridan (New York: Norton, 1977), 147, 166.

12. Lacan, "The Mirror Stage as Formative of the Function of the I as Revealed in Psychoanalytic Experience," *Écrits,* 1, 2.

13. See Bruce Fink, *The Lacanian Subject: Between Language and Jouissance* (Princeton, N.J.: Princeton Univ. Press, 1995), 49–68.

14. Tom Shippey, *J.R. R. Tolkien: Author of the Century* (Boston: Houghton Mifflin, 2001), 118.

15. Ibid., 119.

16. William James, "The Moral Philosopher and the Moral Life," *Pragmatism and Other Writings,* ed. Giles Gunn (New York: Penguin, 2000), 253.

17. Søren Kierkegaard, *The Sickness unto Death,* ed. and trans. Alastair Hannay (New York: Penguin Books, 1989), 83.

18. Kierkegaard, *Concluding Unscientific Postscript to "Philosophical Fragments,"* vol. 1, ed. and trans. Howard V. Hong and Edna H. Hong (Princeton, N.J.: Princeton Univ. Press, 1992), 253.

19. Ibid., 254.

20. See, for instance, Molly's account on pages 792–95. Another (possibly unreliable) reference to Joelle's disfiguring, this one from

Hal's point of view, reads: "This was after the girl Orin had been wildly in love with and Himself had compulsively used in films had been disfigured" (634).

21. Ibid., 243–54.

22. Kierkegaard, *Either/Or II*, ed. and trans. Walter Lowrie (Princeton, N.J.: Princeton Univ. Press, 1992), 183.

23. Wallace Stevens, *Opus Posthumous*, ed. Samuel French Morse (New York: Knopf, 1957), 159.

24. Ibid., 162, 163, 206, 237; Wallace, "An Interview," 134.

25. Lacan, "Agency of the Letter in the Unconscious," 167.

26. Fink, 59.

27. Wallace, "Westward," 330.

28. Cioffi, "An Anguish," 170.

29. Tom LeClair, "The Prodigious Fiction of Richard Powers, William Vollmann, and David Foster Wallace," *Critique* 38, no. 1 (fall 1996): 32; Catherine Nichols, "Dialogizing Postmodern Carnival: David Foster Wallace's *Infinite Jest*," *Critique* 43, no. 1 fall 2001): 5. See also LeClair, "Prodigious Fiction," 38.

30. Wallace, "An Interview," 141; Wallace, "Greatly Exaggerated," *A Supposedly Fun Thing I'll Never Do Again*, 142, 142–43. Wallace concludes the review by arguing, "For those of us civilians who know in our gut that writing is an act of communication between one human being and another, the whole question [of the death of the author] becomes sort of arcane." He then gives the last word to postmodern hero "William (anti-death) Gass," who observes, "One thing which it cannot mean is that *no one did it*" (144–45). As is usually the case with his essays, this review, which he prominently reprinted in *A Supposedly Fun Thing I'll Never Do Again*, functions as somewhat more direct exploration of themes and ideas he expresses in his novels and short stories.

31. Wallace, "Derivate Sport," 14.

32. Nichols, "Dialogizing Postmodern Carnival," 14.

## 5. *Brief Interviews with Hideous Men*: Interrogations and Consolidations

1. Wallace, "*Quo Vadis*—Introduction," *Review of Contemporary Fiction* 16 (spring 1996): 7.

2. Wallace, *Brief Interviews with Hideous Men* (Boston: Back Bay Books, 2000), 229. Further references will be noted parenthetically.

3. Wallace, "An Interview with David Foster Wallace," interview by Larry McCaffery, *Review of Contemporary Fiction* 13 (summer 1993): 127.

4. John Barth, *Chimera* (Greenwich, Conn.: Fawcett Crest Books, 1972), 207–8.

5. Vladimir Nabokov, *Lolita* (New York: Vintage Books, 1955), 314–15; Nabokov, *Nikolay Gogol,* as quoted in Brian Boyd's *Vladimir Nabokov: The American Years* (London: Vintage, 1993), 57.

6. Wallace, "*Quo Vadis*—Introduction," *Review of Contemporary Fiction* 16 (spring 1996): 8.

# Bibliography

## Books as Author

*The Broom of the System.* New York: Viking, 1987.

*Girl with Curious Hair.* New York: Norton, 1989.

*Signifying Rappers: Rap and Race in the Urban Present.* With Mark Costello. New York: Ecco Press, 1990.

*Infinite Jest.* Boston: Little, Brown, 1996

*A Supposedly Fun Thing I'll Never Do Again: Essays and Arguments.* Boston: Little, Brown, 1997.

*Brief Interviews with Hideous Men: Stories.* Boston: Little, Brown, 1999.

*Up, Simba! Seven Days on the Trail of an Anticandidate.* iPublish.com, 2000. (Microsoft Reader eBook)

## Selected Periodical Publications (Uncollected)

### Fiction

"Order and Flux in Northampton." *Conjunctions* 17 (fall 1991): 91–118.

"Yet Another Example of the Porousness of Certain Borders (VIII)." *McSweeney's Quarterly Concern* 1 (1998):

"Yet Another Example of the Porousness of Various Borders (VI): Projected But Not Improbable Transcript of Author's Parents' Marriage's End, 1971." *McSweeney's Quarterly Concern* 3 (1999): Printed along the spine.

"Mr. Squishy." [Writing as Elizabeth Klemm.] *McSweeney's Quarterly Concern* 5 (2000): 199–248.

"Incarnations of Burned Children." *Esquire,* November 2000, 196.

"Good Old Neon." *Conjunctions* 37 (fall 2001): 105–40. Reprinted in *The O. Henry Prize Stories 2002,* ed. Larry Dark (New York: Anchor Books, 2002), 371–407.

"Another Pioneer." *Colorado Review* 28 (summer 2001): 179–204.

"Peoria {4}." *TriQuarterly* 112 ( June 2002): 131.

"Peoria {9} 'Whispering Pines.'" *TriQuarterly* 112 ( June 2002): 132–33.

"Oblivion." *Esquire,* November 2002,

*Articles*

"The Empty Plenum: David Markson's *Wittgenstein's Mistress.*" *Review of Contemporary Fiction* 10 (summer 1990): 217–39.

"Rabbit Resurrected." *Harper's,* August 1992, 39–41.

"Democracy and Commerce at the U.S. Open." *Tennis,* September 1996, 70–75.

"John Updike, Champion Literary Phallocrat, Drops One; Is This Finally the End for Magnificent Narcissists?" *New York Observer,* 13 October 1997.

"F/X Porn." *Waterstone's,* winter/spring 1998.

"Laughing with Kafka." *Harper's,* July 1998, 57–64.

"Neither Adult Nor Entertainment." [Writing as Willem R. deGroot and Matt Rundlet.] *Premier,* September 1998, 88–93.

"The Weasel, Twelve Monkeys, and the Shrub: Seven Days in the Life of the Late, Great John McCain." *Rolling Stone,* 16 April 2000, 53–68, 144–45.

"Rhetoric and the Math Melodrama." *Science,* 22 December 2000, 2263–67.

"Tense Present: Democracy, English, and the Wars over Usage." *Harper's,* April 2001, 39–58.

"The View from Mrs. Thompson's." *Rolling* Stone, 25 October 2001, 92–95, 132–33.

*Works Edited*

"The Future of Fiction: A Forum Edited by David Foster Wallace." *Review of Contemporary Fiction* 16 (spring 1996).

Selected Works about David Foster Wallace

*Profiles and Interviews*

Bruni, Frank. "The Grunge American Novel." *New York Times Magazine,* 24 March 1996, 38–41.

Costello, Mark. "Fighting to Write: A Short Reminiscence of D. F. Wallace." *Review of Contemporary Fiction* 13 (summer 1993): 235–36.

McCaffery, Larry. "An Interview with David Foster Wallace." *Review of Contemporary Fiction* 13 (summer 1993): 127–50.

Passaro, Vincent. "The Last Laugh." *Harper's Bazaar,* February 1996, 104.

Sawhill, Robert. "I Was a Voyeur at AA Meetings." *Newsweek,* 12 February 1996, 80.

Sheppard, R. Z. "712,000 Typos!" *Time,* 19 February 1996, 70.

———. "Fiction's New Fab Four." *Time,* 14 April 1997, 89.

Stein, Lorin. "David Foster Wallace: In the Company of Creeps." *Publishers Weekly,* 3 May 1999, 52–53.

Van Sant, Gus. "A Fun Thing They'll Never Do Again: Gus Van Sant meets David Foster Wallace." *Dazed and Confused,* May 1998.

*Scholarly Essays*

Cioffi, Frank Louis. "'An Anguish Become a Thing': Narrative As Performance in David Foster Wallace's *Infinite Jest.*" *Narrative* 8, no. 2 (May 2000): 161–81.

Hayles, N. Katherine. "The Illusion of Autonomy and the Fact of Recursivity: Virtual Ecologies, Entertainment, and Infinite Jest." *New Literary History* 30, no. 3 (1999 summer): 675–97.

Jacobs, Timothy. "Wallace's *Infinite Jest.*" *Explicator* 58, no. 3 (spring 2000): 172–75.

LeClair, Tom. "The Prodigious Fiction of Richard Powers, William Vollmann, and David Foster Wallace." *Critique: Studies in Contemporary Fiction* 38, no. 1 (fall 1996): 12–37.

Mortenson, Erik R. "Xmas Junkies: Debasement and Redemption in the Work of William S. Burroughs and David Foster Wallace." *TriQuarterly* 9, no. 2 (summer 1999): 37–46.

Nichols, Catherine. "Dialogizing Postmodern Carnival: David Foster Wallace's *Infinite Jest.*" *Critique* 43, no. 1 (fall 2001): 3–16.

Olsen, Lance. "Termite Art, or Wallace's Wittgenstein." *Review of Contemporary Fiction* 13, no. 2 (summer 1993): 199–215.

Rother, James. "Reading and Riding the Post-Scientific Wave: The Shorter Fiction of David Foster Wallace." *Review of Contemporary Fiction* 13, no. 2 (summer 1993): 216–34.

Scott, A. O. "The Panic of Influence." *New York Review of Books* 47, no. 2: 39–34.

Other Works Cited

Altieri, Charles. *Act and Quality: A Theory of Literary Meaning and Humanistic Understanding.* Amherst: Univ. of Massachusetts Press, 1981.

Ashbery. John. *Self-Portrait in a Convex Mirror.* New York: Viking, 1975.

Augustine. *Confessions.* Translated by R. S. Pine-Coffin. New York: Viking Penguin, 1961.

Barth, John. *Chimera.* Greenwich, Conn.: Fawcett Crest Books, 1972.

———. "The Literature of Exhaustion." In *The Friday Book: Essays and Other Nonfiction,* 62–76. New York: Putnam, 1984.

———. *Lost in the Funhouse: Fiction for Print, Tape, Live Voice.* New York: Doubleday, 1967.

Bloom, Harold. *The Anxiety of Influence: A Theory of Poetry.* New York: Oxford Univ. Press, 1973.

Boyd, Brian. *Vladimir Nabokov: The American Years.* London: Vintage Books, 1993.

Brown, Norman O. *Life against Death: The Psychoanalytic Meaning of History.* Middletown, Conn.: Wesleyan Univ. Press, 1959.

———. *Love's Body.* New York: Random House, 1966.

Calinescu, Matei. *Five Faces of Modernity: Modernism, Avant-Garde, Decadence, Kitsch, Postmodernism.* Durham, N.C.: Duke Univ. Press, 1987.

Derrida, Jacques. *"Différance."* In *Critical Theory since 1965,* edited by Hazard Adams and Leroy Searle, 120–36. Tallahassee: Univ. Press of Florida, 1986.

Eliot, T. S. *"Ulysses,* Order, and Myth." In *The Selected Prose of T. S. Eliot,* edited by Frank Kermode, 175–78. New York: Harcourt Brace Jovanovich, 1975.

Ferris, Timothy. *The Whole Shebang: A State-of-the-Universe(s) Report.* New York: Touchstone Books, 1977.

Fink, Bruce. *The Lacanian Subject: Between Language and Jouissance.* Princeton, N.J.: Princeton Univ. Press, 1995.

Hadas, Moses. *Ancilla to Classical Learning.* New York: Columbia Univ. Press, 1954.

Harris, Charles. *Passionate Virtuosity: The Fiction of John Barth.* Chicago: Univ. of Illinois Press, 1983.

Hartnack, Justus. *Wittgenstein and Modern Philosophy.* Translated by Maurice Cranston. New York: Doubleday, 1965.

James, William. "The Moral Philosopher and the Moral Life." In *Pragmatism and Other Writings,* edited by Giles Gunn, 242–63. New York: Penguin, 2000.

Kierkegaard, Søren. *Concluding Unscientific Postscript to "Philosophical Fragments."* Vol. 1. Edited and translated by Howard V. Hong and Edna H. Hong. Princeton, N.J.: Princeton Univ. Press, 1992.

———. *Either/Or II.* Edited and translated by Walter Lowrie. Princeton, N.J.: Princeton University Press, 1992.

———. *The Sickness unto Death.* Edited and translated by Alastair Hannay. New York: Penguin Books, 1989.

Lacan, Jacques. *Écrits: A Selection.* Translated by Alan Sheridan. New York: Norton, 1977.

McHale, Brian. *Postmodernist Fiction.* New York: Methuen, 1987.

McLuhan, Marshall. *The Gutenberg Galaxy: The Making of Typographic Man.* Toronto: Univ. of Toronto Press, 1962.

Morris, Christopher D. "Barth and Lacan: The World and the Moebius Strip." *Critique: Studies in Modern Fiction* 17, no. 1 (fall 1975): 69–77.

Ozick, Cynthia. "Usurpation (Other People's Stories)." *Bloodshed and Three Novellas*. New York: Knopf, 1976.

Pynchon, Thomas. *The Crying of Lot 49*. New York: Harper and Row, 1966.

Scott, A. O. "The Panic of Influence." *New York Review of Books* 47, no.2 (February 10, 2000): 39–43.

Sedgwick, Eve Kosofsky. *Between Men: English Literature and Male Homosocial Desire*. New York: Columbia Univ. Press, 1985.

Shannon, Claude E. and Warren Weaver. *The Mathematical Theory of Communication*. Urbana: Univ. of Illinois Press, 1964.

Shapiro, David. *John Ashbery: An Introduction to the Poetry*. New York: Columbia Univ. Press, 1979.

Shippey, Tom. *J .R. R. Tolkien: Author of the Century*. Boston: Houghton Mifflin, 2001.

Spaten, Henry. *Wittgenstein and Derrida*. Lincoln: Univ. of Nebraska Press, 1986.

Steiner, George. *Real Presences*. Chicago: Univ. of Chicago Press, 1989.

Stevens, Wallace. *Opus Posthumous*. Edited by Samuel French Morse. New York: Knopf, 1957.

Updike, John. *Rabbit, Run*. New York: Fawcett Crest Books, 1960.

Weston, Michael. *Kierkegaard and Modern Continental Philosophy: An Introduction*. New York: Routledge, 1994.

Wittgenstein, Ludwig. *The Philosophical Investigations*. Translated by G. E. M. Anscombe. New York: Macmillan, 1953.

———. *Tractatus Logico-Philosophicus*. Translated by D. F. Pears and B. F. McGuinness. New York: Routledge & Kegan Paul, 1961.

Woolley, Deborah. "Empty 'Text,' Fecund Voice: Self-Reflexivity in Barth's *Lost in the Funhouse*." *Contemporary Literature* 26, no. 4 (winter 1985): 460–81.

# Index

*This index does not include references to material contained in the notes.*